James

Preaching Verse-by-Verse

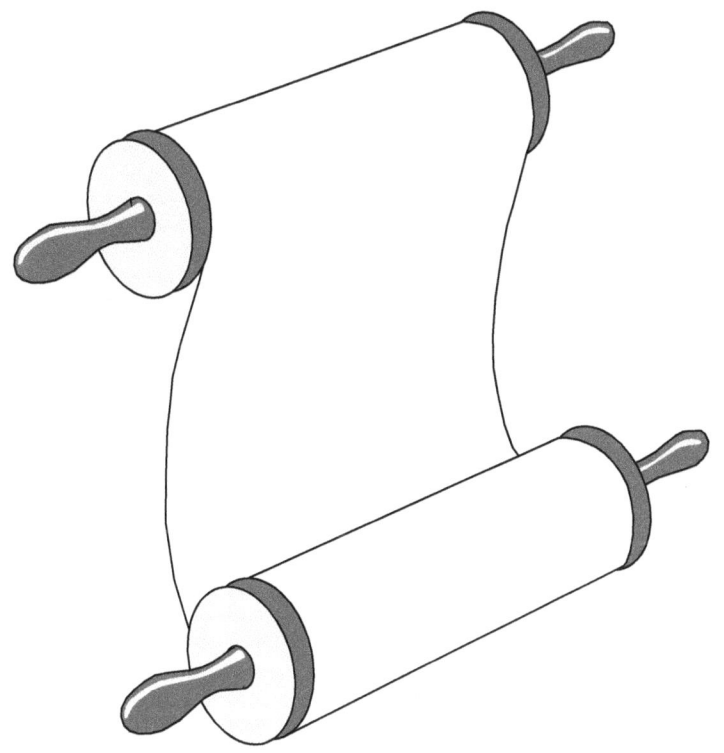

Pastor D. A. Waite, Th.D., Ph.D.

Published by
THE BIBLE FOR TODAY PRESS

Published by
THE BIBLE FOR TODAY PRESS
900 Park Avenue
Collingswood, New Jersey 08108 U.S.A.
Pastor D. A. Waite, Th.D., Ph.D.
𝔅𝔦𝔟𝔩𝔢 𝔉𝔬𝔯 𝔗𝔬𝔡𝔞𝔶 𝔅𝔞𝔭𝔱𝔦𝔰𝔱 ℭ𝔥𝔲𝔯𝔠𝔥
Church Phone: 856-854-4747
BFT Phone: 856-854-4452
Orders: 1-800-John 10:9
e-mail: BFT@BibleForToday.org
Website: www.BibleForToday.org
FAX: 856-854-2464

We Use and Defend
the King James Bible

Copyright, 2017
All Rights Reserved
May, 2017

BFT #4165

ISBN #978-1-56848-113-5

Acknowledgments

I wish to thank and to acknowledge the assistance of the following people:

- **The Congregation** of the **Bible For Today Baptist Church**–for whom these messages were prepared, to whom they were delivered, and by whom they were published. They listened attentively and encouraged their Pastor.
- **Yvonne Sanborn Waite**–my wife, who encouraged the publication of these sermons, read the manuscript, developed the various boxes, and gave other helpful suggestions and comments. The boxes help the reader to see some of the more important topics that are covered in the various chapters.
- **Pastor Daniel Waite**–our church's Assistant Pastor for helping to keep our computers up-to-date and working properly day by day so that this book could be written and published.
- **Patricia Canter**–a friend of Mrs. Waite and me who volunteered to take the cassette tapes of the verse-by-verse exposition of the book of James and put these words into digital format to be used for this book. She also volunteered to proofread the final copy.
- **Dr. Kirk DiVietro**–a friend for many years, one of our Dean Burgon Society faithful Vice Presidents, who is an expert on the use of computers. He has helped in various ways to make the computer work easier when performing the needed tasks.

James–Preaching Verse By Verse

Foreword

- **The Beginning.** This book is the **fourteenth** in a series of verse-by-preaching from various New Testament books of the Bible. It is an attempt to bring to the minds of the readers two things: (1) the **meaning** of the words in the verses, and (2) some practical **applications** of those words to the lives of both genuine Christians and non-Christians.
- **Preached Sermons.** These were messages that I preached to our **Bible For Today Baptist Church** in Collingswood, New Jersey. They were broadcast over the radio, and over the Internet by computer streaming around the world. I took half a chapter each Sunday as the messages were preached. All verses are from the King James Bible.
- **Other Verses.** In connection with both the **meaning** and **application** of the verses in this book, there are many verses from other places in the Bible that have been quoted for further elaboration on the teachings in this book. All the verses of Scripture that were used to illustrate further truth are written out in full for easy reference.
- **A Transcription.** This entire book was typed into computer format by Patricia Canter from the tape recordings of the messages as they were preached. In addition to the words used as I preached these sermons, I have added other words for clarification as needed.
- **The Audience.** The intended audience for this book is the same as the audience that listened to the messages in the first place. These studies are not meant to be overly scholarly, though there are some references to various Greek Words used. My aim and burden is to try to help genuine Christians to understand and follow the Words of God. It is also my hope that my children, grandchildren, great grandchildren, and others might profit from this study. There is an 18-page INDEX of words and phrases.

Yours For God's Words,

D. A. Waite

Pastor D. A. Waite, Th.D., Ph.D.
Bible For Today Baptist Church

Table of Contents

Publisher's Data. I
Acknowledgments. iii
Foreword.. iv
Table of Contents. v
James Chapter One. 1
James Chapter Two. 45
James Chapter Three.. 83
James Chapter Four. 117
James Chapter Five. 147
Index of Words and Phrases.. 187
About the Author. 205
Order Blank Pages. 289
Defined King James Bible Orders. 297

James
Chapter One

James 1:1

"James, a servant of God and of the Lord Jesus Christ, to the twelve tribes which are scattered abroad, greeting."

The book of James was probably written about 60 A.D. There are several people named "James" in the New Testament. I believe this James was the son of Zebedee. <u>He was the brother of the Apostle John.</u>

James was a *"servant of God and the Lord Jesus Christ."*

THE MEANING OF THE GREEK WORD, "DOULOS"

The Greek Word for *"servant"* is DOULOS.

Some of the meanings of that Greek Word are:

"1) a slave, bondman, man of servile condition; 1a) a slave; 1b) metaph., one who gives himself up to another's will, those whose service is used by Christ in extending and advancing His cause among men; 1c) devoted to another to the disregard of one's own interests; 2) a servant, attendant."

As a genuine *"servant,"* James was *"one who gives himself up to another's will."* <u>All genuine Christians should be this kind of "servants" for the Lord Jesus Christ and for God the Father.</u>

James was writing *"to the twelve tribes which are scattered abroad."* <u>These were probably twelve different groups that were former Jews who had been converted to Christ and were in the dispersion.</u> They were gathered all over the then-known world. There were twelve tribes of Israel led by Jacob's twelve sons.

- **Matthew 19:28**

"And Jesus said unto them, Verily I say unto you, That ye which have followed me, in the regeneration when the Son of man shall sit in the throne of his glory, ye also shall sit upon twelve thrones, judging <u>the twelve tribes of Israel</u>."

<u>These apostles will judge the twelve tribes of Israel.</u>

- **Acts 26:7**

"Unto which *promise* <u>our twelve tribes</u>, instantly serving *God* day and night, <u>hope to come</u>. For which hope's sake, king Agrippa, I am accused of the Jews."

This refers to the hope of the resurrection. <u>The Old Testament twelve tribes of Israel looked for the resurrection.</u>

- **Revelation 21:12**

"And had a wall great and high, *and* had twelve gates, and at the gates twelve angels, and names written thereon, which are *the names* of the twelve tribes of the children of Israel:"

<u>The names of the twelve apostles will be on the gates of the millennial temple.</u>

Bodily Resurrection In The Old Testament

- **Job 19:26**

"And *though* after my skin *worms* destroy this *body*, <u>yet in my flesh shall I see God</u>:"

These are the twelve tribes that James is writing to. They are saved, born-again Jews that were scattered all over the then-known world after the persecutions in Jerusalem.

James 1:2

"My brethren, count it all joy when ye fall into divers temptations;"

James states that joy should accompany different kinds of temptations. <u>The Greek Word for "*fall*" (PERIPIPTO) implies that these different kinds of temptations are surrounding the person.</u>

THE MEANING OF THE GREEK WORD, "PEIRASMOS"

The Greek Word for "*temptations*" is PEIRASMOS. Some of the meanings of this Greek Word are:

> "*1) an experiment, attempt, trial, proving; 1a) trial, proving: the trial made of you by my bodily condition, since condition served as to test the love of the Galatians toward Paul (Gal. 4:14); 1b) the trial of man's fidelity, integrity, virtue, constancy; 1b1) an enticement to*

> sin, temptation, whether arising from the desires or from the outward circumstances; 1b2) an internal temptation to sin; 1b2a) of the temptation by which the devil sought to divert Jesus the Messiah from his divine errand; 1b3) of the condition of things, or a mental state, by which we are enticed to sin, or to a lapse from the faith and holiness; 1b4) adversity, affliction, trouble: sent by God and serving to test or prove one's character, faith, holiness; 1c) temptation (i.e. trial) of God by men; 1c1) rebellion against God, by which his power and justice are, as it were, put to the proof and challenged to show themselves."

The Greek word, PEIRASMOS, has two meanings in the Scriptures. One meaning is a temptation which is "*an introduction and enticement to sin.*" The second meaning is a "*testing.*" The Lord Jesus Christ was tempted or tested by the Devil in the wilderness. The Lord Jesus Christ was sinless and perfect. As such, He could not be successfully enticed to sin. But He could be and was tested by the Devil.

Verses On Temptation

- **Psalms 95:8**

    "Harden not your heart, as in the provocation, *and* as *in* the day of temptation in the wilderness:"

This testing in the wilderness that happened in the Old Testament involved 600,000 men plus women and children. There were probably two or three million who went out of Egypt into the wilderness. They experienced forty years of testing and temptation. Moses and Aaron were included in this testing. Near the end of the forty years, Moses and Aaron disobeyed the Lord. Because of this, they were forbidden to enter into the land of Canaan.

> **Numbers 20:8-12** *"Take the rod, and gather thou the assembly together, thou, and Aaron thy brother, and speak ye unto the rock before their eyes; and it shall give forth his water, and thou shalt bring forth to them water out of the rock: so thou shalt give the congregation and their beasts drink. And Moses took the rod from before the LORD, as he commanded him. And Moses and Aaron*

*gathered the congregation together before the rock, and he said unto them, Hear now, ye rebels; must we fetch you water out of this rock? And Moses lifted up his hand, and <u>with his rod he smote the rock twice: and the water came out abundantly</u>, and the congregation drank, and their beasts also. And the LORD spake unto Moses and Aaron, Because ye believed me not, to sanctify me in the eyes of the children of Israel, therefore <u>**ye** shall not bring this congregation into the land which I have given them</u>.*"

- **Matthew 6:13**

"And <u>lead us not into temptation</u>, but deliver us from evil: For thine is the kingdom, and the power, and the glory, for ever. Amen."

One of the parts of the disciple's prayer was "*lead us not into temptation.*"

- **Matthew 26:41**

"Watch and pray, <u>that ye enter not into temptation</u>: the spirit indeed is willing, but the flesh is weak."

In the garden of Gethsemane, the Lord Jesus Christ told Peter, James, and John to watch and pray while He prayed. <u>However, three different times, these three disciples did not watch, but fell asleep.</u>

- **1 Corinthians 10:13**

"<u>There hath no temptation taken you</u> but such as is common to man: but God *is* faithful, who will not suffer you to be tempted above that ye are able; <u>but will with the temptation</u> also make a way to escape, that ye may be able to bear *it*."

<u>This verse is speaking about genuine Christians when they fall into different times of testings.</u>

- **1 Timothy 6:9**

"But <u>they that will be rich fall into temptation</u> and a snare, and *into* many foolish and hurtful lusts, which drown men in destruction and perdition."

<u>This verse speaks about those who have a will and a desire to be rich.</u> They will "*fall into temptation and a snare, and into many foolish and hurtful lusts.*"

James 1:3

"**Knowing this, that the trying of your faith worketh patience.**"

The trying of their faith would result in patience.

> **THE MEANING OF THE GREEK WORD, "DOKIMON."**
>
> The Greek Word for *"trying"* is DOKIMON. Some of the meanings of this Greek Word are:
> > *"1) the proving; 2) that by which something is tried or proved, a test."*

This word for *"trying"* is a different Greek Word. <u>It is a testing with the hope that a person will not fail.</u> It's like a person who is testing his parachute that he has folded for himself. He leaves the airplane, pulls the rip chord, and trusts that it will open properly.

> **TESTING BIBLE DOCTRINES**
>
> This verse speaks of a trying of their *"faith."* The Greek Word for *"faith"* here is TEN PISTEN. It has the Greek article with it. When the Word for "faith" has the Greek article, it always refers to the doctrines and the theology of the faith which is found in the Bible. These doctrines were challenged in James' day and they have been and are being and will continually be challenged in the days in which we live.

The result of such trials and tests of the doctrinal faith in James' day and in our day should work *"patience."*

> **THE MEANING OF THE GREEK WORD, "HUPOMONE."**
>
> The Greek Word for *"patience"* is HUPOMONE. Some of the meanings of that Greek Word are:
> > *"1) steadfastness, constancy, endurance; 1a) in the NT the characteristic of a man who is not swerved from his deliberate purpose and his loyalty to faith and piety by even the greatest trials and sufferings; 1b) patiently, and steadfastly; 2) a patient, steadfast waiting for; 3) a patient enduring, sustaining, perseverance; For Synonyms see entry 5861."*

Among many other things, this word means that even in the

greatest trials and sufferings, true Christians should not swerve from their deliberate purpose and his loyalty to their faith and piety, even during the greatest trials and adversities.

Verses On Patience

- **Romans 5:3**

"And not only *so*, but we glory in tribulations also: knowing that tribulation worketh patience;"

TRIBULATION CAN WORK PATIENCE

What genuine Christians really want tribulation? If they want patience, one way to achieve it is by means of tribulation. After repeated tribulation, true Christians will finally realize that they cannot stop it. They must be patient until it is over.

- **Romans 15:4**

"For whatsoever things were written aforetime were written for our learning, that we through patience and comfort of the scriptures might have hope."

The Scriptures give genuine Christians patience, comfort, and hope.

- **Romans 15:5**

"Now the God of patience and consolation grant you to be likeminded one toward another according to Christ Jesus:"

This is one of the titles of the God of the Bible. He is the God of patience. He can patiently wait for judgment of sinners.

- **2 Corinthians 6:4**

"But in all *things* approving ourselves as the ministers of God, in much patience, in afflictions, in necessities, in distresses,"

PAUL HAD MUCH PATIENCE

Paul commented about himself and the other apostles as being *"ministers of God in much patience."* True Christians today should merit that testimony as well.

- **Colossians 1:11**

"Strengthened with all might, according to his glorious power, unto all patience and longsuffering with joyfulness;"

By God's *"glorious power,"* genuine Christians today can be given *"patience"* in the face of anything that comes against them.

James 1:4

"But let patience have her perfect work, that ye may be perfect and entire, wanting nothing."

Patience must be allowed to bring forth her *"perfect"* work.

THE MEANING OF THE GREEK WORD, "TELEIOS."

The Greek Word for *"perfect"* is TELEIOS. Some of the meanings of that Greek Word are:

"1) brought to its end, finished; 2) wanting nothing necessary to completeness; 3) perfect; 4) that which is perfect; 4a) consummate human integrity and virtue; 4b) of men; 4b1) full grown, adult, of full age, mature"

If true Christians permit God the Holy Spirit Who indwells them to make them become full grown and mature in Christ, they will be entire and wanting nothing. This is God's desire for every genuine born-again Christian. This requires reading and obeying the Words of God daily.

Verses On Perfect

- **Romans 12:2**

"And be not conformed to this world: but be ye transformed by the renewing of your mind, that ye may prove what *is* that good, and acceptable, and perfect, will of God."

THE NEED TO FIND THE PERFECT WILL OF GOD

Non-world conformity and being transformed with a new mind by God the Holy Spirit (Who indwells within all true Christians) will cause them to test out and follow the perfect will of God.

- **2 Corinthians 12:9**

"And he said unto me, My grace is sufficient for thee: for <u>my strength is made perfect in weakness</u>. Most gladly therefore will I rather glory in my infirmities, that the power of Christ may rest upon me."

When Paul prayed three times for God to remove his unnamed thorn in his flesh, God didn't remove it; but gave Paul His marvelous grace which enabled him to be made perfect in weakness. <u>For this grace Paul was then able to glory in his infirmities because the power of Christ rested on him.</u>

- **Colossians 4:12**
"Epaphras, who is *one* of you, a servant of Christ, saluteth you, always labouring fervently for you in prayers, that ye may stand perfect and complete in all the will of God."

GOD'S PERFECT WILL IS FOUND IN GOD'S WORDS
The church at Colosse had many good Christian people. Epaphras was one of them. He was a servant of Christ who prayed for others in the Colossian church. He prayed that these genuine Christians stand perfect and complete in all the will of God. That *"will"* is to be found in God's Words. These Words should be constantly read and obeyed.

- **2 Timothy 3:16-17**
"All scripture is given by inspiration of God, and is profitable for doctrine, for reproof, for correction, for instruction in righteousness: That the man of God may be perfect, throughly furnished unto all good works."

The purpose for God's breathing out His Words in the Scripture was that the man of God and all other true Christians might be perfect, being thoroughly furnished with all good works.

- **Hebrews 13:21**
"Make you perfect in every good work to do his will, working in you that which is wellpleasing in his sight, through Jesus Christ; to whom *be* glory for ever and ever. Amen."

Paul's prayer in this verse was that the God of peace might make his readers perfect in every good work to do His will.

- **1 Peter 5:10**
"But the God of all grace, who hath called us unto his eternal glory by Christ Jesus, after that ye have suffered a while, make you perfect, stablish, strengthen, settle *you*."

MADE PERFECT AND MATURE AFTER SUFFERING
The Apostle Peter prayed that his readers might be made *"perfect"* after they have suffered for a while. Suffering by genuine Christians, if properly faced and understood can lead to their maturity.

James 1:5

"If any of you lack wisdom, let him ask of God, that giveth to all men liberally, and upbraideth not; and it shall be given him."

In this verse, James explains to his readers how God's wisdom can be obtained.

James–Preaching Verse By Verse

THE MEANING OF THE GREEK WORD, "SOPHIA."

The Greek Word for "*wisdom*" is SOPHIA. Some of the meanings of that Greek Word are:

"*1) wisdom, broad and full of intelligence; used of the knowledge of very diverse matters; 1a) the wisdom which belongs to men 1a1) spec. the varied knowledge of things human and divine, acquired by acuteness and experience, and summed up in maxims and proverbs; 1a2) the science and learning; 1a3) the act of interpreting dreams and always giving the sagest advice; 1a4) the intelligence evinced in discovering the meaning of some mysterious number or vision; 1a5) skill in the management of affairs; 1a6) devout and proper prudence in intercourse with men not disciples of Christ, skill and discretion in imparting Christian truth; 1a7) the knowledge and practice of the requisites for godly and upright living; 1b) supreme intelligence, such as belongs to God; 1b1) to Christ; 1b2) the wisdom of God as evinced in forming and executing counsels in the formation and government of the world and the scriptures.*"

THE MEANING OF THE GREEK WORD, "AITEO."

To receive God's wisdom, the true Christians must "*ask*" it from God. The Greek Word for "*ask*" is AITEO. Some of the meanings of that Greek Word are:

"*1) to ask, beg, call for, crave, desire, require.*"

This word is not the sense of simply asking a question. It is a begging and a craving for God's wisdom. If asked properly by genuine Christians, God will honor that request liberally. God does not upbraid in this area of His wisdom.

> **THE MEANING OF THE GREEK WORD, "ONEIDIZO."**
> The Greek Word for "up*braid*" is ONEIDIZO. Some of the meanings of that Greek Word are:
> *"1) to reproach, upbraid, revile; 1a) of deserved reproach; 1b) of undeserved reproach, to revile; 1c) to upbraid, cast (favours received) in one's teeth."*

Notice what God does not do when genuine Christians ask Him for His wisdom. He does not revile, reproach, or scold them.

God grants this request for His wisdom when it is properly requested by true Christians who are walking in the will of God.

Verses On Wisdom

- **1 Corinthians 1:20**

"Where *is* the wise? where *is* the scribe? where *is* the disputer of this world? hath not God made foolish the wisdom of this world?"

> **GOD CALLS FOOLISH THE WISDOM OF THIS WORLD**
> There is a false wisdom called in this verse as *"the wisdom of the world."* God has made foolish this kind of wisdom. As far as God is concerned, this worldly wisdom includes all that which is taught in the educational institutions of our world. That which is taught there is foolish when compared with God's wisdom.

- **1 Corinthians 1:21**

"For after that in the wisdom of God the world by wisdom knew not God, it pleased God by the foolishness of preaching to save them that believe."

> **GOD USES THE "FOOLISHNESS" OF PREACHING**
> When the wicked world, by wisdom knew not God, He used the preaching about His Son to save the souls of those who sincerely believe in Him.

- **1 Corinthians 1:30**

"But of him are ye in Christ Jesus, who of God is made unto us wisdom, and righteousness, and sanctification, and redemption:"

> **CHRIST IS MADE WISDOM TO TRUE CHRISTIANS**
> For those who are true Christians God the Father made the Lord Jesus Christ wisdom unto them.

James–Preaching Verse By Verse

- **1 Corinthians 2:4-6**

"And my speech and my preaching *was* <u>not with enticing words of man's wisdom</u>, but in demonstration of the Spirit and of power: That <u>your faith should not stand in the wisdom of men</u>, but in the power of God. Howbeit we speak wisdom among them that are perfect: yet <u>not the wisdom of this world</u>, nor of the princes of this world, that come to nought:"

<u>Paul urged the Christians at Corinth to stand in God's wisdom rather than in the worldly wisdom of men.</u>

- **1 Corinthians 3:19**

"For <u>the wisdom of this world</u> is foolishness with God. For it is written, He taketh the wise in their own craftiness."

GOD CONSIDERS WORLDLY WISDOM FOOLISHNESS

Compared to God's wisdom, the wisdom originating in the world is foolishness when compared to the omniscient wisdom of God. Unfortunately, those in the academic world who are not genuine Christians would dispute this strongly though in error.

I remember going into the book stacks of the library at the University of Michigan. If I remember correctly, there are two or three million books in that library. These books contain the wisdom of this world.

- **Colossians 2:3**

"<u>In whom are hid all the treasures of wisdom</u> and knowledge." This is referring to the Lord Jesus Christ. He has the omniscient treasures of wisdom that only God the Son could have.

- **Colossians 3:16**

"<u>Let the word of Christ dwell in you richly in all wisdom</u>; teaching and admonishing one another in psalms and hymns and spiritual songs, singing with grace in your hearts to the Lord."

<u>The Words of God should dwell richly in every born-again true Christian, in all wisdom. This can only be done by their reading and heeding those Words daily.</u>

- **Colossians 4:5**

"<u>Walk in wisdom</u> toward them that are without, redeeming the time."

CHRISTIANS MUST WALK IN GOD'S WISDOM

Genuine Christians must walk in God's wisdom as they live before the unsaved world. They must redeem and make good use of every minute of their time.

- **James 3:14-15**

"But if ye have bitter envying and strife in your hearts, glory not, and lie not against the truth. <u>This wisdom descendeth not from above</u>, but *is* earthly, sensual, devilish."

God tells us here that there is a wisdom that is earthly, sensual, and devilish. True Christians should agree with God on this, despite the world's denial of it.

Verses On Upbraiding

- **Matthew 11:20**

"<u>Then began he to upbraid the cities</u> wherein most of his mighty works were done, <u>because they repented not</u>:"

CHRIST UPBRAIDED NON-REPENTANT CITIES

The Lord Jesus Christ upbraided and scolded the cities that refused to repent even after they saw His mighty miraculous miracles.

- **Mark 16:14**

"Afterward <u>he appeared unto the eleven as they sat at meat, and upbraided them with their unbelief and hardness of heart</u>, because they believed not them which had seen him after he was risen."

THE APOSTLES DOUBTED CHRIST'S RESURRECTION

After His bodily resurrection, the Lord Jesus Christ appeared unto His eleven remaining apostles. They did not believe he was going to rise bodily from the dead after being crucified. Because of his unbelief, Peter went back to fishing, taking six other apostles with him (John 21:2). Jesus scolded them for their hardness of heart and for going back to fishing for fish.

James 1:6

"But let him ask in faith, nothing wavering. For he that wavereth is like a wave of the sea driven with the wind and tossed."

<u>Prayer must be made to the Lord by genuine Christians without any wavering.</u>

- **Hebrews 10:23**

"Let us hold fast the profession of *our* faith <u>without wavering</u>; (for he *is* faithful that promised;)"

James–Preaching Verse By Verse

> **OUR DOCTRINAL FAITH MUST BE HELD FAST**
> There must be a steadiness in prayer without changing from one thing and then another. The profession of our Bible's faith must be strong and unchanging.

Verses On Unstable Seas

- **Isaiah 57:20**

"But the wicked *are* like the troubled sea, when it cannot rest, whose waters cast up mire and dirt."

The wicked are like the back and forth waves of the sea which have no rest.

- **Matthew 14:24**

"But the ship was now in the midst of the sea, tossed with waves: for the wind was contrary."

Ships in the sea are tossed with the waves.

- **Acts 27:18**

"And we being exceedingly tossed with a tempest, the next *day* they lightened the ship;"

Paul's ship was tossed by the storm when he was going to Rome.

- **Ephesians 4:14**

"That we *henceforth* be no more children, tossed to and fro, and carried about with every wind of doctrine, by the sleight of men, *and* cunning craftiness, whereby they lie in wait to deceive;"

> **THE MEANING OF THE GREEK WORD, "RIPIZO."**
>
> The Greek Word for *"tossed"* is RIPIZO. Some of the meanings of this Greek Word are:
>
> > *"1) to raise a breeze, put air in motion, whether for the sake of kindling a fire or cooling one's self; 1a) to blow up a fire; 1b) to fan, i.e. cool with a fan; 2) to toss to and fro, to agitate; 2a) of the wind 2b) of persons whose mind wavers in uncertainty between hope and fear, between doing and not doing a thing."*

The doctrine of genuine Christians must be stable and firm. It should not change with every new generation or even every time even professed fundamentalists want to modify it or substitute for it some apostate and heretical teachings.

James 1:7

"For let not that man think that he shall receive any thing of the Lord."

True Christians must follow the provisions of verses five and six. Without adhering to these verses, God will not answer their prayers.

> **THE FORM FOR "THINK" MEANS "STOP THINKING"**
>
> The Greek Word for the verb, "think," is in the Greek present tense. It is a negative prohibition. As such, it means stop an action already in process.

James told his readers to stop thinking that they will receive anything from the Lord. Apparently these readers were thinking wrongly about this prayer for God's wisdom.

James 1:8

"A double minded man is unstable in all his ways."

The Greek Word used here indicates that James is speaking of a male.

> **THE MEANING OF THE GREEK WORD, "DIPSUCHOS."**
>
> The Greek Word for *"double minded"* is DIPSUCHOS. Some of the meanings of this Greek Word are:
>
> > *"1) double minded; 1a) wavering, uncertain, doubting; 1b) divided in interest."*

He has literally two souls or a double heart. He is a man who is wavering uncertain, and divided in his interests.

> **MEANING OF THE GREEK WORD, "AKATASTOTOS."**
>
> Not only so, but he is *"unstable"* in all his ways. The Greek Word for that is AKATASTOTOS. Some of the meanings of that Greek Word are:
>
> > *"1) unstable, inconstant, restless."*
>
> James is speaking of a two-faced and unstable man who is trying to lead his wife and family in proper ways. In that condition, his leadership will be in false and erroneous ways.

James–Preaching Verse By Verse

Verses On Double Hearts Or Double Minds
- **1 Chronicles 12:33**

"Of Zebulun, such as went forth to battle, expert in war, with all instruments of war, fifty thousand, which could keep rank: *they were* not of double heart."

Those followers of Zebulun were good soldiers. They were not double hearted.

- **Psalms 12:2**

"They speak vanity every one with his neighbour: *with* flattering lips *and* with a double heart do they speak."

DOUBLE-HEARTEDNESS IS EXPOSED
David exposed those in his day who spoke with a double heart rather than truly and honestly.

- **James 4:8**

"Draw nigh to God, and he will draw nigh to you. Cleanse *your* hands, *ye* sinners; and purify *your* hearts, *ye* double minded."

James again calls some of his readers "*double minded*" with two souls and two minds.

- **Luke 16:13**

"No servant can serve two masters: for either he will hate the one, and love the other; or else he will hold to the one, and despise the other. Ye cannot serve God and mammon."

Trying to serve two masters is also evidence of double mindedness.

1 John 2:16-17

"For all that *is* in the world, the lust of the flesh, and the lust of the eyes, and the pride of life, is not of the Father, but is of the world. And the world passeth away, and the lust thereof: but he that doeth the will of God abideth for ever."

THE WORLD'S AND GOD'S WILL TOTALLY DIFFERENT
There is a great difference between the world and the will of God. Trying to serve both at the same time is being double minded.

Verses On Being Unstable
- **Genesis 49:3-4**

"Reuben, thou *art* my firstborn, my might, and the beginning of my strength, the excellency of dignity, and the excellency of power: Unstable as water, thou shalt not excel; because thou wentest up to thy father's bed; then defiledst thou *it*: he went up to my couch."

Israel's firstborn son, Reuben, was not a strong man. He fluctuated

between right and wrong. He was as unstable as water. He lost his birthright because of his sins.
- **2 Peter 2:14**
"Having eyes full of adultery, and that cannot cease from sin; beguiling unstable souls: an heart they have exercised with covetous practices; cursed children:"

The Apostle Peter wrote about covetous and unstable souls.
- **2 Peter 3:16**
"As also in all *his* epistles, speaking in them of these things; in which are some things hard to be understood, which they that are unlearned and unstable wrest, as *they do* also the other scriptures, unto their own destruction."

THE INSTABILITY OF MODERN BIBLE VERSIONS

One of the dangerous things that unstable people do is to wrest or change and twist the Words of God. Evidence of their wresting is found in the modern Bible translations. Not only do the editors use the false Hebrew, Aramaic, and Greek Words, but they also twist even those false words by either adding, subtracting, or changing in other ways God's Words. They are unstable translators and their translations are unstable as well.

James 1:9

"Let the brother of low degree rejoice in that he is exalted:"

If true Christians are of low degree by the standards of this world, they should rejoice when the Lord Jesus Christ exalts them by giving them eternal life when they receive Him as their Saviour. God can exalt people even if they are considered of low degree by their peers.

James 1:10

"But the rich, in that he is made low: because as the flower of the grass he shall pass away."

REJOICING EVEN WHEN MADE LOW

Those genuine Christians who are rich should rejoice when God makes them low. By being made low, it is hoped that those who are rich will trust in the living God rather than in all their riches.

Those who are rich today might be poor tomorrow. The printing

James–Preaching Verse By Verse 17

of billions of dollars of paper money by our government has made former rich people much less rich. Depending what year you are talking about, what used to be one dollar, is now only 40 or 50 cents. If devaluation continues, it won't be long before it is down to 10 cents or less.

Verses On Things Being Changed And Passing Away
- **Isaiah 2:17**

"And <u>the loftiness of man shall be bowed down</u>, and <u>the haughtiness of men shall be made low</u>: and the LORD alone shall be exalted in that day."

In His own time, God is able to make high things low.

- **Isaiah 40:4**

"Every valley shall be exalted, and <u>every mountain and hill shall be made low</u>: and the crooked shall be made straight, and the rough places plain:"

One day, every mountain and hill shall be made low. They shall be flattened out. <u>The whole typography of this earth will be changed when the Lord Jesus rules and reigns for one thousand years in the millennium</u>.

- **Isaiah 40:6-8**

"The voice said, Cry. And he said, What shall I cry? All flesh *is* grass, and all the goodliness thereof *is* as the flower of the field: <u>The grass withereth, the flower fadeth</u>: because the spirit of the LORD bloweth upon it: surely the people *is* grass. The grass withereth, the flower fadeth: but the word of our God shall stand for ever."

In spite of the grass and flowers fading and passing away, <u>God's Words will remain forever</u>.

- **1 Peter 1:24**

"For all flesh *is* as grass, and all the glory of man as the flower of grass. The grass withereth, and the flower thereof falleth away:"

ADAM'S SIN BROUGHT PHYSICAL DEATH TO ALL

Because of the sin of Adam, the entire human race faces physical death. The picture is that of withering grace and falling flowers. When this happens, all the person's riches remain behind. Only the spirit and soul of the true Christians will abide forever.

- **Psalms 144:4**

"Man is like to vanity: <u>his days *are* as a shadow that passeth away</u>."

Man's days are like a shadow that passes away when the sun goes down.

- **Isaiah 29:5**

"Moreover the multitude of thy strangers shall be like small dust, and the multitude of the terrible ones *shall be* as chaff that passeth away: yea, it shall be at an instant suddenly."

Chaff also passes away as the wind comes and scatters it all around.

- **Jeremiah 13:24**

"Therefore will I scatter them as the stubble that passeth away by the wind of the wilderness."

Stubble is very small. When the wind comes, it blows away.

- **Hosea 13:3**

"Therefore they shall be as the morning cloud, and as the early dew that passeth away, as the chaff *that* is driven with the whirlwind out of the floor, and as the smoke out of the chimney."

All these things pass away as they are driven with the wind.

- **Matthew 24:35**

"Heaven and earth shall pass away, but my words shall not pass away."

HEBREW & GREEK BIBLE WORDS ARE PRESERVED

The Lord Jesus Christ said that even the present heaven and earth shall pass away. Only the Words of the Lord Jesus Christ found in the Hebrew, Aramaic, and Greek will never pass away. Those Words, given by the Lord Jesus Christ to God the Holy Spirit and then passed on to the Bible writers, have been, are being, and will continue to be preserved forever. These are the Words that underlie the King James Bible and have been accurately translated into English.

- **1 Corinthians 7:31**

"And they that use this world, as not abusing *it*: for the fashion of this world passeth away."

All the things of this world will one day pass away.

- **2 Peter 3:10**

"But the day of the Lord will come as a thief in the night; in the which the heavens shall pass away with a great noise, and the elements shall melt with fervent heat, the earth also and the works that are therein shall be burned up."

ONE DAY THE HEAVENS WILL PASS AWAY

Though we don't know when this is going to take place, one day the heavens will pass away.

- 1 John 2:17

"And the world passeth away, and the lust thereof: but he that doeth the will of God abideth for ever."

This old world will also one day pass away.

James 1:11

"For the sun is no sooner risen with a burning heat, but it withereth the grass, and the flower thereof falleth, and the grace of the fashion of it perisheth: so also shall the rich man fade away in his ways."

Once again, James makes clear that the rich man will fade away in his ways just as grass withers and flowers fail.

Things Of Earth That Fail

- Psalms 37:2

"For they shall soon be cut down like the grass, and wither as the green herb."

These earthly plants do not remain for very long. They are cut down and wither.

- Isaiah 19:7

"The paper reeds by the brooks, by the mouth of the brooks, and every thing sown by the brooks, shall wither, be driven away, and be no *more*."

Everything that grows by the brooks shall be driven away and be no more.

- Isaiah 64:6

"But we are all as an unclean *thing*, and all our righteousnesses *are* as filthy rags; and we all do fade as a leaf; and our iniquities, like the wind, have taken us away."

INIQUITIES REMOVE PEOPLE FROM GOD'S WILL

In this verse, people fade as a leaf and their iniquities have taken them away from the fellowship of the Lord.

James 1:12

"Blessed is the man that endureth temptation: for when he is tried, he shall receive the crown of life, which the Lord hath promised to them that love him."

James uses the Greek Word for a male here. He says that he is blessed or happy if he endures temptations.

> **THE MEANING OF THE GREEK WORD, "HUPOMENO."**
> The Greek Word for "*endure*" is HUPOMENO. Some of the meanings of that Greek Word are:
>> "*1) to remain; 1a) to tarry behind; 2) to remain i.e. abide, not recede or flee; 2a) to preserve: under misfortunes and trials to hold fast to one's faith in Christ; 2b) to endure*, bear bravely and calmly: ill treatments."

The trials and tests that come upon this man must be endured in order for him to remain blessed or happy during them. He must bear bravely and calmly all ill treatments. If this is his response to the trials, he will receive a crown of life which the Lord has promised to those who love Him. This is one of the five crowns mentioned in the New Testament. He will receive this crown after he is "*tried*."

> **THE MEANING OF THE GREEK WORD, "DOKIMOS."**
> This Greek Word for "*tried*" is DOKIMOS. Some of the meanings of that Greek Word are:
>> "*1) accepted, particularly of coins and money; 2) accepted, pleasing, acceptable.*"
>
> If the enduring is accepted and pleasing to the Lord, the man will receive the Crown of life.

The Five New Testament Crowns

Here are the five crowns mentioned in the New Testament:

1. **The Crown Of Righteousness**
    2 Timothy 4:8 "*Henceforth there is laid up for me <u>a crown of righteousness</u>, which the Lord, the righteous judge, shall give me at that day: and not to me only, but unto all them also that love his appearing.*"

2. **The Crown Of Glory**
    1 Peter 5:4 "*And when the chief Shepherd shall appear, ye shall receive <u>a crown of glory</u> that fadeth not away.*"

3. **The Incorruptible Crown**
    1 Corinthians 9:25 And every man that striveth for the mastery is temperate in all things. Now they do it to obtain a corruptible crown; but we <u>an incorruptible</u>.

James–Preaching Verse By Verse

4. The Crown of Rejoicing

1 Thessalonians 2:19 *"For what is our hope, or joy, or <u>crown of rejoicing</u>? Are not even ye in the presence of our Lord Jesus Christ at his coming?"*

5. The Crown of Life

James 1:12 *"Blessed is the man that endureth temptation: for when he is tried, he shall receive <u>the crown of life</u>, which the Lord hath promised to them that love him."*

Revelation 2:10 *"Fear none of those things which thou shalt suffer: behold, the devil shall cast some of you into prison, that ye may be tried; and ye shall have tribulation ten days: be thou faithful unto death, and I will give thee <u>a crown of life</u>."*

Verses On Enduring

- **2 Timothy 2:3**

"Thou therefore <u>endure hardness</u>, as a good soldier of Jesus Christ."

ENDURE HARDNESS LIKE GOOD SOLDIERS

Paul told Pastor Timothy to endure hardness. He was to be victorious over any difficulties he might have to go through.

- **2 Timothy 4:5**

"But watch thou in all things, <u>endure afflictions</u>, do the work of an evangelist, make full proof of thy ministry."

<u>Paul also told Pastor Timothy to watch in all things and endure afflictions.</u>

- **Hebrews 12:7**

"<u>If ye endure chastening</u>, God dealeth with you as with sons; for what son is he whom the father chasteneth not?"

PROPER CHASTENING IS OFTEN NECESSARY

Genuine Christians are chastened by God when it is needed. If they endure that Divine chastening, God deals with them as sons and daughters. Fathers, if they are Biblical, chasten their children when it is needed. It is sad that many parents do not properly discipline their children.

- **James 5:10-11**

"Take, my brethren, the prophets, who have spoken in the name of the Lord, for an example of suffering affliction, and of patience. Behold, we count them happy which endure. Ye have heard of the patience of Job, and have seen the end of the Lord; that the Lord is very pitiful, and of tender mercy."

> **ENDURE AFFLICTIONS HAPPILY**
> Though some true Christians who receive suffering and affliction do not properly endure them, those who do so properly are happy in the Lord.

- **1 Corinthians 10:13**

"There hath no temptation taken you but such as is common to man: but God *is* faithful, who will not suffer you to be tempted above that ye are able; but will with the temptation also make a way to escape, that ye may be able to bear *it*."

God can help genuine Christians when afflicted to make a way to escape that they might be able to endure or bear it.

James 1:13

"Let no man say when he is tempted, I am tempted of God: for God cannot be tempted with evil, neither tempteth he any man:"

> **CHRISTIANS' TEMPTATIONS ARE NOT FROM GOD**
> "Let no man say" is a prohibition in the Greek present tense. As such, it means to stop an action already in progress. James is saying to his readers, *"Stop saying when true Christians are tempted that they are tempted by God."* Apparently many of James' readers were saying this. They should not say this. God does not tempt any person to do evil.

Verses On Temptation

- **Matthew 4:1-2**

"Then was Jesus led up of the Spirit into the wilderness to be tempted of the devil. Being forty days tempted of the devil. And in those days he did eat nothing: and when they were ended, he afterward hungered."

James–Preaching Verse By Verse

> **SATAN FAILED IN HIS TEMPTATION OF CHRIST**
> Satan tempted and tested the Lord Jesus Christ when He was in the wilderness for forty days, but he failed miserably in his efforts. On the other hand, Adam and Eve failed when Satan tempted them in the Garden of Eden.

- **1 Corinthians 10:13**

"There hath no temptation taken you but such as is common to man: but <u>God *is* faithful, who will not suffer you to be tempted above that ye are able</u>; but will with the temptation also make a way to escape, that ye may be able to bear *it*."

> **GOD'S WAY TO ESCAPE IN TEMPTATIONS**
> When trials and temptations come to genuine Christians, God has promised to make a way to escape so they may be able to bear it.

- **1 Thessalonians 3:5**

"For this cause, when I could no longer forbear, I sent to know your faith, <u>lest by some means the tempter have tempted</u> you, and our labour be in vain."

> **SATAN'S DESIRE TO TEMPT CHURCHES**
> Paul was concerned that Satan, the tempter, might tempt and test this church. If they fail in such temptations, his labor would be in vain.

- **Galatians 6:1**

"Brethren, if a man be overtaken in a fault, ye which are spiritual, restore such an one in the spirit of meekness; <u>considering thyself, lest thou also be tempted</u>."

<u>If true Christians try to help other Christians who have been overtaken in some fault, they must be very careful lest they also be tempted to sin in the same way. They are to be very careful in all of this.</u>

James 1:14

"But every man is tempted, when he is drawn away of his own lust, and enticed."

> **THE MEANING OF THE GREEK WORD, "PEIRAZO."**
> The Greek Word for "*tempted*" is PEIRAZO. Some of the meanings of that Greek Word are:
> *"1) to try whether a thing can be done;*

> *1a) to attempt, endeavour; 2) to try, make trial of, test: for the purpose of ascertaining his quantity, or what he thinks, or how he will behave himself; 2a) in a good sense; 2b) in a bad sense, to test one maliciously, craftily to put to the proof his feelings or judgments; 2c) to try or test one's faith, virtue, character, by enticement to sin; 2c1) to solicit to sin, to tempt; 1c1a) of the temptations of the devil; 2d) after the OT usage; 2d1) of God: to inflict evils upon one in order to prove his character and the steadfastness of his faith 2d2) men are said to tempt God by exhibitions of distrust, as though they wished to try whether he is not justly distrusted; 2d3) by impious or wicked conduct to test God's justice and patience, and to challenge him, as it were to give proof of his perfections."*

As you can see, this Greek Word has many senses. People are tempted when they are drawn away by their own lust and enticed.

THE MEANING OF THE GREEK WORD, "EXELKO."

The Greek Word for "*drawn away*" is EXELKO. Some of the meanings of that Greek Word are:

> "*1) to draw out; 2) metaph. lure forth: in hunting and fishing as game is lured.*"

The sense is being lured like fish are lured to take the bait. The flesh is very clever and skilled in doing this, even in the lives of genuine Christians.

The Greek Word for "*lusts*" is EPITHUMIA. Some of the meanings of that Greek Word are:

> "*1) desire, craving, longing, desire for what is forbidden, lust. For Synonyms see entry 5845.*"

These lusts are powerful allures to the flesh to do that which is forbidden by the Words of God.

James–Preaching Verse By Verse

THE MEANING OF THE GREEK WORD, "DELEAZO."
The Greek Word for *"enticed"* is DELEAZO. Some of the meanings of that Greek Word are:
> *"1) to bait, catch by a bait; 2) metaph. to beguile by banishments, allure, entice, deceive."*

The evil flesh leads people away to be beguiled and allured by clever means.

Verses On Being Drawn Away
- **Deuteronomy 30:17**

"But if thine heart turn away, so that thou wilt not hear, but shalt be drawn away, and worship other gods, and serve them;"

Many Jews in the Old Testament were drawn away into idolatry.

- **Joshua 8:16**

"And all the people that *were* in Ai were called together to pursue after them: and they pursued after Joshua, and were drawn away from the city."

The tactic of having the enemy drawn away was successfully used by Joshua in the battle for Ai.

Verses On Lust
- **Proverbs 6:24**

"To keep thee from the evil woman, from the flattery of the tongue of a strange woman. Lust not after her beauty in thine heart; neither let her take thee with her eyelids."

LUST BY MEN AND WOMEN SHOULD NOT EXIST
Men should not lust after beautiful women. Nor should women lust after the good looks of men.

- **Matthew 5:28**

"But I say unto you, That whosoever looketh on a woman to lust after her hath committed adultery with her already in his heart."

LOOKING WITH HEART LUST IS ADULTERY
The Lord Jesus Christ defined adultery as not simply for a man to look on a woman, but to look on her with lust in his heart.

- **Galatians 5:16**

"*This* I say then, Walk in the Spirit, and ye shall not fulfil the lust of the flesh."

26 James–Preaching Verse By Verse

> **CHRISTIANS' TWO NATURES–FLESH & HOLY SPIRIT**
> Genuine Christians have two natures, the flesh and God the Holy Spirit. They must walk in the power of the Holy Spirit so as not to walk in the power of their flesh.

- **1 Thessalonians 4:5**
"<u>Not in the lust of concupiscence</u>, even as the Gentiles which know not God:"

> **CHRISTIANS SHOULD DIFFER FROM UNBELIEVERS**
> True Christians must not live their lives in the lust of concupiscence as the unbelievers do. There should be a difference between real Christians and those who are not.

- **1 John 2:16**
"For all that *is* in the world, <u>the lust of the flesh, and the lust of the eyes</u>, and the pride of life, is not of the Father, but is of the world. And <u>the world passeth away, and the lust thereof</u>: but he that doeth the will of God abideth for ever."

> **TRUE CHRISTIANS WILL ABIDE FOREVER**
> The lust of the flesh and of the eyes will pass away, but the genuine Christian who does the will of God will abide forever.

Verses On Entice

- **Deuteronomy 13:6**
"If thy brother, the son of thy mother, or thy son, or thy daughter, or the wife of thy bosom, or thy friend, which *is* as thine own soul, <u>entice thee secretly, saying, Let us go and serve other gods</u>, which thou hast not known, thou, nor thy fathers;"

Here is a case of secret enticement. It is just as dangerous and wrong as if it were open enticement.

- **Judges 14:15**
"And it came to pass on the seventh day, that they said unto Samson's wife, <u>Entice thy husband, that he may declare unto us the riddle</u>, lest we burn thee and thy father's house with fire: have ye called us to take that we have? *is it* not *so*?"

When the Philistines couldn't find out Samson's strength, they said to his wife, Delilah, "*entice thy husband*" to find out the source of his strength.

- **2 Chronicles 18:19**
"And the LORD said, <u>Who shall entice Ahab king of Israel, that he may go up and fall at Ramothgilead</u>? And one spake saying after this manner, and another saying after that manner."

James–Preaching Verse By Verse

God wanted someone to entice wicked Ahab to go to Ramothgilead and die there. This was a proper use of enticement by the Lord Himself.

- **Proverbs 1:10**

"My son, if sinners entice thee, consent thou not."

This is a verse that my wife's Grandmother Barker used to tell to her young son who was in the military.

James 1:15

"Then when lust hath conceived, it bringeth forth sin: and sin, when it is finished, bringeth forth death."

Lust once conceived, brings forth sin and sin brings forth death.

MEANING OF THE GREEK WORD, "SULLAMBANO."

The Greek Word for *"conceived"* is SULLAMBANO. Some of the meanings of that Greek Word are:

"1) to seize, take: one as prisoner; 2) to conceive, of a woman; 2a) metaph. of lust whose impulses a man indulges; 3) to seize for one's self; 3a) in a hostile sense, to make (one a permanent) prisoner; 4) to take hold together with one, to assist, help, to succour."

Lust conceives sin which is evil like a mother conceives a child which is good. Because of Adam's sin all will end up in death, even this little baby one day.

Verses On Death

- **Romans 6:16**

"Know ye not, that to whom ye yield yourselves servants to obey, his servants ye are to whom ye obey; whether of sin unto death, or of obedience unto righteousness?"

Sin leads to death. It should not be engaged in by any genuine Christians.

Paul said to the Christians in Rome,

- **Romans 6:21**

"What fruit had ye then in those things whereof ye are now ashamed? for the end of those things *is* death."

There is no good fruit in the practice of sin. There is only evil fruit.

- **Romans 6:23**

"For the wages of sin *is* death; but the gift of God *is* eternal life through Jesus Christ our Lord."

> **THE LAKE OF FIRE FOR CHRIST-REJECTERS**
> The wages of sin leads to an eternal death in the Lake of Fire for those who have rejected the Lord Jesus Christ as their Saviour.

- **Romans 7:5**

"For when we were in the flesh, the motions of sins, which were by the law, did work in our members to bring forth fruit unto death."

Repeatedly, God says that sin leads to death. That's the end of it all.

Romans 8:6

"For to be carnally minded is death; but to be spiritually minded is life and peace."

> **SPIRITUAL MINDEDNESS BRINGS LIFE AND PEACE**
> Being carnally minded is desiring things of our flesh. True Christians are indwelt by God the Holy Spirit. Yielding to Him brings life and peace.

James 1:16

"Do not err, my beloved brethren."

The verb "*err*" is in the Greek present tense. It is a prohibition which means to stop an action already in progress. It means "*stop erring*"!

> **THE MEANING OF THE GREEK WORD, "PLANAO."**
> The Greek Word for "*err*" is PLANAO. Some of the meanings of that Greek Word are:
>
> *"1) to cause to stray, to lead astray, lead aside from the right way; 1a) to go astray, wander, roam about; 2) metaph.; 2a) to lead away from the truth, to lead into error, to deceive; 2b) to be led into error; 2c) to be led aside from the path of virtue, to go astray, sin; 2d) to sever or fall away from the truth; 2d1) of heretics; 2e) to be led away into error and sin."*

Verses On Erring

- **Psalms 95:10**

"Forty years long was I grieved with *this* generation, and said, It is a people that do err in their heart, and they have not known my ways:"

IN THE WILDERNESS ISRAEL ERRED IN HEART

This verse shows the heart of God regarding His people, Israel. He was grieved because they erred in their hearts and have not known His ways.

- Isaiah 9:16

"For the leaders of this people cause *them* to err; and *they that are* led of them *are* destroyed."

CHURCH LEADERS OFTEN CAUSE PEOPLE TO ERR

This is very true of many church leaders as well. When they err from the truth, their church followers often follow them in their errors.

- Matthew 22:29

"Jesus answered and said unto them, Ye do err, not knowing the scriptures, nor the power of God."
The Lord Jesus Christ was talking to His disciples and the Pharisees. These Pharisees thought they knew everything. The Lord Jesus told them that they erred not knowing either the Scriptures or the power of God.

- Hebrews 3:10

"Wherefore I was grieved with that generation, and said, They do alway err in *their* heart; and they have not known my ways."
Israel erred against the Lord in their heart. They did not know His ways. This grieved the Lord greatly.

- James 5:19-20

"Brethren, if any of you do err from the truth, and one convert him; Let him know, that he which converteth the sinner from the error of his way shall save a soul from death, and shall hide a multitude of sins."

BRETHREN SOMETIMES ERR FROM THE TRUTH

This verse shows that even the brethren might err from the truth. They must not only know the Words of God, but they must follow them completely.

James 1:17

"Every good gift and every perfect gift is from above, and cometh down from the Father of lights, with whom is no variableness, neither shadow of turning."

Every good and perfect gift comes from God Himself. He is called here *"the Father of Lights."* He is without any darkness or sin at all. Notice also one of His attributes. He has no *"variableness, neither shadow of turning."* He does not change. He is unchangeable.

> **MEANING OF THE GREEK WORD, "PARALLAGAY."**
> The Greek Word for *"variableness"* is PARALLAGAY. Some of the meanings of that Greek Word are:
> *"1) variation, change"*
> The God of the Bible does not change His ways, His doctrines, or His procedures. He has *"no variableness."* We can depend on Him and His Words that He will do as He has promised.

Verses On Change
- Proverbs 24:21

"My son, fear thou the LORD and the king: *and* meddle not with them that are given to change:"

> **DON'T MEDDLE WITH PEOPLE WHO CHANGE**
> Our God does not change. The Scriptures do not change. Truth does not change. God commands us to keep away from people who are given to change. Don't meddle with them. They will lead you astray from God's Words and will.

- Jeremiah 2:36

"Why gaddest thou about so much to change thy way? thou also shalt be ashamed of Egypt, as thou wast ashamed of Assyria."
Jeremiah the prophet condemned Israel for changing their ways against the ways of God.
- Malachi 3:6

"For I am the LORD, I change not; therefore ye sons of Jacob are not consumed."
The God of the Bible does not change. Because He doesn't change, he is merciful to sinful Israel.

James 1:18
"Of his own will begat he us with the word of truth, that we should be a kind of firstfruits of his creatures."

> **CHRISTIANS ARE GOD'S FIRSTFRUITS**
> By His own will God begat those who truly trust His Son, the Lord Jesus Christ, as their Saviour. They heard about this Saviour from the Words of God. Being born-

James–Preaching Verse By Verse

again, these genuine Christians become *"a kind of firstfruits of His creatures."* The word *"begat"* refers to being born. In this case it is being spiritually born *"of His own will."*

Verses On Being Born Of God

- **John 1:10-13**

"He was in the world, and the world was made by him, and the world knew him not. He came unto his own, and his own received him not. But <u>as many as received him, to them gave he power to become the sons of God</u>, *even* to them that believe on his name: <u>Which were born</u>, not of blood, nor of the will of the flesh, nor of the will of man, but <u>of God</u>."

GENUINE CHRISTIANS ARE BORN OF GOD

When people become genuine Christians, they are born by God. This is a new spiritual birth.

- **John 3:3**

"Jesus answered and said unto him, Verily, verily, I say unto thee, <u>Except a man be born again, he cannot see the kingdom of God</u>."

Those are the words of the Lord Jesus Christ. <u>"Born-again" is a good and Scriptural term to use.</u>

- **John 3:7**

"Marvel not that I said unto thee, <u>Ye must be born again</u>."

This is what the Lord Jesus Christ told Nicodemus. He applied it to him (*"thou"*) as well as to all the other Pharisees (*"ye"*).

- **1 Peter 1:23**

"<u>Being born again</u>, not of corruptible seed, but of incorruptible, <u>by the word of God</u>, which liveth and abideth for ever."

<u>The source that tells how to be born-again is the Words of God.</u>

- **1 John 5:1**

"<u>Whosoever believeth that Jesus is the Christ is born of God</u>: and every one that loveth him that begat loveth him also that is begotten of him."

<u>People are born of God who genuinely trust the Lord Jesus Christ as their Saviour.</u>

- **1 John 5:4**

"For <u>whatsoever is born of God overcometh the world</u>: and this is the victory that overcometh the world, *even* our faith."

This verse also refers to a person being *"born of God."*

Verses On Firstfruits

This verse says of the true Christians *"that we should be a kind*

of firstfruits of his creatures."
- **Proverbs 3:9**
"Honour the LORD with thy substance, and with <u>the firstfruits of all thine increase:</u>"

This refers to giving to the Lord the firstfruits of what we have received.
- **Romans 8:23**
"And not only *they*, but <u>ourselves also, which have the firstfruits of the Spirit</u>, even we ourselves groan within ourselves, waiting for the adoption, *to wit*, the redemption of our body."

> **CHRISTIANS HAVE THE FIRSTFRUITS OF THE SPIRIT**
>
> Those who have become genuine Christians receive immediately the "firstfruits of the Spirit," that is, they receive God the Holy Spirit indwelling them.

- **1 Corinthians 15:20**
"But now is <u>Christ</u> risen from the dead, *and* <u>become the firstfruits of them that slept.</u>"

> **THREE STAGES OF CHRISTIANS' RESURRECTIONS**
>
> The bodily resurrection of saved Christians is in three different stages:
>
> (1) The Lord Jesus Christ's resurrection as the firstfruits;
>
> (2) The true Christians at their rapture to Heaven;
>
> (3) Probably at the end of the Tribulation for those who are saved.

- **1 Corinthians 15:23**
"<u>But every man in his own order: Christ the firstfruits</u>; afterward they that are Christ's at his coming."

> **CHRIST THE FIRST TO BE BODILY RESURRECTED**
>
> The Lord Jesus Christ was the first to be raised bodily with a resurrected body.

James 1:19

"Wherefore, my beloved brethren, let every man be swift to hear, slow to speak, slow to wrath:"

Notice these three things.
(1) "*Swift to hear*" is the first thing.
(2) "*Slow to speak*" is the second thing.
(3) "*Slow to wrath*" is the third thing.

It is important to hear before anything is done about what you hear.

Verses On Hearing

- **Luke 8:21**

"And he answered and said unto them, My mother and my brethren are these which hear the word of God, and do it."

The Lord Jesus Christ defines who his mother and brethren are. It is those who hear and do God's Words.

- **Luke 9:35**

"And there came a voice out of the cloud, saying, This is my beloved Son: hear him."

WE CAN HEAR CHRIST THROUGH ACCURATE BIBLES

God the Father wants everyone to hear His Son, the Lord Jesus Christ. The only way people can hear the Words of the Lord Jesus Christ today is by reading, if English-speaking, the King James Bible. If speaking another language people should use an accurate translation from the proper Hebrew, Aramaic, and Greek Bible Words.

- **John 5:25**

"Verily, verily, I say unto you, The hour is coming, and now is, when the dead shall hear the voice of the Son of God: and they that hear shall live."

HEARING CHRIST'S WORDS USING SOUND BIBLES

Those who are spiritually dead can receive spiritual life by hearing the Son of God Whose Words are found in a sound Bible.

- **John 10:27**

"My sheep hear my voice, and I know them, and they follow me:"

Those who are genuine Christians are Christ's sheep. They hear and follow His voice found in sound Bibles.

- **Hebrews 3:15**

"While it is said, To day if ye will hear his voice, harden not your hearts, as in the provocation."

GOD SPEAKS TODAY THROUGH ACCURATE BIBLES

Hearing God's voice is only possible today by reading and heeding a sound Bible like the King James Bible in English.

- **Revelation 2:7**

"He that hath an ear, let him hear what the Spirit saith unto the churches; To him that overcometh will I give to eat of the tree of

life, which is in the midst of the paradise of God."
Hearing what the Spirit says today is found in sound Bibles.
- **Revelation 3:20**
"Behold, I stand at the door, and knock: if any man hear my voice, and open the door, I will come in to him, and will sup with him, and he with me."

People must hear the Words of the Lord Jesus Christ by reading the King James Bible or some other sound Bible in another language.

Verses On Speaking

James 1:19 says that true Christians, after they hear God's Words, must be "*slow to speak.*"
- **Matthew 6:7**
"But when ye pray, use not vain repetitions, as the heathen *do*: for they think that they shall be heard for their much speaking."

When speaking, genuine Christians should not use vain repetitions.
- **1 Timothy 5:13**
"And withal they learn *to be* idle, wandering about from house to house; and not only idle, but tattlers also and busybodies, speaking things which they ought not."

CHRISTIANS' MOUTHS MUST BE GUARDED

True Christians must not speak things that they should not speak. They must be careful and guarded in their speech.

A Verse On Wrath
- **Ephesians 4:26**
"Be ye angry, and sin not: let not the sun go down upon your wrath:"

Wrath is uncontrolled anger. This should be used only sparingly if at all.

MEANING OF THE GREEK WORD, "ORGE."

The Greek Word for "*wrath*" is ORGE. Some of the meanings of this Greek Word are:

> "*1) anger, the natural disposition, temper, character; 2) movement or agitation of the soul, impulse, desire, any violent emotion, but esp. anger; 3) anger, wrath, indignation; 4) anger exhibited in punishment, hence used for punishment itself; 4a) of punishments inflicted by magistrates.*"

James 1:20

"For the wrath of man worketh not the righteousness of God."

Man's wrath does not have anything to do with God's righteousness.

Verses On Righteousness

- **Romans 3:22-24**

"Even the righteousness of God *which is* by faith of Jesus Christ unto all and upon all them that believe: for there is no difference: For all have sinned, and come short of the glory of God; Being justified freely by his grace through the redemption that is in Christ Jesus:"

God's righteousness is received only by genuine faith in the Lord Jesus Christ as Saviour.

- **Romans 3:26**

"To declare, *I say*, at this time his righteousness: that he might be just, and the justifier of him which believeth in Jesus."

TRUE FAITH IN CHRIST BRINGS RIGHTEOUSNESS

God's righteousness is bestowed by His grace when people genuinely believe on the Lord Jesus Christ as their Saviour. This verse shows clearly how God the Father made His Son, the Lord Jesus Christ, to be sin for everyone in the world so that those who truly trust in His Son, might receive God's perfect righteousness.

James 1:21

"Wherefore lay apart all filthiness and superfluity of naughtiness, and receive with meekness the engrafted word, which is able to save your souls."

James urged his readers to "*lay apart*" all filthiness and naughtiness.

MEANING OF THE GREEK WORD, "RUPARIA."

The Greek Word for "*filthiness*" is RUPARIA. Some of the meanings of that Greek Word are:

"*1) to make filthy, befoul; 2) to defile, dishonour; 3) to make filthy.*"

> **MEANING OF THE GREEK WORD, "KAKIA."**
> The Greek Word for "*naughtiness*" is KAKIA. Some of the meanings of that Greek Word are:
>> "*1) malignity, malice, ill-will, desire to injure; 2) wickedness, depravity; 2a) wickedness that is not ashamed to break laws; 3) evil, trouble.*"

Both of these sins are to be laid away and rejected. On the contrary, they are to receive with meekness the "*engrafted*" Word which is able to save their souls.

> **MEANING OF THE GREEK WORD, "EMPHUTOS."**
> The Greek Word for "*engrafted*" is EMPHUTOS. Some of the meanings of that Greek Word are:
>> "*1) inborn, implanted by nature, implanted by others instruction*"

- **Romans 10:17**

"So then <u>faith *cometh* by hearing, and hearing by the word of God</u>."

Once people exercise genuine faith in the Lord Jesus Christ they receive the engrafted Word of God.

Verses On Filthiness

- **Proverbs 30:12**

"*There is* a generation *that are* pure in their own eyes, and *yet* is not washed from their filthiness."

> **PURITY IN OUR OWN EYES DOESN'T MEAN PURITY**
> Though people might think they are pure in their own eyes, if they're still not genuine Christians, they are not washed from their filthiness. The Pharisees in the Lord Jesus day were pure in their own eyes, but they were in much filthiness in their hearts and lives.

- **Ezekiel 36:25**

"Then will I sprinkle clean water upon you, and <u>ye shall be clean: from all your filthiness</u>, and from all your idols, will I cleanse you."

> **CONVERTED JEWS WILL BE CLEAN WITH GOD**
> When they come back to the Lord in the future, the Jews will be clean from all their filthiness.

James–Preaching Verse By Verse

- 2 Corinthians 7:1

"Having therefore these promises, dearly beloved, <u>let us cleanse ourselves from all filthiness of the flesh and spirit</u>, perfecting holiness in the fear of God."

CHRISTIANS SHOULD CLEANSE FROM FILTHINESS

These are true Christians. They are urged to cleanse themselves from all filthiness of both the flesh and the spirit.

- Ephesians 5:3-4

"But fornication, and all uncleanness, or covetousness, <u>let it not be once named among you</u>, as becometh saints; <u>Neither filthiness</u>, nor foolish talking, nor jesting, which are not convenient: but rather giving of thanks."

CHRISTIANS SHOULD PLEASE CHRIST

Those who are genuine Christians should not live a life of filthiness or other sins. They should live to please the Lord Jesus Christ Who died to save their souls.

James 1:22

"**But be ye doers of the word, and not hearers only, deceiving your own selves.**"

CHRISTIANS MUST BE HEARERS AND DOERS ALSO

It is necessary for all true Christians to be hearers of God's Words day by day. Throughout their lives, there must also be a doing of these Words in addition to the hearing of them. <u>It is a sad thing when many of these Christians know the Scriptures and the doctrines taught therein, but they lack the doing and the practice of the doctrines they know very well. This is hypocrisy.</u>

James 1:23

"**For if any be a hearer of the word, and not a doer, he is like unto a man beholding his natural face in a glass:**"

This is an illustration of the preceding verse about hearing but not doing. <u>If genuine Christians are only hearers, it is like those who look in a mirror to see if their hair and clothing are in place</u>. Yet, they leave the mirror and refuse to straighten their hair and their

James–Preaching Verse By Verse

clothing. If this is the case, it would be a waste of time for them to even bother to look at that mirror.

> **SOME CHRISTIANS REFUSE TO OBEY GOD'S WORDS**
> So, some true Christians look into God's Words and see what God expects of them and yet refuse to obey those Words.

Verses On Mirrors

- **Job 37:18**

"Hast thou with him spread out the sky, *which is* strong, *and* <u>as a molten looking glass</u>?"

The question is asked here about the sky. It is strong and like a looking glass.

- **1 Corinthians 13:12**

"For <u>now we see through a glass, darkly</u>; but then face to face: now I know in part; but then shall I know even as also I am known."

> **THE BIBLE IS LIKE A MIRROR**
> Genuine Christians look in their Bibles as in a looking glass. They see some things, but they are not completely clear. One day, when they get their new resurrected bodies, they will see things perfectly.

- **2 Corinthians 3:18**

"But we all, <u>with open face beholding as in a glass the glory of the Lord</u>, are changed into the same image from glory to glory, *even* as by the Spirit of the Lord."

> **GOD'S WORDS SHOW HIS GLORY**
> <u>True Christians can behold God's glory in His Words.</u> As those Words are applied by them, God the Holy Spirit is able to change them from glory to glory as they yield to His will.

James 1:24

"For he beholdeth himself, and goeth his way, and straightway forgetteth what manner of man he was."

These people who look into this looking glass behold themselves and go their way forgetting what they looked like.

MEANING OF THE GREEK WORD, "KATANOEO."

The Greek Word for *"behold"* is KATANOEO. Some of the meanings of that Greek Word are:

"1) to perceive, remark, observe, understand; 2) to consider attentively, fix one's eyes or mind upon."

Even though this beholding is very attentive, if nothing is done to correct the faults that are discovered by the use of this mirror, it is a complete waste of time to use the mirror in the first place. As genuine Christians look into the mirror of God's Words, God expects them to line up their lives with the teachings of those Words.

James 1:25

"But whoso looketh into the perfect law of liberty, and continueth therein, he being not a forgetful hearer, but a doer of the work, this man shall be blessed in his deed."

Here is the application to looking into God's Words, the perfect law of liberty.

MEANING OF THE GREEK WORD, "PARAKUPTO."

The Greek Word for *"look"* is PARAKUPTO. Some of the meanings of this Greek Word are:

"1) to stoop to a thing in order to look at it; 2) to look at with head bowed forward; 3) to look into with the body bent; 4) to stoop and look into; 5) metaph. to look carefully into, inspect curiously; 5a) of one who would become acquainted with something."

This is a Word that means to stoop down to something in order to look at and inspect it very carefully.

OBEDIENCE TO GOD'S WORDS IS BLESSED BY GOD

Once the Words of God are examined carefully and obeyed by these genuine Christians, they will be blessed by their obedience to what they have found in God's Words. This is why I stand for the King James Bible and the underlying Hebrew, Aramaic, and Greek Words which it faithfully and carefully translate. I believe it is the only accurate, faithful, and true English translation of the proper Hebrew, Aramaic, Greek words.

> Looking into and continuing in God's faithful Words will make for blessed, content, and happy Christians.

James 1:26

"If any man among you seem to be religious, and bridleth not his tongue, but deceiveth his own heart, this man's religion is vain."

Here is the case of people who seem to be religious or who worship God and yet refuse to bridle their tongues. If this is the case, they deceive their hearts and their religion is vain.

> **MEANING OF THE GREEK WORD, "CHALINAGOGEO."**
> The Greek Word for *"bridle"* is CHALINAGOGEO. Some of the meanings of this Greek Word are:
> *"1) to lead by a bridle, to guide; 2) to bridle, hold in check, restrain."*

The tongue must be under control of the person who has it. It must be held in check and restrained to avoid deception of the heart and vain religion.

Verses On The Tongue And Mouth

- **Psalms 39:1**

"I said, I will take heed to my ways, that I sin not with my tongue: I will keep my mouth with a bridle, while the wicked is before me."

David was conscious of the possibility of sinning with his tongue. For this reason, He wanted to keep his mouth with a bridle.

- **Psalms 34:13**

"Keep thy tongue from evil, and thy lips from speaking guile."

The tongue can be evil as well as the mind and the actions. To please the Lord, the true Christians' tongues should be kept from evil words.

- **Psalms 35:28**

"And my tongue shall speak of thy righteousness *and* of thy praise all the day long."

> **TONGUES SHOULD TALK OF GOD'S RIGHTEOUSNESS**
> Our tongues should talk of God's righteousness and be used to praise the Lord rather than to speak unprofitable things.

- **Psalms 52:2**

"Thy tongue deviseth mischiefs; like a sharp razor, working

deceitfully."

> **BAD USE OF THE TONGUE IS LIKE A SHARP RAZOR**
> The tongue can be used wrongly like a sharp razor. As such, it divides and rips to shreds. It also deceives mischiefs and works deceitfully.

- **Psalms 57:4**
"My soul *is* among lions: *and* I lie *even among* them that are set on fire, *even* the sons of men, whose teeth *are* spears and arrows, and their tongue a sharp sword."

This verse speaks of evil people who use their tongues like a sharp sword rather than properly.

- **Psalms 120:2**
"Deliver my soul, O LORD, from lying lips, *and* from a deceitful tongue."

The Psalmist wanted to be delivered from lying lips and a deceitful tongue. This is an excellent wish of us today.

- **Proverbs 15:2**
"The tongue of the wise useth knowledge aright: but the mouth of fools poureth out foolishness."

When we know a thing and we use it in a right way, you are wise—you should be wise as far as your tongue.

- **Proverbs 18:21**
"Death and life *are* in the power of the tongue: and they that love it shall eat the fruit thereof."

The tongue has the power of death and life. It is a powerful and an important part of our bodies.

- **Proverbs 21:23**
"Whoso keepeth his mouth and his tongue keepeth his soul from troubles."

> **CONTROL OF THE TONGUE KEEPS FROM TROUBLE**
> Genuine Christians must learn how to keep their tongues from trouble. This is not easy.

- **Proverbs 31:26**
"She openeth her mouth with wisdom; and in her tongue *is* the law of kindness."

> **A VIRTUOUS WOMAN HAS A KIND TONGUE**
> The virtuous woman opens her mouth with wisdom and in her tongue is the law of kindness. It would be wonderful to have thousands of such virtuous women.

- **James 3:5**

"Even so <u>the tongue is a little member</u>, and boasteth great things. Behold, how great a matter a little fire kindleth!"

THE SMALL TONGUE CAN BRING BIG TROUBLE

Though the tongue is a small part of our body, it can bring a lot of trouble when improperly used. It is like the small rudder on a big ship that guides the whole vessel. The tongue is like a fire. It doesn't take much to burn down great buildings.

- **James 3:6**

"And <u>the tongue *is* a fire, a world of iniquity</u>: so is the tongue among our members, that <u>it defileth the whole body</u>, and setteth on fire the course of nature; and it is set on fire of hell."

<u>The tongue is a fire and a world of iniquity. It can defile the entire body. It is set on the fire of hell. Be careful with your tongue.</u>

- **James 3:8**

"But <u>the tongue can no man tame; *it is*</u> an unruly evil, full of deadly poison."

The tongue is untamable. It is full of deadly poison. Only if genuine Christians walk moment by moment in the power and control of God the Holy Spirit (Who indwells them) can they keep their tongues in proper control. Only the Lord is able to tame the tongue. <u>If true Christians walk in the power of the Spirit of God, they will not fulfil the lust of their flesh and the wickedness of their tongues.</u>

James 1:27

"Pure religion and undefiled before God and the Father is this, To visit the fatherless and widows in their affliction, and to keep himself unspotted from the world."

<u>This is a verse that defines an important aspect of pure religion. It is to visit those in affliction, and keep unspotted from the world.</u>

THE MEANING OF THE GREEK WORD, "KATHAROS."

The Greek Word for *"pure"* is KATHAROS. Some of the meanings of that Greek Word are:

> *"1) clean, pure; 1a) physically; 1a1) purified by fire; 1a2) in a similitude, like a vine cleansed by pruning and so fitted to bear fruit; 1b) in a levitical sense; 1b1) clean, the use of which is not forbidden,*

> imparts no uncleanness; 1c) ethically; 1c1) free from corrupt desire, from sin and guilt; 1c2) free from every admixture of what is false, sincere genuine; 1c3) blameless, innocent; 1c4) unstained with the guilt of anything."

> **MEANING OF THE GREEK WORD, "EPISKEPTOMAI."**
> The Greek Word for *"visit"* is EPISKEPTOMAI. Some of the meanings of that Greek Word are:
>> *"1) to look upon or after, to inspect, examine with the eyes; 1a) in order to see how he is, i.e. to visit, go to see one; 1a1) the poor and afflicted, the sick' 1b) to look upon in order to help or to benefit; 1b1) to look after, have care for, provide for: of God' 1c) to look (about) for, look out (one to choose, employ, etc.)"*

This certainly is a very descriptive and detailed word for visiting the fatherless and widows in their affliction. We have four widows attending our church presently. We want to help them all we can and also keep ourselves unspotted from the world.

Verses On Widows And The Fatherless
- **Exodus 22:22**

"Ye shall not afflict any widow, or fatherless child."
God is concerned for the safety and care of both of these groups of people.

- **Deuteronomy 10:18**

"**He doth execute the judgment of the fatherless and widow**, and loveth the stranger, in giving him food and raiment."
God is the One Who judges regarding the fatherless and widows.

- **Deuteronomy 24:17**

"Thou shalt not pervert the judgment of the stranger, *nor of the fatherless*; nor take a widow's raiment to pledge:"

> **PROTECT THE FATHERLESS AND WIDOWS**
> When people are either fatherless or widows, no one should attempt anything illegal regarding them. They are more defenseless than others. They should be protected.

- **Deuteronomy 27:19**

"Cursed be he that perverteth the judgment of the stranger,

fatherless, and widow. And all the people shall say, Amen."
No one should pervert their judgment. They should help them.
- **Psalms 68:5**
"A father of the fatherless, and a judge of the widows, *is* God in his holy habitation."

> **GOD IS A FATHER TO FATHERLESS AND WIDOWS**
> God helps both the fatherless and the widows as a father and as a judge.

- **Psalms 94:6**
"They slay the widow and the stranger, and murder the fatherless."

The wicked slay the widow and the strangers and murder the fatherless. These are terrible things to do to these people.

- **Psalms 146:9**
"The LORD preserveth the strangers; he relieveth the fatherless and widow: but the way of the wicked he turneth upside down."

God is concerned for the fatherless and the widows.

- **Isaiah 1:17**
"Learn to do well; seek judgment, relieve the oppressed, judge the fatherless, plead for the widow."

Isaiah pled for the fatherless and widows in his day.

- **Zechariah 7:10**
"And oppress not the widow, nor the fatherless, the stranger, nor the poor; and let none of you imagine evil against his brother in your heart."

> **DON'T OPPRESS THE WIDOWS AND FATHERLESS**
> The widows and fatherless were not to be oppressed. God is concerned about both these groups of needy people.

James
Chapter Two

James 2:1

"My brethren, have not the faith of our Lord Jesus Christ, the Lord of glory, with respect of persons."

THE MEANING OF THE GREEK PRESENT TENSE

This is a negative prohibition in the Greek present tense. When the Greek present tense is used in such a prohibition, it means to stop an action already in progress. If it were in the Greek aorist tense, it would mean to not even begin such an action.

Therefore, James is telling his readers to stop having the faith in our Lord Jesus Christ with respect of persons. Since the Greek Word for *"faith"* is preceded by the Greek article, it is referring to the doctrines and teachings of the Bible. They should treat everyone alike in regard to these doctrines concerning the Lord Jesus Christ.

MEANING OF THE GREEK WORD, "PROSOPOLEPSIA."

The Greek Word for *"respect of persons"* is PROSOPOLEPSIA. Some of the meanings of that Greek Word are:

> *"1) respect of persons; 2) partiality; 2a) the fault of one who when called on to give judgment has respect of the outward circumstances of man and not to their intrinsic merits, and so prefers, as the more worthy, one who is rich, high born, or powerful, to another who does not have these qualities."*

The term would refer to a person having respect to the outward circumstances of men or women. James commanded his readers to stop such favoritism.

Verses On Respect Of Persons
- **2 Chronicles 19:7**

"Wherefore now let the fear of the LORD be upon you; take heed and do *it*: for *there is* no iniquity with the LORD our God, nor respect of persons, nor taking of gifts."

> **GOD IS NO RESPECTER OF PERSONS**
> The Lord does not sin or have any respect of persons. He sees all the people of the world on the same level.

- **Proverbs 24:23**

"These *things* also *belong* to the wise. *It is* not good to have respect of persons in judgment."

To have respect of persons in matters of judgment is not good.

- **Proverbs 28:21**

"To have respect of persons *is* not good: for for a piece of bread *that* man will transgress."

Solomon repeats the fact that it is not good to have respect of persons. For a piece of bread that kind of a person will transgress.

- **Romans 2:11**

"For there is no respect of persons with God."

> **CHRISTIANS SHOULD NOT RESPECT PERSONS**
> God Himself is no respecter of persons. Genuine Christians should follow His example in this.

- **Ephesians 6:9**

"And, ye masters, do the same things unto them, forbearing threatening: knowing that your Master also is in heaven; neither is there respect of persons with him."

> **GOD RECOGNIZES ALL PERSONS ALIKE**
> The Christians' Master in Heaven does not use respect of persons. He recognizes all people as sinners who need to trust His Son as their Saviour in order to have His forgiveness and salvation.

- **Colossians 3:25**

"But he that doeth wrong shall receive for the wrong which he hath done: and there is no respect of persons."

People who do wrong should receive the penalty of doing that wrong without exceptions for highly ranked people.

- **1 Peter 1:17**

"And if ye call on the Father, who without respect of persons judgeth according to every man's work, pass the time of your sojourning *here* in fear:"

God the Father judges every person according to their work without any respect of persons.

James 2:2

"For if there come unto your assembly a man with a gold ring, in goodly apparel, and there come in also a poor man in vile raiment;"

Here's an illustration of having a respect of persons. One man has a goodly apparel and the other man is dressed in vile raiment. The first man is rich, but the second man is poor.

THE MEANING OF THE GREEK WORD, "PTOKOS."

The Greek Word for *"poor"* is PTOKOS. Some of the meanings of that Greek Word are:

"1) reduced to beggary, begging, asking alms; 2) destitute of wealth, influence, position, honour; 2a) lowly, afflicted, destitute of the Christian virtues and eternal riches; 2b) helpless, powerless to accomplish an end; 2c) poor, needy; 3) lacking in anything; 3a) as respects their spirit; 3a1) destitute of wealth of learning and intellectual culture which the schools afford (men of this class most readily give themselves up to Christ's teaching and proved themselves fitted to lay hold of the heavenly treasure)."

This is a very clear meaning of what James is writing about.

Verses On Rich And Poor

- **Proverbs 10:4**

"He becometh poor that dealeth *with* a slack hand: but the hand of the diligent maketh rich."

THE RESULTS OF LAZINESS AND DILIGENCE

Laziness often leads to poverty and diligence often leads to being rich.

- **Proverbs 10:22**

"The blessing of the LORD, it maketh rich, and he addeth no sorrow with it."

There is a spiritual richness made possible by the blessings of the Lord.

- **Proverbs 13:7**
"There is that <u>maketh himself rich, yet</u> *hath* <u>nothing</u>: *there is* that <u>maketh himself poor, yet</u> *hath* <u>great riches.</u>"

WEALTH AND SPIRITUAL VALUES

Richness in wealth and goods might go with it a person who has nothing spiritually. On the other hand, a person who is poor in worldly goods, yet has the Lord Jesus Christ, has great spiritual riches.

- **Proverbs 14:20**
"<u>The poor is hated</u> even of his own neighbour: but <u>the rich</u> *hath* <u>many friends.</u>"

THE INFLUENCE OF MONEY AND FRIENDS

Many poor people are hated by their neighbors and others, but often the rich have many friends, especially if they give them money.

- **Proverbs 18:23**
"<u>The poor useth intreaties; but the rich answereth roughly.</u>"

THE SPEECH OF THE POOR AND THE RICH

The poor try to get along with people in a kind manner, but often the rich answer people roughly because they don't need them to be their friends.

- **Proverbs 21:17**
"<u>He that loveth pleasure</u> *shall be* <u>a poor man</u>: he that loveth wine and oil shall not be rich."

THE HIGH COST OF PLEASURES

The price of pleasures is usually very high. This will lead to poverty. Just consider the cost of narcotics, horse racing, gambling, sex, and other pleasures of this world.

- **Proverbs 22:2**
"<u>The rich and poor meet together</u>: the LORD *is* the maker of them all."

God puts the rich and poor all together. He made them all and they are treated fairly by Him.

- **Proverbs 22:7**
"<u>The rich ruleth over the poor</u>, and the borrower *is* servant to the lender."

<u>The poor who borrow money from the rich becomes subject to the rules of the rich in paying that money back.</u>

James–Preaching Verse By Verse

- **Proverbs 23:4**

"<u>Labour not to be rich</u>: cease from thine own wisdom."

The main goal in a person's life should not to be rich. To have this as a goal, there is often a sacrifice of many valuable things.

- **Proverbs 28:6**

"<u>Better *is* the poor that walketh in his uprightness, than *he that is* perverse *in his* ways, though he *be* rich</u>."

Righteous and being poor is far better with God than the perverse and the rich.

- **Proverbs 28:20**

"A faithful man shall abound with blessings: but <u>he that maketh haste to be rich shall not be innocent</u>."

Often those who are hasty to be rich cut corners and do evil in such pursuits. If so, they will not be innocent.

- **Ecclesiastes 5:12**

"The sleep of a labouring man *is* sweet, whether he eat little or much: but <u>the abundance of the rich will not suffer him to sleep</u>."

THE SLEEP PROBLEMS OF THE RICH

Sleep often goes from the rich people because they might be concerned for what they have and might be thinking of how they can become even richer.

- **Luke 12:21**

"So *is* he that layeth up treasure for himself, and <u>is not rich toward God</u>."

Here is a contrast between worldly riches and having poverty toward the things of the Lord.

- **2 Corinthians 8:9**

"For ye know the grace of our Lord Jesus Christ, that, though he was rich, yet for your sakes he became poor, that <u>ye through his poverty might be rich</u>."

CHRIST BECAME POOR TO MAKE CHRISTIANS RICH

What a majestic verse is this! The Lord Jesus Christ was rich in Heaven, yet became poor by coming down to earth, being crucified for the sins of the world so that sinners who trust Him as their Saviour might be rich in eternal life and God's grace.

1 Timothy 6:17-18
"Charge them that are <u>rich in this world, that they be not highminded, nor trust in uncertain riches</u>, but in the living God, who giveth us richly all things to enjoy; That they do good, that they be <u>rich in good works</u>, ready to distribute, willing to communicate;"

If true Christians are rich in this world, they are neither to be highminded about it, nor are they to trust in uncertain riches, but in the living God. Our U. S. Dollar is very uncertain. President Obama has printed BILLIONS of paper dollars every month, thus inflated that dollar and made it go down and down and down. It will very soon cease to be the standard for oil and the world because of its depleted value.

James 2:3

"And ye have respect to him that weareth the gay clothing, and say unto him, Sit thou here in a good place; and say to the poor, Stand thou there, or sit here under my footstool:"

It is wrong to have respect on the one in gay clothing and not care for the poor person who enters the church. The homosexuals have polluted the word, "*gay*" in our day.

THE MEANING OF THE GREEK WORD, "LAMPROS."

The Greek Word for "*gay*" is LAMPROS. Some of the meanings of that Greek Word are:

"*1) shining; 1a) brilliant; 1b) clear, transparent; 2) splendid, magnificent; 2a) splendid things i.e. luxuries or elegancies in dress or style.*"

<u>So this is an illustration in respect of persons between the rich and the poor.</u> There should be equal treatment of all parties, whether rich or poor.

James 2:4

"Are ye not then partial in yourselves, and are become judges of evil thoughts?"

These people were accused by James of being "*partial.*" They were making a distinction, discriminating, and preferring one above another. They have also become judges of evil thoughts.

THE BIBLE AND EVIL THOUGHTS

The Words of God should be the standard against all evil thoughts. People should not take the place of God's Words regarding "*evil thoughts.*" The Lord Himself is the only one Who can be the proper judge on these matters. He alone can read and expose evil thoughts. It is not possible for human beings to know what evil thoughts are in the minds of others.

James 2:5

"**Hearken, my beloved brethren, Hath not God chosen the poor of this world rich in faith, and heirs of the kingdom which he hath promised to them that love him?**"

THE POOR IN THE WORLD CAN BE RICH IN FAITH

James wants his readers especially to listen to what he is talking about here. It concerns the poor in this world who are rich in faith. Peter, Andrew, James and John were all poor fishermen that God called to be His servants.

God gave them the riches of faith in the Lord Jesus Christ. Though funds are needed to care for our needs, the riches of eternal life by genuine faith in the Lord Jesus Christ as our Saviour is of paramount importance.

Verses On The Poor

- **Psalms 72:12**

"For he shall deliver the needy when he crieth; the poor also, and *him* that hath no helper."

The Lord is concerned for the poor and needy both physically poor and spiritually poor.

- **Psalms 74:21**

"O let not the oppressed return ashamed: let the poor and needy praise thy name."

Just because people might be poor and needy doesn't mean they shouldn't praise the Name of the Lord.

- **Proverbs 14:31**

"He that oppresseth the poor reproacheth his Maker: but he that honoureth him hath mercy on the poor."

God honors those who have mercy on the poor. He is concerned about them.

James–Preaching Verse By Verse

- **Matthew 11:5**

"The blind receive their sight, and the lame walk, the lepers are cleansed, and the deaf hear, the dead are raised up, and the poor have the gospel preached to them."

DISCIPLES PREACHED THE GOSPEL TO THE POOR
The disciples reported that, in their journeys the poor had the gospel preached to them.

- **Matthew 26:9-11**

"For this ointment might have been sold for much, and given to the poor. When Jesus understood *it*, he said unto them, Why trouble ye the woman? for she hath wrought a good work upon me. For ye have the poor always with you; but me ye have not always."

JUDAS ISCARIOT WANTED MONEY TO STEAL
Judas Iscariot was the treasurer of the disciples. He had the bag of money and wanted the money that the expensive perfume would bring. He didn't care for the poor, but wanted the money for himself.

- **Luke 6:20**

"And he lifted up his eyes on his disciples, and said, Blessed *be ye* poor: for yours is the kingdom of God."

The Lord Jesus Christ said His disciples were blessed though they were poor, they were part of the kingdom of God.

- **Luke 14:13-14**

"But when thou makest a feast, call the poor, the maimed, the lame, the blind: And thou shalt be blessed; for they cannot recompense thee: for thou shalt be recompensed at the resurrection of the just."

Invite the poor to the feasts in addition to the maimed, the lame, and the blind. God will recompense you for doing this.

- **Romans 15:26**

"For it hath pleased them of Macedonia and Achaia to make a certain contribution for the poor saints which are at Jerusalem."

CHRISTIANS SUPPORTED POOR CHRISTIANS
Those genuine Christians living in the provinces of Macedonia and Achaia made a contribution to those at Jerusalem who were poor Christians. They were part of God's family, so other members of that body tried to help them in their poverty.

- 1 Corinthians 13:3

"And though I bestow all my goods to feed *the poor*, and though I give my body to be burned, and have not charity, it profiteth me nothing."

Giving goods to the poor is fine, but it must be accompanied by genuine charity or Christian love.

- 2 Corinthians 6:10

"As sorrowful, yet alway rejoicing; as poor, yet making many rich; as having nothing, and *yet* possessing all things."

THE APOSTLES-POOR AND MAKING MANY RICH

Paul describes his missionary life. He and the other missionaries in his day were poor, yet making many rich in the treasures of the Lord Jesus Christ. They themselves had practically nothing, but they possessed all things in Christ.

- 2 Corinthians 8:9

"For ye know the grace of our Lord Jesus Christ, that, though he was rich, yet for your sakes he became poor, that ye through his poverty might be rich."

CHRIST BECAME POOR TO MAKE PEOPLE RICH

Our rich Saviour, the Lord Jesus Christ became poor by coming to this earth in a perfect human body to take the sins of the world in His own body. Through genuinely trusting in this Saviour people can be made rich.

- Galatians 2:10

"Only *they would* that we should remember the poor; the same which I also was forward to do."

True Christians should never forget the poor, but should remember them. Paul did this.

James 2:6

"But ye have despised the poor. Do not rich men oppress you, and draw you before the judgment seats?"

According to James, his readers have despised the poor yet the rich men oppress them and take them to court.

> **THE MEANING OF THE GREEK WORD, "ATIMAZO."**
> The Greek Word for *"despise"* is ATIMAZO. Some of the meanings of that Greek Word are:
>> *"1) to dishonour, insult, treat with contempt; 1a) whether in word, deed or thought"*
>
> These people have insulted and expressed contempt for the poor.

> **MEANING OF GREEK WORD, "KATADUNASTEUO."**
> The Greek Word for *"oppress"* is KATADUNASTEUO. Some of the meanings of that Greek Word are:
>> *"1) to exercise harsh control over one, to use one's power against one;* 2) to oppress one."

These rich men had very harsh control over these people James is addressing.

Verses On Oppression
- **Exodus 3:9**

"Now therefore, behold, the cry of the children of Israel is come unto me: and I have also seen the oppression wherewith the Egyptians oppress them."

Because of the oppression of the children of Israel by the evil Egyptians, God took action to deliver His people.

- **Exodus 22:21**

"Thou shalt neither vex a stranger, nor oppress him: for ye were strangers in the land of Egypt."

Israel was not to vex or oppress any strangers. They themselves were strangers in Egypt.

- **Leviticus 25:17**

"Ye shall not therefore oppress one another; but thou shalt fear thy God: for I *am* the LORD your God."

The Israelites were not to oppress one another, but were to serve the Lord their God.

- **Deuteronomy 24:14**

"Thou shalt not oppress an hired servant *that is* poor and needy, *whether he be* of thy brethren, or of thy strangers that *are* in thy land within thy gates:"

The Israelites were not to oppress their hired servants who is poor and needy.

- **Proverbs 22:22**

Rob not the poor, because he *is* poor: <u>neither oppress the afflicted in the gate:"</u>

<u>No one should oppress those who are afflicted people.</u>

- **Zechariah 7:10**

"<u>And oppress not the widow, nor the fatherless, the stranger, nor the poor</u>; and let none of you imagine evil against his brother in your heart."

<u>There was to be no oppression of widows, fatherless, strangers, or poor.</u> They should all be treated kindly and fairly.

James 2:7

"Do not they blaspheme that worthy name by the which ye are called?"

These rich people blaspheme the worthy Name of the Lord Jesus Christ.

MEANING OF THE GREEK WORD, "BLASPHEMEO."

The Greek Word for *"blaspheme"* is BLASPHEMEO. Some of the meanings of this Greek Word are:

"1) to speak reproachfully, rail at, revile, calumniate, blaspheme; 2) to be evil spoken of, reviled, railed at."

The object of this blasphemy by the rich is the *"worthy Name"* of the Lord Jesus Christ.

THE MEANING OF THE GREEK WORD, "KALOS."

The Greek Word for "worthy" is KALOS. Some of the meanings of that Greek Word are:

"1) beautiful, handsome, excellent, eminent, choice, surpassing, precious, useful, suitable, commendable, admirable; 1a) beautiful to look at, shapely, magnificent; 1b) good, excellent in its nature and characteristics, and therefore well adapted to its ends; 1b1) genuine, approved; 1b2) precious; 1b3) joined to names of men designated by their office, competent, able, such as one ought to be; 1b4) praiseworthy, noble; 1c) beautiful by reason of purity of heart and life, and hence praiseworthy; 1c1)

> *morally good, noble; 1d) honourable, conferring honour; 1e) affecting the mind agreeably, comforting and confirming."*

The Name of the Lord Jesus Christ is certainly a beautiful, excellent, choice, and precious Name! Shame on these rich people, or any people in the world, to blaspheme that worthy Name!

Verses On Name And Blaspheme

- **Isaiah 9:6**

"For unto us a child is born, unto us a son is given: and the government shall be upon his shoulder: and his name shall be called Wonderful, Counsellor, The mighty God, The everlasting Father, The Prince of Peace."

Isaiah prophesied of all these titles of the Name of the Lord Jesus Christ. His name, worthy name, by the which you are called.

- **2 Samuel 12:14**

"Howbeit, because by this deed thou hast given great occasion to the enemies of the LORD to blaspheme, the child also *that is* born unto thee shall surely die."

David's adultery with Bathsheba caused people to blaspheme God's Name.

- **Psalms 74:10**

"O God, how long shall the adversary reproach? shall the enemy blaspheme thy name for ever?"

This is a good question. How long will God's adversaries blaspheme His Name? Will it be forever? I hope not.

- **Acts 26:11**

"And I punished them oft in every synagogue, and compelled *them* to blaspheme; and being exceedingly mad against them, I persecuted *them* even unto strange cities."

PAUL MADE CHRISTIANS BLASPHEME CHRIST

Before he became a genuine Christian, Paul compelled Christians to blaspheme His Name.

- **Revelation 13:6**

"And he opened his mouth in blasphemy against God, to blaspheme his name, and his tabernacle, and them that dwell in heaven."

The political beast during the seven year Tribulation period will blaspheme the Name of God and His Son, the Lord Jesus Christ.

James 2:8

"If ye fulfil the royal law according to the scripture, Thou shalt love thy neighbour as thyself, ye do well:"

To fulfil the royal law means to perform and follow it. If you love your neighbor as yourself, you do well.

> **THE MEANING OF THE GREEK WORD, "PLESION."**
> The Greek Word for "*neighbor*" is PLESION. Some of the meanings of this Greek Word are:
>> "*1) a neighbour; 1a) a friend; 1b) any other person, and where two are concerned, the other (thy fellow man, thy neighbour), according to the Jews, any member of the Hebrew race and commonwealth; 1c) according to Christ, any other man irrespective of race or religion with whom we live or whom we chance to meet.*"

Verses On Loving Neighbors

- **Leviticus 19:18**

"Thou shalt not avenge, nor bear any grudge against the children of thy people, but thou shalt love thy neighbour as thyself: I *am* the LORD."

This is the first time this expression is used in the Bible.

- **Matthew 5:43**

"Ye have heard that it hath been said, Thou shalt love thy neighbour, and hate thine enemy."

This is the first time this is used in the New Testament. The Lord Jesus Christ didn't tell people to hate their enemies.

- **Matthew 19:19**

"Honour thy father and *thy* mother: and, Thou shalt love thy neighbour as thyself."

> **CHRISTIANS--LOVE OTHERS AS THEMSELVES**
> People's love for the neighbors should be to the same level as their love for themselves. That's a very high standard that the Lord Jesus Christ laid down.

- **Matthew 22:35-40**

"Then one of them, *which was* a lawyer, asked *him a question*, tempting him, and saying, Master, which *is* the great commandment in the law? Jesus said unto him, Thou shalt love the Lord thy God with all thy heart, and with all thy soul, and with all thy mind. This is the first and great commandment. And the second is like unto it, Thou shalt love thy neighbour as thyself. On these two commandments hang all the law and the prophets."

This was a good answer by the Lord Jesus Christ to this lawyer's question.

- **Romans 13:9**

"For this, Thou shalt not commit adultery, Thou shalt not kill, Thou shalt not steal, Thou shalt not bear false witness, Thou shalt not covet; and if *there be* any other commandment, it is briefly comprehended in this saying, namely, Thou shalt love thy neighbour as thyself."

IF YOU LOVE PEOPLE, YOU WON'T HURT THEM

If you love your neighbor as yourself you don't kill them; you don't commit adultery with them; you don't covet what they have; you don't steal from them; and you don't bear false witness against him. This is the summation of that second half of the ten commandments.

- **Galatians 5:14**

"For all the law is fulfilled in one word, *even* in this; Thou shalt love thy neighbour as thyself."

This is the summation of love for people's neighbors. It must be as strong as their love for themselves.

James 2:9

"But if ye have respect to persons, ye commit sin, and are convinced of the law as transgressors."

James brought up having respect of persons as he mentioned in the first verse of this chapter. The people who practice this commit sin and are transgressors.

MEANING OF THE GREEK WORD, "PROSOPOLEPSIA."

Remember some of the meanings of the Greek Word for that expression (PROSOPOLEPSIA):

> *"1) respect of persons; 2) partiality; 2a) the fault of one who when called on to give judgment has respect of the outward circumstances of man and not to their intrinsic merits, and so prefers, as the more worthy, one who is rich, high born, or powerful, to another who does not have these qualities."*

James–Preaching Verse By Verse   59

The Greek Word for "*commit*" is in the Greek present tense. It means that the person who is guilty of respecting persons is committing continuous and uninterrupted sin.

Two Verses On Respect Of Persons
- **Deuteronomy 1:17**

"Ye shall not respect persons in judgment; *but* ye shall hear the small as well as the great; ye shall not be afraid of the face of man; for the judgment *is* God's: and the cause that is too hard for you, bring *it* unto me, and I will hear it."

Justice must be blind. It must be fair to all concerned.
- **Deuteronomy 16:19**

"Thou shalt not wrest judgment; thou shalt not respect persons, neither take a gift: for a gift doth blind the eyes of the wise, and pervert the words of the righteous."

The sin of respecting persons is listed along with twisting proper judgment and taking gifts that blind the minds.

James 2:10

" For whosoever shall keep the whole law, and yet offend in one point, he is guilty of all."

This is quite an indictment. For a person to seek to keep the entire law of Moses and yet to fail to keep just one part of it, is guilty of it all.

Verses On The Law Of Moses
- **Romans 3:19**

"Now we know that what things soever the law saith, it saith to them who are under the law: that every mouth may be stopped, and all the world may become guilty before God."

DEEDS CANNOT SAVE THE SOUL OF ANYONE

The deeds of the law cannot save the soul of anyone. The law of Moses should stop the mouths of those who attempt to keep it but fail to do so.

- **Romans 3:21**

"But now the righteousness of God without the law is manifested, being witnessed by the law and the prophets;"

James–Preaching Verse By Verse

> **RIGHTEOUSNESS IS ONLY BY FAITH IN CHRIST**
>
> Righteousness with God is only through genuine faith in the Lord Jesus Christ like it states clearly in Romans 3:23-24
>
> > *"For all have sinned, and come short of the glory of God; <u>Being justified freely by his grace through the redemption that is in Christ Jesus</u>:"*
>
> <u>Not by the law, not by doing anything but by His grace are people saved</u>. God gives them something they don't deserve so that God may be just and the justifier of those who genuinely trust the Lord Jesus Christ as their Saviour.

- **Romans 3:28**

"Therefore we conclude that <u>a man is justified by faith without the deeds of the law</u>."

<u>This verse makes it clear that justification is by faith without any deeds of the law at all.</u>

James 2:11

"For he that said, Do not commit adultery, said also, Do not kill. Now if thou commit no adultery, yet if thou kill, thou art become a transgressor of the law."

> **SINNING IN ANY AREA MAKES YOU A SINNER**
>
> James is saying here that genuine Christians must be very careful. If you kill but don't commit adultery, you are a transgressor of the law. As far as adultery is concerned, it is a command not only in the Old Testament, but it is repeated many places also in the New Testament.

Verses On Adultery

- **Exodus 20:14**

"<u>Thou shalt not commit adultery</u>."

This is one of the ten commandments given in the Old Testament.

- **Leviticus 20:10**

"And the man that committeth adultery with *another* man's wife, *even he* that committeth adultery with his neighbour's wife, <u>the adulterer and the adulteress shall surely be put to death</u>."

> **OLD TESTAMENT ADULTERERS WERE SLAIN**
> With the way people are living today, if the Old Testament law of Moses were still in effect today, we'd have a very great multitude of dead people all around the world.

Deuteronomy 5:18
"Neither shalt thou commit adultery."
This is one of the ten commandments repeated to the new generation of Israelites.

- **Proverbs 6:32**
"*But* whoso committeth adultery with a woman lacketh understanding: he *that* doeth it destroyeth his own soul."
The adulterer as well as the adulteress are both fools.

- **Jeremiah 7:9**
"Will ye steal, murder, and commit adultery, and swear falsely, and burn incense unto Baal, and walk after other gods whom ye know not;"
Jeremiah speaks out clearly against adultery.

- **Jeremiah 23:14**
"I have seen also in the prophets of Jerusalem an horrible thing: they commit adultery, and walk in lies: they strengthen also the hands of evildoers, that none doth return from his wickedness: they are all of them unto me as Sodom, and the inhabitants thereof as Gomorrah."

> **SOME FALSE PROPHETS WERE ADULTERERS**
> This verse seems to indicate that even some of the prophets were committing adultery. These were men of God supposedly. We have some preachers, evangelists, and members even of Bible-believing churches who are committing adultery. It's a terrible thing against the Words of God.

- **Jeremiah 29:23**
"Because they have committed villany in Israel, and have committed adultery with their neighbours' wives, and have spoken lying words in my name, which I have not commanded them; even I know, and *am* a witness, saith the LORD."
The verse before this one is speaking about "*the captivity of Judah which are in Babylon.*" The Jews practiced adultery during the 70 years of captivity in Babylon. It was a disgusting thing to the Lord.

- **Matthew 5:27-28**
"Ye have heard that it was said by them of old time, Thou shalt not commit adultery: But I say unto you, That whosoever looketh on a woman to lust after her hath committed adultery with her already in his heart."

> **CHRIST SAID LOOKING WITH LUST IS ADULTERY**
> The Lord Jesus Christ adds to the sense of physical adultery by referring to adultery of the heart if a man looks on a woman to lust after her. This could be applied to women looking on men to lust after them.

- **Galatians 5:19**
"Now the works of the flesh are manifest, which are *these*; Adultery, fornication, uncleanness, lasciviousness,"

The first of the many works of the flesh mentioned in Galatians 5 is adultery. Genuine Christians still have their sinful flesh and must rely upon God the Holy Spirit Who is living within them to overcome adultery or any of the other fleshly works mentioned in Galatians 5.

2 Peter 2:14
"Having eyes full of adultery, and that cannot cease from sin; beguiling unstable souls: an heart they have exercised with covetous practices; cursed children:"

> **SOME HAVE EYES FULL OF HEART-ADULTERY**
> Peter spoke of people having eyes that lusted after other people and thus would be committing adultery of the heart as mentioned by the Lord Jesus Christ in Matthew 5:27-28 above.

- **Jeremiah 7:9**
"Will ye steal, murder, and commit adultery, and swear falsely, and burn incense unto Baal, and walk after other gods whom ye know not;"

Verses On Murder

- **Hosea 6:9**
"And as troops of robbers wait for a man, *so* the company of priests murder in the way by consent: for they commit lewdness."

Old Testament priests are accused here of committing murder.

- **Matthew 19:18**
"He saith unto him, Which? Jesus said, Thou shalt do no murder, Thou shalt not commit adultery, Thou shalt not steal, Thou shalt not bear false witness,"

James–Preaching Verse By Verse

The Lord Jesus Christ summed up some of the Old Testament ten commandments, including not committing murder. When the Jewish leaders instructed the people to crucify the Lord Jesus Christ and release Barabbas, they were asking for the release of a murderer and thought nothing of it.

- **Luke 23:25**

"And he released unto them him that for sedition and murder was cast into prison, whom they had desired; but he delivered Jesus to their will."

Pilate released Barabbas who was in prison for murder.

- **Romans 1:29**

"Being filled with all unrighteousness, fornication, wickedness, covetousness, maliciousness; full of envy, murder, debate, deceit, malignity; whisperers,"

THIS WORLD IS FILLED WITH MURDER

The godless world in the past and even now was and is filled with murder along with many of these other things.

- **Matthew 5:21-22**

"Ye have heard that it was said by them of old time, Thou shalt not kill; and whosoever shall kill shall be in danger of the judgment: But I say unto you, That whosoever is angry with his brother without a cause shall be in danger of the judgment: and whosoever shall say to his brother, Raca, shall be in danger of the council: but whosoever shall say, Thou fool, shall be in danger of hell fire."

CHRIST SAID ANGER IS OFTEN SPIRITUAL MURDER

The Lord Jesus Christ speaks of spiritual murder when someone is angry with his brother without a cause.

James 2:12

"So speak ye, and so do, as they that shall be judged by the law of liberty."

James was saying to these true Christians that they should speak and do things that would pass judgment by the law of liberty. This would be a reference to the Judgment Seat of Christ.

NON-CHRISTIANS ARE JUDGED AND SENT TO HELL

Those who are not genuine Christians will be judged at the Great White Throne Judgment and be sent into the fires of everlasting Hell. The Judgment Seat of Christ is spoken about in 2 Corinthians 3 and 5.

Verses On The Judgment Seat Of Christ
- **2 Corinthians 5:10**

"For <u>we must all appear before the judgment seat of Christ</u>; that every one may receive the things *done* in *his* body, according to that he hath done, whether *it be* good or bad."

<u>The "*we*" in this verse is a reference only to true Christians.</u> This judgment is for all of these Christians. It is for the things done in their bodies, whether good or bad.

- **1 Corinthians 3:9-15**

"For we are labourers together with God: ye are God's husbandry, *ye are* God's building. According to the grace of God which is given unto me, as a wise masterbuilder, I have laid the foundation, and another buildeth thereon. But <u>let every man take heed how he buildeth thereupon. For other foundation can no man lay than that is laid, which is Jesus Christ</u>. Now if any man build upon this foundation gold, silver, precious stones, wood, hay, stubble; Every man's work shall be made manifest: for the day shall declare it, because it shall be revealed by fire; and the fire shall try every man's work of what sort it is. If any man's work abide which he hath built thereupon, he shall receive a reward."

Paul is talking about genuine Christians who have trusted the Lord Jesus Christ as their Saviour and have been placed upon Him as their Foundation. They must take heed to the materials they build upon Him, their Foundation.

JUDGMENT SEAT OF CHRIST'S SIX MATERIALS

There are six different building materials in two categories. The first category of three materials are small, very valuable, and are made more pure by fire–gold, silver, and precious stones. The second category of three materials can be quite large, not very valuable, and are consumed by fire–hay, wood, and stubble.

<u>The basis of this judgment is not by quantity, but by quality.</u> It will not be by how much is involved, but of what sort of materials are involved. It seems like those things that are done for themselves are illustrated by the wood, hay, and stubble. Those things that are done for the Lord Jesus Christ are illustrated by gold, silver, and precious stones.

HAY, WOOD, AND STUBBLE WORKS ARE BURNED UP

If their works are like hay, wood, and stubble, the fire will burn them up and be destroyed. They will not go to

> Hell, but they will suffer the loss of any rewards. There will be no rewards given to them. If their works are like gold, silver, and precious stones, the fire will purify them and they will receive a reward.

James 2:13

"For he shall have judgment without mercy, that hath shewed no mercy; and mercy rejoiceth against judgment."

If people do not use mercy in their judgment, they themselves will not have mercy shown to them. God is a merciful God.

> **THE MEANING OF THE GREEK WORD, "ELEOS."**
> The Greek Word for *"mercy"* is ELEOS. Some of the meanings of that Greek Word are:
>> *"1) mercy: kindness or good will towards the miserable and the afflicted, joined with a desire to help them; 1a) of men towards men: to exercise the virtue of mercy, show one's self merciful; 1b) of God towards men: in general providence; the mercy and clemency of God in providing and offering to men salvation by Christ; 1c) the mercy of Christ, whereby at his return to judgment he will bless true Christians with eternal life."*

Verses On Mercy And Merciful

- **Exodus 34:6**

"And the LORD passed by before him, and proclaimed, The LORD, The LORD God, merciful and gracious, longsuffering, and abundant in goodness and truth,"

One of the many attributes of the God of the Bible is that He is merciful.

- **Psalms 18:25-26**

"With the merciful thou wilt shew thyself merciful; with an upright man thou wilt shew thyself upright; With the pure thou wilt shew thyself pure; and with the froward thou wilt shew thyself froward."

Those who show mercy will receive mercy from the Lord.

- **Luke 6:36**

"*Be ye therefore merciful, as your Father also is merciful.*"
That's a command for true Christians. They should be merciful just like their Heavenly Father is merciful.
- **Luke 18:13**
"And the publican, standing afar off, would not lift up so much as *his* eyes unto heaven, but smote upon his breast, saying, <u>God be merciful to me a sinner.</u>"
And God did show him mercy in answer to his prayer. We must realize that God is the One that dispenses mercy. He takes note of our miserable condition here upon this earth and only through the Lord Jesus Christ, God's Son, at Calvary, did God show the ultimate act of His mercy.

GOD SENT CHRIST FOR PEOPLE TO TRUST IN HIM
God could have sent every person who ever lived to Hell's fires for all eternity. Instead, He sent His Son to die for the sins of the world so that those who sincerely trust Him as their Saviour might receive eternal life and go to God's Heaven for all eternity.

James 2:14
"**What doth it profit, my brethren, though a man say he hath faith, and have not works? can faith save him?**"

In Paul's books such as Romans and all others, <u>it is clear that people must become genuine Christians by true faith in the Lord Jesus Christ alone without any kind of works</u>. This genuine faith is seen by God.

FAITH THAT LACKS WORKS IS FALSE FAITH
James, on the other hand speaks of the fruits of that faith that can be seen by other people. If that faith lacks proper fruit and works to go with it, that faith is false and spurious faith and cannot save such an individual. This distinction must be understood throughout the book of James to understand it properly.

Verses on Salvation By Faith Not By Works
- **Ephesians 2:8-10**
"For <u>by grace are ye saved through faith</u>; and that not of yourselves: *it is* the gift of God: <u>Not of works</u>, lest any man should boast. For we are his workmanship, <u>created in Christ Jesus unto good works</u>, which God hath before ordained that we should walk in them."
These verses make clear that people are saved by sincere faith in

the Lord Jesus Christ, and not by any works they might have done. After they are genuine Christians, God wants them to walk in good works by God's saving power and assistance.
- **Titus 3:8**
"*This is* a faithful saying, and these things I will that thou affirm constantly, that they which have believed in God might be careful to maintain good works. These things are good and profitable unto men."

TRUE FAITH IN CHRIST SAVED-NOT GOOD WORKS
Good works should always follow genuine faith in the Lord Jesus Christ. No one can be saved by good works, but only by true faith in the Lord Jesus Christ the Saviour.

- **Titus 3:14**
"And let ours also learn to maintain good works for necessary uses, that they be not unfruitful."

Genuine Christians should maintain good works after being saved.
- **Matthew 5:16**
"Let your light so shine before men, that they may see your good works, and glorify your Father which is in heaven."

By the good works of true Christians which others can see, they can glorify God the Father.
- **Acts 15:9**
"And put no difference between us and them, purifying their hearts by faith."

The words, "*us and them*" refer to both Jews and Gentiles.

HEARTS CAN BE PURIFIED BY FAITH IN CHRIST
In order for any of them to become genuine Christians, they must have their hearts purified by true faith in the Lord Jesus Christ as their Saviour.

- **Romans 1:17**
"For therein is the righteousness of God revealed from faith to faith: as it is written, The just shall live by faith."

Genuine faith in the Lord Jesus Christ as their Saviour is the only way people can receive the righteousness of God.
- **Romans 3:22**
"Even the righteousness of God *which is* by faith of Jesus Christ unto all and upon all them that believe: for there is no difference:"

The righteousness of God is only by sincere faith in the Lord Jesus Christ as Saviour.

- **Romans 3:26**
"To declare, *I say*, at this time his righteousness: that he might be just, and the justifier of him which believeth in Jesus."

> **JUSTIFIED IN THE EYES OF GOD IS NEEDED**
> People are justified in the eyes of God only by those who truly believe in the Lord Jesus Christ. It is never by means of people's works.

- **Romans 4:5**
"But to him that worketh not, but believeth on him that justifieth the ungodly, his faith is counted for righteousness."

This verse is crystal clear on the relationship between genuine faith in the Lord Jesus Christ versus people's works.

- **Romans 5:1**
"Therefore being justified by faith, we have peace with God through our Lord Jesus Christ:"

All people must be justified or declared righteous in God's sight by true faith, not by their works.

- **Galatians 2:16**
"Knowing that a man is not justified by the works of the law, but by the faith of Jesus Christ, even we have believed in Jesus Christ, that we might be justified by the faith of Christ, and not by the works of the law: for by the works of the law shall no flesh be justified."

- **Galatians 3:26**
"For ye are all the children of God by faith in Christ Jesus."

Faith in the Lord Jesus Christ is the only way people can become children of God. It is not by their works.

- **Ephesians 2:8-9**
"For by grace are ye saved through faith; and that not of yourselves: *it is* the gift of God: Not of works, lest any man should boast."

These are very clear verses on this subject of faith versus works for salvation.

James 2:15

"If a brother or sister be naked, and destitute of daily food,"

This is an illustration of a genuine Christian man or woman who have neither proper clothing or proper food.

James 2:16

"And one of you say unto them, Depart in peace, be ye warmed and filled; notwithstanding ye give them not those things which are needful to the body; what doth it profit?"

It's not enough to say, be warmed and be filled with food. There must follow proper deeds to care for and help with these necessary needs. Just talking about these needs without assisting these people are without profit.

James 2:17

"Even so faith, if it hath not works, is dead, being alone."

James then explains this illustration. There must be genuine and real faith which is evidenced by good and properly motivated works that follow that genuine faith. If this faith is not followed by Biblical and sound works and deeds, that faith is dead faith.

THE MEANING OF THE GREEK WORD, "NEKROS."

The Greek Word for *"dead"* is NEKROS. Some of the meanings of that Greek Word are:

"1) properly; 1a) one that has breathed his last, lifeless; 1b) deceased, departed, one whose soul is in Hades; 1c) destitute of life, without life, inanimate; 2) metaph.; 2a) spiritually dead; 2a1) destitute of a life that recognises and is devoted to God, because given up to trespasses and sins; 2a2) inactive as respects doing right; 2b) destitute of force or power, inactive, inoperative."

Biblical faith cannot be dead faith. That kind of faith is phony faith. It is not genuine.

James 2:18

"Yea, a man may say, Thou hast faith, and I have works: shew me thy faith without thy works, and I will shew thee my faith by my works."

Here's a man who says someone has faith in the Lord Jesus Christ as Saviour and he has works. But is this man's *"faith"* genuine or spurious? It might not be genuine faith, but just faith in the head and the intellect, but not true faith from the heart.

TRUE FAITH IN CHRIST RESULTS IN GODLY WORKS

The other man says that he will show his faith in the Lord Jesus Christ by the godly and Christian works that he does. This does not teach that salvation is by good works, but it teaches that genuine faith should produce godly and Spirit-led works. Without such works, that kind of false and fake faith is vain and worthless.

When people live for the Devil, for the world, and for the flesh and yet say they have faith in the Lord Jesus Christ, we have every reason to doubt the genuineness of that person's faith. They are lying when they say they have faith in the Lord Jesus Christ and yet evidence these evil works. Sound faith should lead to sound results and sound works.

WHEN I BECAME A CHRISTIAN MY LIFE CHANGED

When I became a born-again Christian as a senior at Berea High School in Berea, Ohio, my classmates saw the fruit in my life. My life changed. My faith in the Lord Jesus Christ produced a difference in my life. I didn't do the things I used to do. I didn't go with the same crowd I used to go with.

This is what James is talking about. Show me your genuine faith in the Lord Jesus Christ by the Christian fruits displayed in your lives. Dead works are the result of dead and phony faith.

James 2:19

"Thou believest that there is one God; thou doest well: the devils also believe, and tremble."

James tells us that the devils believe, but how do they believe. Does this mean that they have true faith in the Lord Jesus Christ as their Saviour? Of course it does not. If not, what does it mean? It means that they have phony faith, not true faith. Perhaps they believe that Jesus was a real person, but they would never accept Him as their Saviour. That type of belief is dead. The devils have no Christian fruit or works.

Verses About Devils

- Mark 1:32-34

"And at even, when the sun did set, they brought unto him all that were diseased, and them that were possessed with devils. And all the city was gathered together at the door. And he healed many that were sick of divers diseases, and cast out many

James–Preaching Verse By Verse 71

devils; and suffered not the devils to speak, because they knew him."
The Lord Jesus Christ did not allow the devils to speak after He had cast them out of the people. They knew Him, but not as their Saviour from sin.

- **Mark 5:2-13**
"And when he was come out of the ship, immediately there met him out of the tombs a man with an unclean spirit. Who had *his* dwelling among the tombs; and no man could bind him, no, not with chains: Because that he had been often bound with fetters and chains, and the chains had been plucked asunder by him, and the fetters broken in pieces: neither could any *man* tame him. And always, night and day, he was in the mountains, and in the tombs, crying, and cutting himself with stones. But when he saw Jesus afar off, he ran and worshipped him, And cried with a loud voice, and said, What have I to do with thee, Jesus, *thou* Son of the most high God? I adjure thee by God, that thou torment me not. For he said unto him, Come out of the man, *thou* unclean spirit. And he asked him, What *is* thy name? And he answered, saying, My name *is* Legion: for we are many. And he besought him much that he would not send them away out of the country. Now there was there nigh unto the mountains a great herd of swine feeding. And all the devils besought him, saying, Send us into the swine, that we may enter into them. And forthwith Jesus gave them leave. And the unclean spirits went out, and entered into the swine: and the herd ran violently down a steep place into the sea, (they were about two thousand;) and were choked in the sea."

When I was on active duty as a Naval Chaplain, I preached on this event spoken of in the Gospels. I entitled it *"Taming the Untamed"* because the Lord Jesus Christ had miraculously healed this man who was untamed by anyone even though he was bound with chains.

The Senior Chaplain on the base was an apostate Presbyterian chaplain. He was in the chapel during my sermon. When the sermon was over, he was furious with me because of it. He said: *"Chaplain Waite, that sermon was intellectually barren and spiritually sterile."* He then removed me from preaching any longer in the morning services at that Navy Chapel. This he did despite the motto of the Navy Chaplaincy at this time which was "COOPERATION WITHOUT COMPROMISE." My Baptist endorsing agency would have stood with me in that sermon. The Senior Chaplain should not have violated the Navy Chaplain Corps' motto by being angry at this sermon.

This chaplain warned me that I would be called to Washington and would be rebuked. As it turned out, he was called to Washington, not me, and was ordered to have me returned to the morning Navy Chapel services like before. God led the Chaplaincy leaders of that day to do the right thing. I'm sure all would be changed for the worse in today's Navy Chaplain Corps.

When the devils entered into the swine, they all went into the sea and were destroyed. No wonder that the compromised Jews who tended the unclean swine were more concerned and angry at the loss of their animals rather than being happy that this man was finally clothed and in his right mind. They ordered the Lord Jesus Christ to leave their area.

- **Luke 4:41**

"And devils also came out of many, crying out, and saying, Thou art Christ the Son of God. And he rebuking *them* suffered them not to speak: for they knew that he was Christ."

The devils believe, but it is fake and phony "*belief.*" It is not true and sincere at all. They have a belief. True Bible belief is sincere and from the heart of people. It is not superficial like that of the devils that James is speaking about.

THE MEANING OF THE GREEK WORD, "PHRISSO."

The Greek Word for "*tremble*" is PHRISSO. Some of the meanings of that Greek Word are:

"*1) to bristle, stiffen, stand up; 2) to shudder, to **be struck with extreme fear, to be horrified.**"*

They are struck with extreme fear and horrified because of the Divine power ot the Lord Jesus Christ over them. In Him, they have met their match—and then much more!

James 2:20

"**But wilt thou know, O vain man, that faith without works is dead?**"

James is talking about "*man*" which is the Greek Word ANTHROPOS which means a human being person whether a man or a woman. He refers to these individuals as being "vain."

THE MEANING OF THE GREEK WORD, "KENOS."

The Greek Word for "*vain*" is KENOS. Some of the meanings of that Greek Word are:

"*1) empty, vain, devoid of truth; 1a) of places, vessels, etc., which contain nothing; 1b) of men; 1b1) empty handed;*

James–Preaching Verse By Verse

> 1b2) *without a gift* 1c) metaph. *destitute of spiritual wealth, of one who boasts of his faith as a transcendent possession, yet is without the fruits of faith* 1d) metaph. *of endeavours, labours, acts, which result in nothing, vain, fruitless, without effect;* 1d1) *vain of no purpose."*

All that such people do result in nothing. Their ideas and work is fruitless and with no valid purpose. The kind of faith that does not result in Christian works is dead faith. It is not genuine. It is the kind that the devils possess.

- **Matthew 5:16**
"Let your light so shine before men, that they may see your good works, and glorify your Father which is in heaven."

The Lord Jesus Christ told His disciples to let their Christian light shine so that others may see their Christian works and glorify their Father Who is in Heaven.

James 2:21

"Was not Abraham our father justified by works, when he had offered Isaac his son upon the altar?"

Here is another illustration that James gives. It speaks of how people are "justified" before other human beings. It is by their godly works and deeds. Justification before God is by sincere heart faith which God can see. Justification before people must be by their deeds and works which others can behold.

Verses On Being Justified Before By People By Works

> **ABRAHAM'S ACTIONS–AN EVIDENCE OF HIS FAITH**
> Abraham's actions and works were an evidence of his faith in God's instructions to sacrifice his son, Isaac. He passed God's test by what he did thus, by this action, clearly declaring his faith in God's previous promises concerning his son, Isaac.

- **Genesis 22:1-14**
"And it came to pass after these things, that God did tempt Abraham, and said unto him, Abraham: and he said, Behold, *here* I *am*. And he said, Take now thy son, thine only *son* Isaac, whom thou lovest, and get thee into the land of Moriah; and offer him there for a burnt offering upon one of the mountains which I will tell thee of. And Abraham rose up early in the morning, and saddled his ass, and took two of his young men with him, and Isaac his son, and clave the wood for the burnt

offering, and rose up, and went unto the place of which God had told him. Then <u>on the third day</u> Abraham lifted up his eyes, and saw the place afar off. And Abraham said unto his young men, Abide ye here with the ass; and <u>I and the lad will go yonder and worship, and come again to you</u>. And Abraham took the wood of the burnt offering, and laid *it* upon Isaac his son; and he took the fire in his hand, and a knife; and they went both of them together. And Isaac spake unto Abraham his father, and said, My father: and he said, Here *am* I, my son. And he said, Behold the fire and the wood: but <u>where *is* the lamb for a burnt offering? And Abraham said, My son, God will provide himself a lamb</u> for a burnt offering: so they went both of them together. And they came to the place which God had told him of; and Abraham built an altar there, and laid the wood in order, and bound Isaac his son, and laid him on the altar upon the wood. And Abraham stretched forth his hand, and took the knife to slay his son. And the angel of the LORD called unto him out of heaven, and said, Abraham, Abraham: and he said, Here *am* I. And he said, <u>Lay not thine hand upon the lad, neither do thou any thing unto him: for now I know that thou fearest God, seeing thou hast not withheld thy son, thine only *son* from me</u>. And Abraham lifted up his eyes, and looked, and behold <u>behind *him* a ram caught in a thicket by his horns: and Abraham went and took the ram, and offered him up for a burnt offering in the stead of his son</u>. And Abraham called the name of that place Jehovahjireh: as it is said *to* this day, In the mount of the LORD it shall be seen."

> **GOD PROMISED ABRAHAM SEED AS THE STARS**
> **God had promised that his seed would be as the stars of heaven, as the sand of the sea. Then he told Abraham go up on Mount Moriah and offer him up as a sacrifice.**

In obedience to God's command, Abraham went three days journey to Mount Moriah. I wonder what he was thinking about during this three-day journey. What was Isaac thinking about? What were Abraham's two young servants who were him thinking about?

Notice Abraham's solid faith in the promises of God when he said to his two young men who accompanied him:

>"*I and the lad will go yonder and worship, and <u>come again</u> to you.*"

It is very clear in the Hebrew text that the verb, "come again," is in the first person plural form–"***WE** will come again.*" That means both Abraham and Isaac would come down from mount Moriah again.

James–Preaching Verse By Verse

> **FAITH IN GOD LED ABRAHAM TO OBEDIENCE**
> How could Abraham be so certain that both he and Isaac would come down from the mount alive when God had told him to sacrifice him? Hebrews 11: 19 speaks about Abraham's firm faith in the Lord and in the bodily resurrection of Isaac if need be:

- **Hebrews 11:19**
"Accounting that <u>God was able to raise him up, even from the dead; from whence also he received him in a figure.</u>"

God told Abraham not to lay his hand upon his son, Isaac. Isaac asked Abraham earlier: *"where is the lamb for a burnt offering?"* Abraham replied that *"God will provide himself a lamb."* <u>God provided a male lamb for a sacrifice instead of his son, Isaac. This is a picture of the Lord Jesus Christ's offering of Himself as the Lamb of God.</u>

Here is the context of Hebrews 11:19 which shows God's promises to Abraham about his *"seed"* and the many generations of children would be born to Isaac.

- **Hebrews 11:17-19**
"By faith Abraham, when he was tried, offered up Isaac: and he that had received the promises offered up his only begotten *son*, Of whom it was said, That in Isaac shall thy seed be called: <u>Accounting that God *was* able to raise *him* up, even from the dead; from whence also he received him in a figure.</u>"

> **THOUSANDS OF DESCENDANTS PROMISED**
> Abraham's faith that God would raise up a seed of thousands of descendants of children was proved by his obedience to be obedient to God in the sacrifice of his son, Isaac.

James 2:22

"Seest thou how faith wrought with his works, and by works was faith made perfect?"

In the case of Abraham, his faith was established by his works and by those works his faith was made perfect or mature.

> **THE MEANING OF THE GREEK WORD, "TELEIOO."**
> The Greek Word for *"perfect"* is TELEIOO. Some of the meanings of that Greek Word are:
> "1) *to make perfect, complete; 1a) to carry through completely, to accomplish,*

> *finish, bring to an end; 2) to complete (perfect); 2a) add what is yet wanting in order to render a thing full; 2b) to be found perfect; 3) to bring to the end (goal) proposed; 4) to accomplish; 4a) bring to a close or fulfilment by event; 4a1) of the prophecies of the scripture"*

Verses On Being Perfect Or Mature

- **2 Corinthians 13:11**

"Finally, brethren, farewell. <u>Be perfect</u>, be of good comfort, be of one mind, live in peace; and the God of love and peace shall be with you."

<u>The true Christians in the church at Corinth were to be mature and grown up in their faith and knowledge of God's Words.</u>

- **Colossians 1:28**

"Whom we preach, warning every man, and teaching every man in all wisdom; <u>that we may present every man perfect in Christ Jesus:</u>"

<u>God wants all genuine Christians to be mature and grown up children rather than remaining babes in Christ.</u>

- **Colossians 4:12**

"Epaphras, who is *one* of you, a servant of Christ, saluteth you, always labouring fervently for you in prayers, <u>that ye may stand perfect and complete in all the will of God.</u>"

GOD WANTS CHRISTIANS TO BE MATURE

God wants all true Christians to stand mature and complete in all of God's will. His will is found in His Words. His Words must be read, studied, and followed day by day.

- **2 Timothy 3:17**

"<u>That the man of God may be perfect</u>, throughly furnished unto all good works."

SCRIPTURES PRESERVED TO ENABLE MATURITY

This is why the Scriptures were produced and preserved. It was to enable genuine Christians to be mature and complete by being thoroughly furnished with all good works that please the Lord Jesus Christ.

- **Hebrews 13:21**

"<u>Make you perfect in every good work to do his will</u>, working in you that which is wellpleasing in his sight, through Jesus Christ; to whom *be* glory for ever and ever. Amen."

Only the Lord Himself can make true Christians perfect and mature in the Lord Jesus Christ's will.

- **1 Peter 5:10**
"But <u>the God of all grace</u>, who hath called us unto his eternal glory by Christ Jesus, after that ye have suffered a while, <u>make you perfect</u>, stablish, strengthen, settle *you*."

The God of all grace, after some suffering, can make genuine Christians mature and grown up by His power.

James 2:23

"And the scripture was fulfilled which saith, Abraham believed God, and it was imputed unto him for righteousness: and he was called the Friend of God."

It is very clear that when Abraham believed God that God imputed righteousness unto him, calling him his friend.

THE MEANING OF THE GREEK WORD, "LOGIZOMAI."

The Greek Word for *"impute"* is LOGIZOMAI. Some of the meanings of that Greek Word are:

"1) to reckon, count, compute, calculate, count over; 1a) to take into account, to make an account of; 1a1) metaph. to pass to one's account, to impute; 1a2) a thing is reckoned as or to be something, i.e. as availing for or equivalent to something, as having the like force and weight; 1b) to number among, reckon with; 1c) to reckon or account; 2) to reckon inward, count up or weigh the reasons, to deliberate; 3) by reckoning up all the reasons, to gather or infer; 3a) to consider, take into account, weigh, meditate on; 3b) to suppose, deem, judge; 3c) to determine, purpose, decide. [This word deals with reality. If I "logizomai" or reckon that my bank book has $25 in it, it has $25 in it. Otherwise I am deceiving myself. This word refers to facts not suppositions.]"

<u>Biblical righteousness before God</u> is by genuine belief and faith in the Lord Jesus Christ as people's Saviour. **<u>Practical and observable righteousness before men</u>** is when true Christians practice Biblical good works in the power of the Holy Spirit. This

demonstrates and shows their sincere faith in the Lord Jesus Christ as their Saviour.
- **Genesis 15:1-6**
"After these things the word of the LORD came unto Abram in a vision, saying, Fear not, Abram: I *am* thy shield, *and* thy exceeding great reward. And Abram said, Lord GOD, what wilt thou give me, seeing I go childless, and the steward of my house *is* this Eliezer of Damascus? And Abram said, Behold, to me thou hast given no seed: and, lo, one born in my house is mine heir. And, behold, the word of the LORD *came* unto him, saying, This shall not be thine heir; but he that shall come forth out of thine own bowels shall be thine heir. And <u>he brought him forth abroad, and said, Look now toward heaven, and tell the stars, if thou be able to number them: and he said unto him, So shall thy seed be. And he believed in the LORD; and he counted it to him for righteousness.</u>"

God saw Abraham's genuine faith in His promise of a multitude of descendants and counted it to him for righteousness.
- **Romans 4:3**
"For what saith the scripture? <u>Abraham believed God, and it was counted unto him for righteousness.</u>"

This is a reference to Genesis 15:1-6 above. It corroborates God's method of imputing righteousness to those who trust Him by genuine faith.
- **Romans 4:5**
"But <u>to him that</u> worketh not, but <u>believeth on him that justifieth the ungodly, his faith is counted for righteousness.</u>"

Once again, righteousness with God is not by works, but by people's true and sincere faith in the Lord Jesus Christ as their Saviour.
- **Romans 4:11**
"And he received the sign of circumcision, a seal of the <u>righteousness of the faith which</u> *he had* <u>yet</u> being uncircumcised: that he might be the father of all them that believe, though they be not circumcised; that righteousness might be imputed unto them also:"

Righteousness by faith is taught here clearly.
- **Galatians 3:6**
"Even as <u>Abraham believed God, and it was accounted to him for righteousness.</u>"

ABRAHAM AND IMPUTED RIGHTEOUSNESS

Abraham is used repeatedly to illustrate God's imputed righteousness on a person because of his genuine faith in God's promises.

James 2:24

"Ye see then how that by works a man is justified, and not by faith only."

Remember that this "justification" is in the eyes of people. People have to see the works of these Christians to know whether or not they are genuine. "Justification" in the sight of God is by genuine faith in the Lord Jesus Christ as Saviour. God doesn't need to see people's works to know if they are true Christians. He can see their sincere faith in their Saviour, but people need works to "justify" people who profess to be Christians.

Verses On Justification

- **Acts 13:39**

"And by him all that believe are justified from all things, from which ye could not be justified by the law of Moses."
Genuine believing in the Lord Jesus Christ is what justifies people.

- **Romans 3:24**

"Being justified freely by his grace through the redemption that is in Christ Jesus:"
Justification is by God's grace through the Lord Jesus Christ's redemption. Justification is an act of God whereby a person is declared righteous in His sight.

- **Romans 3:26**

"To declare, *I say*, at this time his righteousness: that he might be just, and the justifier of him which believeth in Jesus."
Because of what the Lord Jesus Christ did on the cross of Calvary, God is both just and also is the "justifier" of all those who genuinely believe in the Lord Jesus Christ.

- **Romans 3:28**

"Therefore we conclude that a man is justified by faith without the deeds of the law."

JUSTIFICATION BEFORE GOD BY FAITH

Justification before God is by true faith in the Lord Jesus Christ, not by any deeds that people might do.

- **Romans 4:5**

"But to him that worketh not, but believeth on him that justifieth the ungodly, his faith is counted for righteousness."
In this verse, justification by God of every ungodly person in the world is not by their works, but by their true faith in the Lord Jesus Christ.

- **Galatians 3:24**

"Wherefore the law was our schoolmaster *to bring us* unto

Christ, that we might be justified by faith."
Justification before God is by genuine faith in the Lord Jesus Christ alone.

- **Romans 5:1**
  "Therefore being justified by faith, we have peace with God through our Lord Jesus Christ:"

Justification before God by faith in the Lord Jesus Christ brings peace with God.

James 2:25

"Likewise also was not Rahab the harlot justified by works, when she had received the messengers, and had sent them out another way?"

Joshua sent two men to search out the land before Israel entered into Canaan. They went into Jericho and entered the house of Rahab the harlot. Apparently, she was a former harlot. She had repented and trusted the Lord God of Israel. In fact, she is in the line of our Saviour. She received the messengers and sent them on their way. These works showed her inner faith which justified her in the eyes of people.

Verses About Rahab

- **Joshua 2:1**
  "And Joshua the son of Nun sent out of Shittim two men to spy secretly, saying, Go view the land, even Jericho. And they went, and came into an harlot's house, named Rahab, and lodged there."

The two spies stayed in Rahab's house.

- **Joshua 2:6**
  "But she had brought them up to the roof of the house, and hid them with the stalks of flax, which she had laid in order upon the roof."

They were hidden on Rahab's roof under stalks of flax.

- **Joshua 2:8-15**
  "And before they were laid down, she came up unto them upon the roof; And she said unto the men, I know that the LORD hath given you the land, and that your terror is fallen upon us, and that all the inhabitants of the land faint because of you. For we have heard how the LORD dried up the water of the Red sea for you, when ye came out of Egypt; and what ye did unto the two kings of the Amorites, that were on the other side Jordan, Sihon and Og, whom ye utterly destroyed. And as soon as we had heard *these things*, our hearts did melt, neither did there remain any more courage in any man, because of you: for the LORD

your God, he *is* God in heaven above, and in earth beneath. Now therefore, I pray you, swear unto me by the LORD, since I have shewed you kindness, that ye will also shew kindness unto my father's house, and give me a true token: And *that* ye will save alive my father, and my mother, and my brethren, and my sisters, and all that they have, and deliver our lives from death. And the men answered her, Our life for yours, if ye utter not this our business. And it shall be, when the LORD hath given us the land, that we will deal kindly and truly with thee. Then <u>she let them down by a cord through the window</u>: for her house *was* upon the town wall, and she dwelt upon the wall."

Jericho's wall just fell flat. The only thing that did not fall down was that harlot's house where the father and the mother and the family were safe. <u>The scarlet cord that was let down is a picture of the blood of Christ. Rehab was justified in the eyes of people who saw her good works in saving the two spies.</u>

James 2:26

"For as the body without the spirit is dead, so faith without works is dead also."

DEATH DEFINED-THE BODY WITHOUT THE SPIRIT

That is a good definition of death. Death is the body without the spirit. When the spirit and soul leave this body, our body is dead. So faith without works is dead also. Dead faith we don't need. True Christians need vibrant, genuine faith that brings forth fruit that others may see.

Verses On Good Works

- **Titus 3:14**

"And <u>let ours also learn to maintain good works</u> for necessary uses, that they be not unfruitful."

CHRISTIANS MUST BEAR GOOD FRUIT

Genuine Christian believers must bear fruit. That's what James is going after. Paul declared in Romans that people can be justified before God by genuine faith in the Lord Jesus Christ. Good works should result in that justifying faith in the Saviour.

- **2 Peter 1:8**

"For if these things be in you, and abound, they make *you that ye shall* neither *be* barren nor unfruitful in the knowledge of our Lord Jesus Christ."

God does not want true Christians barren or unfruitful in their lives. He wants them to produce fruit.

- **John 15:5**

"I am the vine, ye *are* the branches: He that abideth in me, and I in him, the same bringeth forth much fruit: for without me ye can do nothing."

Genuine Christians who abide in Christ the True Vine will bring forth much fruit.

- **John 15:8**

"Herein is my Father glorified, that ye bear much fruit; so shall ye be my disciples."

God wants true Christians to bear much fruit.

- **John 15:16**

"Ye have not chosen me, but I have chosen you, and ordained you, that ye should go and bring forth fruit, and *that* your fruit should remain: that whatsoever ye shall ask of the Father in my name, he may give it you."

CHRISTIANS SHOULD BEAR PERMANENT FRUIT

This is why the Lord Jesus Christ chose His disciples–to bear much permanent fruit. That should be the result of sincere faith in the Lord Jesus Christ as their Saviour.

James Chapter Three

James 3:1

"My brethren, be not many masters, knowing that we shall receive the greater condemnation."

James cautions his many readers to stop trying to be *"masters"* which means *"teachers"* in this verse.

> **HOW TO STOP AN ACTION ALREADY IN PROGRESS**
>
> This action comes from the fact that the Greek verb for *"be"* is in the Greek present tense. This negative prohibition indicates a present action that should be stopped. If these teachers make mistakes, they will receive greater condemnation because they have led their pupils astray.

There are many theological modernists, liberals, and apostates preaching in churches and teaching people doctrinal errors. God says there's going to be great judgment and condemnation for erroneous teaching.

> **THE MEANING OF THE GREEK WORD, "KRIMA."**
>
> The Greek Word for *"condemnation"* is KRIMA. Some of the meanings of that Greek Word are:
>
> *"1) a decree, judgments; 2) judgment; 2a) condemnation of wrong, the decision (whether severe or mild) which one passes on the faults of others; 2b) in a forensic sense; 2b1) the sentence of a judge; 2b2) the punishment with which one is sentenced; 2b3) condemnatory sentence, penal judgment, sentence; 3) a matter to be judicially decided, a lawsuit, a case in court."*

It is better not to have any teaching at all rather than to teach error

Verses Using The Word, Master
- **Luke 6:40**

"<u>The disciple is not above his master</u>: but every one that is perfect shall be as his master."

In other words, learners are not above their teachers.

- **John 3:10**

"Jesus answered and said unto him, <u>Art thou a master of Israel, and knowest not these things</u>?"

As a teacher, Nicodemus should have known these things.

- **2 Timothy 2:2**

"And the things that thou hast heard of me among many witnesses, <u>the same commit thou to faithful men, who shall be able to teach others also</u>."

Teachers must be good students. They must know the Scriptures and teach others what they know.

James 3:2

"For in many things we offend all. If any man offend not in word, the same is a perfect man, and able also to bridle the whole body."

This verse highlights the importance of the proper use of the tongue. Offending others by our words is a common occurrence. If people do not offend in their words, they are called "*perfect*."

THE MEANING OF THE GREEK WORD, "TELEIOS."

The Greek Word for "*perfect*" is TELEIOS. Some of the meanings of this Greek Word are:

"*1) brought to its end, finished; 2) wanting nothing necessary to completeness; 3) perfect; 4) that which is perfect; 4a) consummate human integrity and virtue; 4b) of men; 4b1) full grown, adult, of full age, mature*"

Control of the tongue indicates a maturity in the person involved. Such control would lead also in the "bridling" of the entire body.

MEANING OF THE GREEK WORD, "CHALINAGOGEO."

The Greek word for "*bridle*" is CHALINAGOGEO. Some of the meanings of that Greek Word are:

"*1) to lead by a bridle, to guide; 2) to*

> *bridle, hold in check, restrain.*"

People might be able to run a mile in very few minutes, to high jump or pole vault very high, or do other feats, but the measure of perfect, complete, mature people is not to offend in word and being able to bridle the entire body.

Verses On Offend
- **Psalms 119:165**

"Great peace have they which love thy law: and <u>nothing shall offend them</u>."

If people love God's Words, they will be able to handle offensive words and behavior.

- **1 Corinthians 8:13**

"Wherefore, <u>if meat make my brother to offend</u>, I will eat no flesh while the world standeth, <u>lest I make my brother to offend</u>."

In the New Testament time (and also today), eating certain foods offended some people.

Verses On Perfect
- **Matthew 5:48**

"<u>Be ye therefore perfect</u>, even as <u>your Father which is in heaven is perfect</u>."

The goal of genuine Christians should be to be perfect or mature Christians by studying and living out the Words of God.

- **2 Corinthians 12:9**

"And he said unto me, My grace is sufficient for thee: for <u>my strength is made perfect</u> in weakness. Most gladly therefore will I rather glory in my infirmities, that the power of Christ may rest upon me."

GOD'S STRENGTH IS MADE PERFECT IN WEAKNESS

God's strength is made perfect in the weakness of true Christians who, though weak, trust in that strength.

- **Ephesians 4:13**

"<u>Till we all come</u> in the unity of the faith, and of the knowledge of the Son of God, <u>unto a perfect man</u>, unto the measure of the stature of the fulness of Christ:"

When genuine Christians get to Heaven, they will be absolutely mature and perfect.

- **Colossians 1:28**

"Whom we preach, warning every man, and teaching every man in all wisdom; that we may <u>present every man perfect in Christ Jesus</u>:"

> **CHRISTIANS SHOULD BE MATURE IN CHRIST**
> Again, this refers to Paul's desire for true Christians to be mature in the Lord Jesus Christ.

- Colossians 4:12

"Epaphras, who is *one* of you, a servant of Christ, saluteth you, always labouring fervently for you in prayers, that ye may stand perfect and complete in all the will of God."

Genuine Christians should be mature and complete in God's will.

- 2 Timothy 3:17

"That the man of God may be perfect, throughly furnished unto all good works."

> **THE BIBLE CAN MAKE CHRISTIANS MATURE**
> The Scriptures can make true Christians perfect and mature if they study them and follow them.

Verses On Bridle

- Psalms 32:9

"Be ye not as the horse, *or* as the mule, *which* have no understanding: whose mouth must be held in with bit and bridle, lest they come near unto thee."

Genuine Christians should bridle and control their tongues as bridles control horses and mules.

- Psalms 39:1

"I said, I will take heed to my ways, that I sin not with my tongue: I will keep my mouth with a bridle, while the wicked is before me."

> **THE TONGUE NEEDS TO BE BRIDLED**
> Putting a bridle on the tongue will prevent speaking wrong and harmful words.

- Isaiah 37:29

"Because thy rage against me, and thy tumult, is come up into mine ears, therefore will I put my hook in thy nose, and my bridle in thy lips, and I will turn thee back by the way by which thou camest."

Isaiah said that he also needed a bridle in his lips to restrain his tongue.

James 3:3

"Behold, we put bits in the horses' mouths, that they may obey us; and we turn about their whole body."

The bits in the mouth of horses are used to control the horse's actions and direction. Bits are about four inches long and yet they can control a very large horse. Having been given a horse when I was a young man, I know about the use of bits. There is a straight bit which is used to stop most horses. There is also a curved bit that when used is more painful to the horse and is used to stop frisky horses. My horse was very frisky so I used both bits for my Arabian five-gaited mare. She obeyed me very well with the use of the bit that might be needed at the time.

James 3:4

"Behold also the ships, which though they be so great, and are driven of fierce winds, yet are they turned about with a very small helm, whithersoever the governor listeth."

Here is another illustration of small things that guide larger things. A very small helm or rudder, by comparison, can direct a very large ship. We have the bit which is small that controls the whole horse and so the rudder, the helm, controls a huge ship. You need a little bit to control the big things. The ships, though they be so great and huge, are driven by fierce stormy winds. In like manner, our little tongue can control our entire bodily actions if it gets out of line.

James 3:5

"Even so the tongue is a little member, and boasteth great things. Behold, how great a matter a little fire kindleth!"

THE SMALL TONGUE CAN DO HUGE DAMAGE

So a very small tongue can boast of very large and great things. The tongue here is likened to a little part of our body that can kindle huge fires if not kept in control. It's like the literal fires that, as this is written, burned down thousands of acres of a forest and also scores of homes that were in its path.

Verses On The Tongue
- **Psalms 10:7**

"His mouth is full of cursing and deceit and fraud: <u>under his tongue *is* mischief and vanity</u>."

MANY UNCHRISTIAN MOUTHS ARE FILTHY
Worldly unsaved people often have filthy mouths filled with cursing, mischief, vanity, and filth. More and more television that used to censor certain bad or cursing words now permits them to spue out of actors' mouths.

- **Psalms 12:3**

"The LORD shall cut off all flattering lips, *and* <u>the tongue that speaketh proud things</u>:"

Flattering, proud, and arrogant words proceed forth from the tongue of many.

- **Psalms 15:3**

"<u>*He that* backbiteth not with his tongue</u>, nor doeth evil to his neighbour, nor taketh up a reproach against his neighbour."

It is good not to backbite with the tongue, yet many use their tongues for this purpose against their enemies.

- **Psalms 34:13**

"Keep thy tongue from evil, and thy lips from speaking guile."

Just keep it from evil. That's all.

- **Psalms 35:28**

"And <u>my tongue shall speak of thy righteousness *and* of thy praise all the day long</u>."

MAY OUR TONGUES SPEAK OF PRAISE TO GOD
This is a proper use of the tongue which is used to speak of God's righteousness and praise.

- **Psalms 39:1**

"I said, I will take heed to my ways, <u>that I sin not with my tongue</u>: I will keep my mouth with a bridle, while the wicked is before me."

King David did not want to sin with his tongue. He wanted to bridle his tongue and mouth.

- **Psalms 50:19**

"Thou givest thy mouth to evil, and <u>thy tongue frameth deceit</u>."

David was talking about an evil man whose tongue framed deceit. There are many such people in our world today.

- **Psalms 52:2**

"<u>Thy tongue deviseth mischiefs; like a sharp razor, working deceitfully</u>."

James–Preaching Verse By Verse

THE UNBRIDLED TONGUE DOES THREE THINGS
This description of the tongue is clear: (1) it devises mischiefs; (2) it is like a sharp razor; and (3) it works deceitfully.

- **Psalms 57:4**

"My soul *is* among lions: *and* I lie *even among* them that are set on fire, *even* the sons of men, whose teeth *are* spears and arrows, and their tongue a sharp sword."

The tongue can be turned into a sharp sword that pierces and kills people's honor and reputation.

- **Psalms 64:3**

"Who whet their tongue like a sword, *and* bend *their bows to shoot* their arrows, *even* bitter words:"

Here again the tongue is likened to a dangerous aggressive sword.

- **Psalms 66:17**

"I cried unto him with my mouth, and he was extolled with my tongue."

The Lord can be extolled and lifted up with the tongue.

- **Psalms 71:24**

"My tongue also shall talk of thy righteousness all the day long: for they are confounded, for they are brought unto shame, that seek my hurt."

This is a good use of the tongue by talking of God's righteousness all day.

- **Psalms 73:9**

"They set their mouth against the heavens, and their tongue walketh through the earth."

These tongues speak against God and His heavens throughout the whole world.

- **Psalms 119:172**

"My tongue shall speak of thy word: for all thy commandments *are* righteousness."

OUR TONGUES SHOULD EXALT GODS WORDS
The psalmist uses his tongue to exalt God's righteous Words.

- **Psalms 126:2**

"Then was our mouth filled with laughter, and our tongue with singing: then said they among the heathen, The LORD hath done great things for them."

Here is singing with the tongue.

- **Psalms 139:4**
"For *there is* not a word in my tongue, *but*, lo, O LORD, thou knowest it altogether."

God, because of His omniscience, knows every word on the tongue of everyone.

- **Proverbs 6:24**
"To keep thee from the evil woman, from the flattery of the tongue of a strange woman."

DON'T SUCCUMB TO LYING HARLOTS

God does not want His children to succumb to the lying flattery of any strange harlot women.

- **Proverbs 10:20**
"The tongue of the just *is as* choice silver: the heart of the wicked *is* little worth."

Just people have tongues that are like choice silver.

- **Proverbs 12:18-19**
"There is that speaketh like the piercings of a sword: but the tongue of the wise *is* health. The lip of truth shall be established for ever: but a lying tongue *is* but for a moment."

The tongue of those who are wise is healthy.

- **Proverbs 15:2**
"The tongue of the wise useth knowledge aright: but the mouth of fools poureth out foolishness."

Wise people use their tongues in right ways.

- **Proverbs 15:4**
"A wholesome tongue *is* a tree of life: but perverseness therein *is* a breach in the spirit."

A wholesome tongue is like a tree that gives life-giving benefits.

- **Proverbs 16:1**
"The preparations of the heart in man, and the answer of the tongue, *is* from the LORD."

If people are asking for it, God can give proper answers to their questions.

- **Proverbs 18:21**
"Death and life *are* in the power of the tongue: and they that love it shall eat the fruit thereof."

The tongue is capable of pronouncing either death or life in certain situations.

- **Proverbs 21:23**
"Whoso keepeth his mouth and his tongue keepeth his soul from troubles."

James–Preaching Verse By Verse

A CONTROLLED TONGUE AVOIDS MUCH TROUBLE
If the tongue is controlled, it will keep people out of many troubles.

- **Proverbs 26:28**

"A lying tongue hateth *those that are* afflicted by it; and a flattering mouth worketh ruin."

A tongue that lies hates those who are harmed by it.

- **Proverbs 31:26**

"She openeth her mouth with wisdom; and in her tongue *is* the law of kindness."

The virtuous woman speaks out kindness with her tongue rather than wickedness.

- **Romans 14:11**

"For it is written, As I live, saith the Lord, every knee shall bow to me, and every tongue shall confess to God."

BOTH SAVED AND LOST WILL CONFESS TO CHRIST
One day in the future, God will make every person in the world confess to Him. This includes the genuine Christians who will confess that the Lord Jesus Christ is their Saviour. It also includes the lost, unsaved who have never trusted in the Lord Jesus Christ as their Saviour. At the Great White Throne judgment, they will have to agree with God that they are without excuse for their rejection of His Son.

- **Philippians 2:11**

"And *that* every tongue should confess that Jesus Christ *is* Lord, to the glory of God the Father."

Every tongue of the true Christians should confess that Jesus Christ is Lord.

- **James 1:26**

"If any man among you seem to be religious, and bridleth not his tongue, but deceiveth his own heart, this man's religion *is* vain."

If people do not bridle their tongues, their religion is vain and useless.

- **1 Peter 3:10**

"For he that will love life, and see good days, let him refrain his tongue from evil, and his lips that they speak no guile:"

To have a good life and good days, people should refrain their tongues from speaking evil.

- **1 John 3:18**

"My little children, let us not love in word, neither in tongue; but in deed and in truth."

CHRISTIAN LOVE SHOWN BY WORDS AND DEEDS

True Christian love cannot be evidenced only by the use of the tongue, but must be followed by both deeds and truth. Genuine Christians must take diligent heed to how they use their tongues when speaking to other Christians as well as when speaking to people who are not true Christians.

James 3:6

"And the tongue is a fire, a world of iniquity: so is the tongue among our members, that it defileth the whole body, and setteth on fire the course of nature; and it is set on fire of hell."

The tongue is a fire. This is a metaphor which likens the tongue to a fire. Hell has real and literal fire, though many are denying it these days. It is called the "*Lake of Fire.*" (Revelation 19:20; 20:10; 20:14-15.)

A DIRTY TONGUE CAN DEFILE THE WHOLE BODY

But the tongue has the potential of being a "*world of iniquity*" if used wrongly. It can defile the whole body. You might say that your body is clean because you take a shower or a bath. A dirty talking tongue can make your whole body defiled and dirty from God's standpoint. God says here that, when misused, it is "*set on fire of hell.*"

Verses On Fire

- **Proverbs 6:27**

"Can a man take fire in his bosom, and his clothes not be burned?"

The result of fire in your chest is that your clothes will be burned as well as your flesh. You could die.

- **Matthew 3:12**

"Whose fan *is* in his hand, and he will throughly purge his floor, and gather his wheat into the garner; but he will burn up the chaff with unquenchable fire."

THE LOST WILL BE SENT TO EVERLASTING FIRE

The Lord Jesus Christ is speaking about the non-Christians who will be sent to the Lake of Fire in Hell and like chaff will suffer in the fire.

- **Matthew 5:22**
"But I say unto you, That whosoever is angry with his brother without a cause shall be in danger of the judgment: and whosoever shall say to his brother, Raca, shall be in danger of the council: but whosoever shall say, Thou fool, shall be in danger of hell fire."

The fires of Hell are real. Though the Lord Jesus speaks of literal fire in Hell, many (even some Bible-believing Christians) are denying it.

- **Matthew 13:42**
"And shall cast them into a furnace of fire: there shall be wailing and gnashing of teeth."

The Lord Jesus Christ is speaking of a furnace of real fire in Hell.

- **Matthew 18:8-9**
"Wherefore if thy hand or thy foot offend thee, cut them off, and cast *them* from thee: it is better for thee to enter into life halt or maimed, rather than having two hands or two feet to be cast into everlasting fire. And if thine eye offend thee, pluck it out, and cast *it* from thee: it is better for thee to enter into life with one eye, rather than having two eyes to be cast into hell fire."

The fires of Hell are not only literal, but they are also everlasting.

- **Matthew 25:41**
"Then shall he say also unto them on the left hand, Depart from me, ye cursed, into everlasting fire, prepared for the devil and his angels:"

EVERLASTING HELL FIRE AWAITS THE LOST PEOPLE

God did not prepare the everlasting fires of Hell for people. He prepared it for the Devil and his angels. Those who reject the Saviour will be sent to that everlasting fire at the judgment of the nations.

- **Mark 9:45**
"And if thy foot offend thee, cut it off: it is better for thee to enter halt into life, than having two feet to be cast into hell, into the fire that never shall be quenched:"

Again this is a clear verse that teaches that unquenchable fire will be in Hell.

- **1 Corinthians 3:13**
"Every man's work shall be made manifest: for the day shall declare it, because it shall be revealed by fire; and the fire shall try every man's work of what sort it is."

In this picture of the Judgment Seat Of Christ, fire is described as burning up Christians' bad works which are likened to hay, wood, and stubble.

- **2 Thessalonians 1:8**
"In flaming fire taking vengeance on them that know not God, and that obey not the gospel of our Lord Jesus Christ:"

AT ARMAGEDDON, FLAMING FIRE WILL BE USED
At the battle of Armageddon, flaming fire will be used by the Lord to win the battle against His enemies.

- **Hebrews 12:29**
"For our God is a consuming fire."
God is absolutely Holy and Perfect. Only by genuine faith in the Lord Jesus Christ can a person escape God's consuming fires of Hell.

- **1 Peter 1:7**
"That the trial of your faith, being much more precious than of gold that perisheth, though it be tried with fire, might be found unto praise and honour and glory at the appearing of Jesus Christ:"
Fire removes the dross and impurities that might be in gold.

- **2 Peter 3:7**
"But the heavens and the earth, which are now, by the same word are kept in store, reserved unto fire against the day of judgment and perdition of ungodly men."

HEAVEN AND EARTH WILL PERISH BY FIRE
The scriptures teach clearly that the heavens and earth will not perish by water, but by fire instead.

- **2 Peter 3:12**
"Looking for and hasting unto the coming of the day of God, wherein the heavens being on fire shall be dissolved, and the elements shall melt with fervent heat?"

THE ELEMENTS WILL MELT WITH FERVENT HEAT
This scientific statement, made in the Bible, will one day come true. The elements will melt with fervent heat and we will have a New Heaven and a New Earth.

- **Jude 1:7**
"Even as Sodom and Gomorrha, and the cities about them in like manner, giving themselves over to fornication, and going after strange flesh, are set forth for an example, suffering the vengeance of eternal fire."

The Lord condemned Sodom and Gomorrha with fire and brimstone.

There are many verses on fire. The wayward and uncontrolled tongue is like a fire that just burns and burns and burns.

James 3:7

"For every kind of beasts, and of birds, and of serpents, and of things in the sea, is tamed, and hath been tamed of mankind:"

Though it is difficult, various animals, birds and fish can be tamed. But some people's tongues cannot be tamed by man. Only the Lord can do that.

Taming The Untamed Man
- Mark 5:1-15

"And they came over unto the other side of the sea, into the country of the Gadarenes. And when he was come out of the ship, immediately there met him out of the tombs a man with an unclean spirit, Who had *his* dwelling among the tombs; and <u>no man could bind him, no, not with chains</u>: Because that he had been often bound with fetters and chains, and the chains had been plucked asunder by him, and the fetters broken in pieces: <u>neither could any *man* tame him</u>. And always, night and day, he was in the mountains, and in the tombs, crying, and cutting himself with stones. But when he saw Jesus afar off, he ran and worshipped him, And cried with a loud voice, and said, What have I to do with thee, Jesus, *thou* Son of the most high God? I adjure thee by God, that thou torment me not. For he said unto him, Come out of the man, *thou* unclean spirit. And he asked him, What *is* thy name? And he answered, saying, My name *is* Legion: for we are many. And he besought him much that he would not send them away out of the country. Now there was there nigh unto the mountains a great herd of swine feeding. And all the devils besought him, saying, Send us into the swine, that we may enter into them. And forthwith Jesus gave them leave. And the unclean spirits went out, and entered into the swine: and the herd ran violently down a steep place into the sea, (they were about two thousand;) and were choked in the sea. And they that fed the swine fled, and told *it* in the city, and in the country. And they went out to see what it was that was done. And <u>they come to Jesus, and see him that was possessed with the devil, and had the legion, sitting, and clothed, and in his right mind</u>: and they were afraid."

Just like many tongues. This man was untamed.

As a Navy Chaplain on active duty in Corpus Christi, Texas, I preached a sermon about this passage. I called it "TAMING THE UNTAMED." Though the motto of the Naval Chaplaincy at that time was "COOPERATION WITHOUT COMPROMISE," the senior

Chaplain (Chaplain Carter) who was an apostate Presbyterian, had this to say after the sermon. He said the sermon was *"intellectually barren and spiritually sterile."* He told me that I could no longer preach in the Navy Chapel in the regular morning services. He said that I would be called to Washington and reprimanded for this. As it turned out, HE was called to Washington and reprimanded. He was told to put me back preaching in the regular chapel services. I was grateful to the Lord for the way this turned out.

James 3:8

"**But the tongue can no man tame; it is an unruly evil, full of deadly poison."**

NO HUMAN BEING CAN TAME THE TONGUE
The tongue which is a part of the sinful flesh of people cannot be tamed by man. Only the Lord can do that by the power of the Holy Spirit who indwells every genuine Christian.

Verses On The Flesh And Tongue
- **Romans 3:13-14**

"Their throat *is* an open sepulchre; with their tongues they have used deceit; the poison of asps *is* under their lips: Whose mouth *is* full of cursing and bitterness:"

The tongue can be deceitful like poison.
- **Romans 7:18**

"For I know that in me (that is, in my flesh,) dwelleth no good thing: for to will is present with me; but *how* to perform that which is good I find not."

Even the flesh of the true Christians had no good thing dwelling in it. It is sinful.
- **Romans 13:14**

"But put ye on the Lord Jesus Christ, and make not provision for the flesh, to *fulfil* the lusts *thereof.*"

The flesh must not be given any provision to act in an inappropriate and sinful manner.
- **2 Corinthians 7:1**

"Having therefore these promises, dearly beloved, let us cleanse ourselves from all filthiness of the flesh and spirit, perfecting holiness in the fear of God."

Both the sins that true Christians commit both in their flesh and their human spirit must be cleansed.

- **2 Corinthians 10:3**

"For though we walk in the flesh, we do not war after the flesh:" Though all genuine Christians still have their flesh, it is not to be used in spiritual warfare.

- **Galatians 2:20**

"I am crucified with Christ: nevertheless I live; yet not I, but Christ liveth in me: and the life which I now live in the flesh I live by the faith of the Son of God, who loved me, and gave himself for me."

CHRISTIANS SHOULD BE LED BY THE LORD
So true Christians who live in the flesh must be controlled by the Lord, not their flesh.

- **Galatians 5:16**

"*This* I say then, Walk in the Spirit, and ye shall not fulfil the lust of the flesh."

- **Galatians 5:17**

"For the flesh lusteth against the Spirit, and the Spirit against the flesh: and these are contrary the one to the other: so that ye cannot do the things that ye would."

THE CHRISTIAN BATTLE BETWEEN FLESH & SPIRIT
In the lives of genuine Christians, there is a battle between their flesh and God the Holy Spirit Who indwells them.

- **Galatians 5:19-21**

"Now the works of the flesh are manifest, which are *these*; Adultery, fornication, uncleanness, lasciviousness, Idolatry, witchcraft, hatred, variance, emulations, wrath, strife, seditions, heresies, Envyings, murders, drunkenness, revellings, and such like: of the which I tell you before, as I have also told *you* in time past, that they which do such things shall not inherit the kingdom of God."

There are many and varied works of the flesh mentioned here. Only the Holy Spirit can keep true Christians from manifesting them.

- **Philippians 3:3**

"For we are the circumcision, which worship God in the spirit, and rejoice in Christ Jesus, and have no confidence in the flesh." The genuine Christians should have no confidence in any part of their fleshly nature. Their confidence must be in God the Holy Spirit Who indwells them.

James 3:9

"Therewith bless we God, even the Father; and therewith curse we men, which are made after the similitude of God."

The same tongue is used for both blessing God and sometimes cursing human beings which are made after the similitude of God.

THE MEANING OF THE GREEK WORD, "HOMOIOSIS."
The Greek Word for *"similitude"* is HOMOIOSIS. Some of the meanings of that Greek Word are:
"1) a making like; 2) likeness: after the likeness of God."
This word for *"similitude"* means *"like"* but not the *"same as."* That Greek Word would be something like HOMOOSIS. <u>Human beings (ANTHROPOI) are not identical to God but are like God in that they are tripartite, having three parts: (1) spirit, (2) soul and (3) body. God is also tripartite, existing in three Divine Persons, God the Father, God the Son, and God the Holy Sprit.</u>

Verses On Blessing

THE MEANING OF THE GREEK WORD, "EULOGEO."
The Greek Word for *"bless"* is EULOGEO. Some of the meanings of this Greek Word are:
"1) to praise, celebrate with praises; 2) to invoke blessings; 3) to consecrate a thing with solemn prayers; 3a) to ask God's blessing on a thing; 3b) pray God to bless it to one's use; 3c) pronounce a consecratory blessing on; 4) of God; 4a) to cause to prosper, to make happy, to bestow blessings on; 4b) favoured of God, blessed."

- **Psalms 103:1-2**

"<u>Bless the LORD</u>, O my soul: and all that is within me, *bless* his holy name. <u>Bless the LORD</u>, O my soul, and forget not all his benefits:"

Ths psalmist blessed the Name of the Lord.

- **Psalms 115:18**

"But <u>we will bless the LORD</u> from this time forth and for evermore. Praise the LORD."

James–Preaching Verse By Verse

People are urged to praise the LORD, but many curse and blaspheme Him instead.

- **1 Corinthians 4:12**
"And labour, working with our own hands: being reviled, we bless; being persecuted, we suffer it:"

Paul blessed even though he was reviled by many people. He was truly a converted and changed man.

- **Psalms 62:4**
"They only consult to cast *him* down from his excellency: they delight in lies: they bless with their mouth, but they curse inwardly. Selah."

This is a hypocritical blessing by these people. Inwardly they are cursing though their mouths are blessing.

- **Psalms 109:28**
"Let them curse, but bless thou: when they arise, let them be ashamed; but let thy servant rejoice."

David was to bless, even in the midst of being cursed. That is not easy.

- **Proverbs 27:14**
"He that blesseth his friend with a loud voice, rising early in the morning, it shall be counted a curse to him."

If a person blesses his friend very early in the morning when he is sleeping, it's considered a curse rather than a blessing. It is not the time to bless anyone.

- **Luke 6:28**
"Bless them that curse you, and pray for them which despitefully use you."

If true Christians are walking by the Spirit of God, they are able to bless those who curse them, though it is not easy to do.

- **Romans 12:14**
"Bless them which persecute you: bless, and curse not."

CHRISTIANS WERE TOLD TO BLESS PERSECUTORS

Once again, the genuine Christians in Rome were told to bless their persecutors. The Lord Jesus Christ was an example of this when He said of His persecutors, *"Father, forgive them; for they know not what they do"* (Luke 23:34).

James 3:10
"Out of the same mouth proceedeth blessing and cursing. My brethren, these things ought not so to be."

> **FROM THE SAME MOUTH--BLESSING AND CURSING**
> Out of the same mouth comes both blessing and cursing. This should not be the case with genuine Christians. All the verses given in James 3:9 above about blessing should be reviewed.

James 3:11
"Doth a fountain send forth at the same place sweet water and bitter?"

Like a fountain that doesn't send forth at the same place both sweet water and bitter water, so the tongue should not be used for both blessing and cursing.

> **THE MEANING OF THE GREEK WORD, "PIKROS"**
> The Greek Word for "*bitter*" is PIKROS. Some of the meanings of that Greek Word are:
> "*1) bitter; 2) metaph. harsh, virulent.*"

It's impossible to do.

> **THE MEANING OF THE GREEK WORD, "PEGE."**
> The Greek Word for 'fountain" is PEGE. Some of the meanings of this Greek Word are:
> "*1) fountain, spring; 2) a well fed by a spring.*"

The mouths of true Christians should be bringing forth a great quantity of the sweet water of blessings to those around them.

James 3:12
"Can the fig tree, my brethren, bear olive berries? either a vine, figs? so can no fountain both yield salt water and fresh."

The fig tree doesn't bear grapes and the vine doesn't bring forth figs. Nor can the fountain yield both salt water and fresh water.

Verses On Figs, Grapes And Other Fruit
- Matthew 7:16

"Ye shall know them by their <u>fruits</u>. Do men gather <u>grapes of thorns, or figs of thistles</u>?"

James–Preaching Verse By Verse

The Lord Jesus was talking about people who profess to be true Christians and yet their works do not measure up to their profession.
- **Matthew 7:17-27**
"Even so <u>every good tree bringeth forth good fruit; but a corrupt tree bringeth forth evil fruit</u>. A good tree cannot bring forth evil fruit, neither *can* a corrupt tree bring forth good fruit. Every tree that bringeth not forth good fruit is hewn down, and cast into the fire. Wherefore by their fruits ye shall know them. Not every one that saith unto me, Lord, Lord, shall enter into the kingdom of heaven; but he that doeth the will of my Father which is in heaven. Many will say to me in that day, Lord, Lord, have we not prophesied in thy name? and in thy name have cast out devils? and in thy name done many wonderful works? And then will I profess unto them, I never knew you: depart from me, ye that work iniquity. Therefore whosoever heareth these sayings of mine, and doeth them, I will liken him unto a wise man, which built his house upon a rock: And the rain descended, and the floods came, and the winds blew, and beat upon that house; and it fell not: for it was founded upon a rock. And every one that heareth these sayings of mine, and doeth them not, shall be likened unto a foolish man, which built his house upon the sand: And the rain descended, and the floods came, and the winds blew, and beat upon that house; and it fell: and great was the fall of it."

> **SPIRITUAL FRUIT SHOULD ACCOMPANY SALVATION**
>
> I think the Lord Jesus Christ is talking about those who are truly saved and those who are not saved. ***"By their fruits ye shall know them"* (Matthew 7:20).** Talking mouths do not make genuine Christians. They must be born-again by true faith in the Lord Jesus Christ. <u>If people are saved, they ought to demonstrate it be having spiritual fruit of that salvation.</u>

James 3:13

"Who is a wise man and endued with knowledge among you? let him shew out of a good conversation his works with meekness of wisdom."

A wise and knowledgeable man should have a life that shows his works with meekness of wisdom.

> **MEANING OF THE GREEK WORD, "ANASTROPHE."**
> The Greek Word for *"conversation"* is ANASTROPHE. Some of the meanings of this Greek Word are:
> *"1) manner of life, conduct, behaviour, deportment"*

> **THE MEANING OF THE GREEK WORD, "PRAUTES."**
> The Greek Word for *"meekness."* is PRAUTES. Some of the meanings of this Greek Word are:
> *"1) mildness of disposition, gentleness of spirit, meekness"*

The genuine Christian who is wise and knowledgeable should manifest such knowledge with mildness and gentleness in their daily lives.

Verses On Knowledge

- **1 Corinthians 8:1**

"Now as touching things offered unto idols, we know that we all have knowledge. Knowledge puffeth up, but charity edifieth."
We must be very careful about getting puffed up by knowledge.

- **1 Corinthians 8:11**

"And through thy knowledge shall the weak brother perish, for whom Christ died?"
Some Christians knew much about idolatry, others did not. Their actions should not cause other Christians to be stumbled.

- **Colossians 2:3**

"In whom are hid all the treasures of wisdom and knowledge."
The Lord Jesus Christ has in Himself all the treasures of both wisdom and knowledge.

- **2 Timothy 3:7**

"Ever learning, and never able to come to the knowledge of the truth."

> **GOD'S TRUTH IS FOUND ONLY IN THE RIGHT BIBLE**
> Part of the accumulation of knowledge must be in quest of God's truth as found in the Bible. **Learning that rejects God's truth is serious error.** The Lord Jesus Christ is the way, the truth and the life.

Verses On Wisdom

- **Luke 2:52**

"And Jesus increased in wisdom and stature, and in favour with God and man."

CHRIST WAS BOTH PERFECT GOD & PERFECT MAN
The Lord Jesus Christ came by the miraculous virgin birth as the Perfect Man as well as the Perfect God. He increased in favour with God and man.

- **Acts 6:3**

"Wherefore, brethren, look ye out among you seven men of honest report, full of the Holy Ghost and wisdom, whom we may appoint over this business."

Wisdom was an essential quality for the deacons who would take care of the widows in the congregation.

- **Acts 6:10**

"And they were not able to resist the wisdom and the spirit by which he spake."

Stephen preached the gospel of the Lord Jesus Christ. He had Godly wisdom. Because of that, he was stoned to death because of the wisdom by which he spoke.

- **Acts 7:10**

"And delivered him out of all his afflictions, and gave him favour and wisdom in the sight of Pharaoh king of Egypt; and he made him governor over Egypt and all his house."

God gave Joseph favour and wisdom in the sight of the Pharaoh of Egypt.

- **Ephesians 1:8**

"Wherein he hath abounded toward us in all wisdom and prudence;"

The Lord Jesus Christ abounded toward the Ephesian Christians in all wisdom. Those of us who are saved should have Godly wisdom.

- **Ephesians 1:17**

"That the God of our Lord Jesus Christ, the Father of glory, may give unto you the spirit of wisdom and revelation in the knowledge of him:"

THE EPHESUS CHURCH NEEDED GOD'S WISDOM
Paul was praying for the church at Ephesus that God would give them wisdom in the knowledge about the Lord Jesus Christ.

- **Colossians 1:9**

"For this cause we also, since the day we heard *it*, do not cease to pray for you, and to desire that ye might be filled with the knowledge of his will in all wisdom and spiritual understanding;"

Paul wanted the true Christians in Colosse to be filled with the knowledge of God's will. This is found in a full knowledge of God's Words.
- **Colossians 1:28**
"Whom we preach, warning every man, and teaching every man in all wisdom; that we may present every man perfect in Christ Jesus:"

When teaching the Words of God, people must have God's Divine wisdom. They must study God's Words and pray for God's wisdom to teach them faithfully.
- **Colossians 3:16**
"Let the word of Christ dwell in you richly in all wisdom; teaching and admonishing one another in psalms and hymns and spiritual songs, singing with grace in your hearts to the Lord."

The Words of the Lord Jesus Christ found accurately in our King James Bible must dwell with the genuine Christians in all wisdom. For this to be true, there must be a daily reading, studying, and living of the truths found therein.

READ THE BIBLE IN ONE YEAR=85 VERSES PER DAY

If we read 85 verses per day, the entire Bible can be read each year. I have been doing this since I was 17 years of age. It has been a rich blessing to me now at the age of 89 as this is being written. If you are interested in doing this, you might write me for the 85-verses per day Schedule of Bible verses to read each day of the year.

Colossians 4:5
"Walk in wisdom toward them that are without, redeeming the time."

When we walk through this world, we must use God's wisdom in dealing with those who are unsaved people.
- **James 1:5**
"If any of you lack wisdom, let him ask of God, that giveth to all *men* liberally, and upbraideth not; and it shall be given him."

CHRISTIANS NEED WISDOM FROM GOD'S WORDS

For the true Christian, the wisdom that is needed comes from God and His Words. They should ask Him for this wisdom as they read His Words.

James 3:14

"**But if ye have bitter envying and strife in your hearts, glory not, and lie not against the truth.**"

If genuine Christians lack God's wisdom, they might end up having bitter envying and strife in their hearts.

THE MEANING OF THE GREEK WORD, "ZELOS."

The Greek Word for "*envying*" is ZELOS. Some of the meanings of that Greek Word are:

"*1) excitement of mind, ardour, fervour of spirit; 1a) zeal, ardour in embracing, pursuing, defending anything; 1a1) zeal in behalf of, for a person or thing; 1a2) the fierceness of indignation, punitive zeal 1b) an envious and contentious rivalry, jealousy.*"

These feelings and actions should **not** be a part of the lives of true Christians. There are two commands in this verse. These Christians were not to be glorying or boasting about various things. Since this is a prohibition in the Greek present tense, it means to stop an action already being practiced. (1) They were to "stop their glorying."

The second command is also in the Greek present tense. It means to stop an action already being performed. (2) They were to stop their lying against the truths clearly taught in the Words of God.

Verses On Envy And Envying

- **Romans 13:13**

"Let us walk honestly, as in the day; not in rioting and drunkenness, not in chambering and wantonness, not in strife and envying."

These sins should not be a part of the genuine Christians' walk with the Lord Jesus Christ.

- **1 Corinthians 3:3**

"For ye are yet carnal: for whereas *there is* among you envying, and strife, and divisions, are ye not carnal, and walk as men?"

Envying was present in the lives of those Christians living in Corinth. They lived carnal lives, walking like unregenerate people.

- **Galatians 5:26**

"Let us not be desirous of vain glory, provoking one another, envying one another."

> **PROVOKING AND ENVYING ARE NOT GOOD**
> Those in Galatia were desiring vain glory. They were also provoking and envying one another. James wrote that all these bad things were not to be present.

James 3:15

"This wisdom descendeth not from above, but is earthly, sensual, devilish."

The kind of wisdom that leads to the sins mentioned in the previous verses does not come from above. It is characterized by three adjectives: (1) earthly; (2) sensual; and (3) devilish.

(1) **First**, this sort of wisdom is *"earthly"* because it comes from the earth and those non-Christians living upon it. That's the only kind of "wisdom" that these worldly people know about.

(2) **Second**, this kind of wisdom is sensual.

> **THE MEANING OF THE GREEK WORD, "PSYCHIKOS."**
> The Greek Word for *"sensual"* is PSYCHIKOS. Some of the meanings of that Greek Word are:
>> *"1) of or belonging to breath; 1a) having the nature and characteristics of the breath; 1a1) the principal of animal life, which men have in common with the brutes; 1b) governed by breath; 1b1) the sensuous nature with its subjection to appetite and passion."*

(3) **Third**, this brand of wisdom is devilish.

> **MEANING OF THE GREEK WORD, "DAIMONIODES."**
> The Greek Word for *"devilish"* is DAIMONIODES. Some of the meanings of that Greek Word are:
>> *"1) resembling or proceeding from an evil spirit, demon-like."*

Though genuine Christians cannot be possessed or indwelt by Satan or his minions, they can be influenced by them.

> **PETER WAS BADLY INFLUENCED BY SATAN**
> "*But when he had turned about and looked on his disciples, he rebuked Peter, saying, Get thee behind me, Satan: for thou savourest not the things that be of God, but the things that be of men.*" (Mark 8:33)

See James 3:13 above for various verses on genuine wisdom from God rather than sensual wisdom.

James 3:16

"For where envying and strife is, there is confusion and every evil work."

The results of envying and strife are twofold: (1) confusion; and (2) every evil work. Apparently those to whom James was writing were involved in envying and strife which led to confusion and every evil work.

MEANING OF THE GREEK WORD, "AKATASTASIA."

The Greek Word for "*confusion*" is "AKATASTASIA." Some of the meanings of that Greek Word are:

"*1) instability, a state of disorder, disturbance, confusion.*"

This would destroy the unity that should prevail in local churches.

THE MEANING OF THE GREEK WORD, "PHAULOS."

This Greek Word for "*evil*" is PHAULOS. Some of the meanings of that Greek Word are:

"*1) easy, slight, ordinary, mean, worthless, of no account; 2) ethically, bad, base, wicked.*"

It is very sad, but it is so true that even in many Bible-believing churches there is both envying and strife which lead to confusion and various evil works. These things should not be in these churches. Those attending should be led by God the Holy Spirit and manifest His special gifts (Galatians 5:22-23).

Verses On Confusion

- **Leviticus 18:23**

"Neither shalt thou lie with any beast to defile thyself therewith: neither shall any woman stand before a beast to lie down thereto: it *is* confusion."

GOD CALLS BESTIALITY A WICKED SIN

This describes the sin of bestiality. It is total confusion. God is completely against it. One day those who practice bestiality will try to pass laws that will put pastors in prison who speak out and expose this confusion as sin.

> **HOMOSEXUALITY AND LESBIANISM ARE ALSO SINS**
> They are already considering laws that will seek to imprison pastors who preach against homosexuality and lesbianism. I must preach the whole counsel of God, regardless of what man might do to me.

- **Leviticus 20:12**

"And <u>if a man lie with his daughter in law</u>, both of them shall surely be put to death: <u>they have wrought confusion</u>; their blood *shall be* upon them."

<u>Incest is a sin and also confusion. God's Words are clear regarding this and all other sins.</u>

- **Psalms 35:4**

"Let them be confounded and put to shame that seek after my soul: <u>let them be</u> turned back and <u>brought to confusion</u> that devise my hurt."

David prays that the Lord will bring to confusion those who are seeking to hurt him.

- **Psalms 71:1**

"In thee, O LORD, do I put my trust: <u>let me never be put to confusion</u>."

<u>David does not want to be put to confusion in any way because he puts his trust in the Lord.</u>

- **Isaiah 41:29**

"Behold, they *are* all vanity; their works *are* nothing: <u>their molten images *are* wind and confusion</u>."

<u>Idols and images are confusion.</u> Those who worship them are very confused as well.

- **Jeremiah 3:25**

"We lie down in our shame, and our <u>confusion covereth us</u>: for we have sinned against the LORD our God, we and our fathers, from our youth even unto this day, and have not obeyed the voice of the LORD our God."

<u>The people to whom Jeremiah was preaching were covered with confusion</u> because of their many sins against the Lord.

- **Acts 19:29**

"And <u>the whole city was filled with confusion</u>: and having caught Gaius and Aristarchus, men of Macedonia, Paul's companions in travel, they rushed with one accord into the theatre."

The idolaters at Ephesus did not like Paul's crying out against the goddess Dianna. Because of this, the city was filled with confusion.

- **1 Corinthians 14:33**

"For <u>God is not *the author* of confusion</u>, but of peace, as in all churches of the saints."

James–Preaching Verse By Verse

WHEN IN EXISTENCE, TONGUES WERE ORDERLY
When the gift of speaking foreign languages was in the church before the Bible was completed in 90 to 100 A.D., there had to be an orderly use of this special gift. Otherwise, there would be confusion which is not a part of God's nature.

Verses On Evil Works
- Ecclesiastes 8:11

"Because <u>sentence against an evil work</u> is not executed speedily, therefore the heart of the sons of men is fully set in them to do evil."

<u>This verse speaks of speedy trials and sentencing</u> to those who do evil.
- 2 Timothy 4:18

"And <u>the Lord shall deliver me from every evil work</u>, and will preserve *me* unto his heavenly kingdom: to whom *be* glory for ever and ever. Amen."

PAUL WAS READY TO GO HOME TO HEAVEN
This was Paul's last letter. He was ready to go home to be with the Lord Jesus Christ. He was sure that the Lord would deliver him from every evil work and preserve him for Heaven. He kept being faithful to his Saviour until he was beheaded by Rome.

James 3:17

"But the wisdom that is from above is first pure, then peaceable, gentle, and easy to be intreated, full of mercy and good fruits, without partiality, and without hypocrisy."

In contrast to the fleshly wisdom of the world and of the flesh, the wisdom that is from God has at least the following eight characteristics:

THE MEANING OF THE 8 GREEK WORDS BELOW
The Greek definitions are helpful in the less familiar of these terms.

The Eight Characteristics Of God's Wisdom
1. Pure

The Greek Word for *"pure"* is HAGNOS. Some of the meanings of this Greek Word are:

> "1) exciting reverence, venerable, sacred; 2) pure; 2a) pure from carnality, chaste, modest; 2b) pure from every fault, immaculate; 2c) clean."
>
> 2. Peaceable
>
> The Greek Word for "*peaceable*" is EIRENIKOS. Some of the meanings of this Greek Word are:
>
>> "1) relating to peace; 2) peaceable, pacific, loving peace; 3) bring peace with it, peaceful, salutary."
>
> 3. Gentle
>
> The Greek Word for "*gentle*" is EPIEIKES. Some of the meanings of this Greek Word are:
>
>> "1) seemingly, suitable; 2) equitable, fair, mild, gentle."
>
> 4. Easy to be intreated
>
> The Greek Word for "*easy to be intreated*" is EUPEITHES. Some of the meanings of that Greek Word are:
>
>> "1) easily obeying, compliant"
>
> 5. Full of mercy
> 6. Full of good fruits
> 7. Without partiality
>
> The Greek Word for "*without partiality*" is ADIAKRITOS. Some of the meanings of "*without partiality*" are:
>
>> "1) undistinguished, unintelligible; 2) without dubiousness, or ambiguity."
>
> 8. Without hypocrisy
>
> The Greek Word for "*without hypocrisy*" is ANUPOKRITOS. Some of the meanings of this Greek Word are:
>
>> "1) unfeigned, undisguised, sincere."

Every genuine Christian man and woman need to seek and to find this wisdom that is from above which is given by the God of the Bible. All true Christians need to search God's Words daily and ask Him to help them to understand and use His wisdom.

James 3:18

"And the fruit of righteousness is sown in peace of them that make peace."

The fruit of righteousness is sown in peace.

THE MEANING OF THE GREEK WORD, "DIKAIOSUNE."

The Greek Word for *"righteousness"* is DIKAIOSUNE. Some of the meanings of this Greek Word are:

"1) in a broad sense: state of him who is as he ought to be, righteousness, the condition acceptable to God; 1a) the doctrine concerning the way in which man may attain a state approved of God 1b) integrity, virtue, purity of life, rightness, correctness of thinking, feeling, and acting; 2) in a narrower sense, justice or the virtue which gives each his due."

Righteousness is a very important doctrine of the Bible. It bears much fruit and is sown in peace by them that make peace.

Verses On Righteousness

- **Genesis 15:6**

"And he believed in the LORD; and he counted it to him for righteousness."

HOW GOD'S RIGHTEOUSNESS CAN BE RECEIVED

This verse makes it clear that righteousness before God is received by genuine faith in God's plans and promises. It is not received by the good works of human beings.

- **Psalms 11:7**

"For the righteous LORD loveth righteousness; his countenance doth behold the upright."

God loves righteousness wherever He finds it.

- **Psalms 23:3**

"He restoreth my soul: **he leadeth me in the paths of righteousness** for his name's sake."

For those who are seeking it, God can lead them in the paths of righteousness.

- **Acts 17:31**
  "Because he hath appointed a day, in the which he will judge the world in righteousness by *that* man whom he hath ordained; *whereof* he hath given assurance unto all *men*, in that he hath raised him from the dead."

GOD ALWAYS JUDGES RIGHTEOUSLY
God's judgments are always righteous. The Lord Jesus Christ has been given the task of all final judgment. He will judge righteously.

- **Romans 4:3**
  "For what saith the scripture? Abraham believed God, and it was counted unto him for righteousness."
Abraham's faith brought him righteousness with God.
- **Romans 4:5**
  "But to him that worketh not, but believeth on him that justifieth the ungodly, his faith is counted for righteousness."
Genuine faith in God's promises and purposes brings His righteousness to the person.
- **Romans 6:19**
  "I speak after the manner of men because of the infirmity of your flesh: for as ye have yielded your members servants to uncleanness and to iniquity unto iniquity; even so now yield your members servants to righteousness unto holiness."

CHRISTIANS SHOULD BE RIGHTEOUS AND HOLY
After salvation, genuine Christians should yield the members of their bodies to righteousness and holiness.

- **Romans 10:10**
  "For with the heart man believeth unto righteousness; and with the mouth confession is made unto salvation."
True and genuine heart-belief in the Lord Jesus Christ as Saviour brings God's righteousness.
- **1 Corinthians 1:30**
  "But of him are ye in Christ Jesus, who of God is made unto us wisdom, and righteousness, and sanctification, and redemption:"
One of the four things the Lord Jesus Christ made unto the true Christians is righteousness.
- **2 Corinthians 9:10**
  "Now he that ministereth seed to the sower both minister bread for *your* food, and multiply your seed sown, and increase the fruits of your righteousness;)"

James–Preaching Verse By Verse

Once people have God's righteousness by true faith in the Lord Jesus Christ, God wants to have produced some fruits of that righteousness.
- **Ephesians 5:9**
"(For the fruit of the Spirit is in all goodness and righteousness and truth;)"

The Spirit of God is interested in helping true Christians to manifest God's righteous principles.
- **Philippians 1:11**
"Being filled with the fruits of righteousness, which are by Jesus Christ, unto the glory and praise of God."

CHRISTIANS SHOULD BE RIGHTEOUS
God wants genuine Christians to be filled with the fruits of righteousness which are made possible by the Lord Jesus Christ.

- **2 Timothy 3:16-17**
"All scripture is given by inspiration of God, and is profitable for doctrine, for reproof, for correction, for instruction in righteousness: That the man of God may be perfect, throughly furnished unto all good works."

The Bible gives true Christians instruction in righteousness. That's the only source for God's righteousness.
- **Titus 3:5**
"Not by works of righteousness which we have done, but according to his mercy he saved us, by the washing of regeneration, and renewing of the Holy Ghost;"

No one is saved by their own works of righteousness, but by God's washing them by regeneration.
- **Hebrews 1:9**
"Thou hast loved righteousness, and hated iniquity; therefore God, even thy God, hath anointed thee with the oil of gladness above thy fellows."

This is speaking of the Lord Jesus Christ Who loves righteousness.
- **Hebrews 12:11**
"Now no chastening for the present seemeth to be joyous, but grievous: nevertheless afterward it yieldeth the peaceable fruit of righteousness unto them which are exercised thereby."

PEOPLE SHOULD BE EXERCISED BY CHASTENING
God's chastening of His genuine Christians yields the fruit of righteousness to those who are exercised by it.

- **1 John 3:10**
"In this the children of God are manifest, and the children of the devil: whosoever doeth not righteousness is not of God, neither he that loveth not his brother."

Those who don't do righteousness are not of God. This is clear.

In James 3:18 above, it mentions that the fruit of righteousness is sown in peace.

THE MEANING OF THE GREEK WORD, "EIRENE."

The Greek Word for *"peace"* is EIRENE. Some of the meanings of this Greek Word are:

"1) a state of national tranquillity; 1a) exemption from the rage and havoc of war; 2) peace between individuals, i.e. harmony, concord; 3) security, safety, prosperity, felicity, (because peace and harmony make and keep things safe and prosperous); 4) of the Messiah's peace; 4a) the way that leads to peace (salvation); 5) of Christianity, the tranquil state of a soul assured of its salvation through Christ, and so fearing nothing from God and content with its earthly lot, of whatsoever sort that is; 6) the blessed state of devout and upright men after death."

Verses On Peace

- **Romans 5:1**
"Therefore being justified by faith, we have peace with God through our Lord Jesus Christ:"

Peace with God is only by being justified by genuine faith in the Lord Jesus Christ.

- **2 Corinthians 13:11**
"Finally, brethren, farewell. Be perfect, be of good comfort, be of one mind, live in peace; and the God of love and peace shall be with you."

This is one of the attributes of God. He's called the God of love and of peace.

- **Galatians 5:22**
"But the fruit of the Spirit is love, joy, peace, longsuffering, gentleness

The Spirit of God, indwells all born-again Christians. One of His fruits that He manifests, when they are controlled by Him, is peace.

- **Ephesians 4:3**
"Endeavouring to keep <u>the unity of the Spirit in the bond of peace</u>."

<u>God wants peace in His obedient churches</u>. The unity of the Spirit brings the bond of peace.

- **Philippians 4:7**
"And <u>the peace of God</u>, which passeth all understanding, <u>shall keep your hearts and minds</u> through Christ Jesus."

The peace of God keeps the hearts and minds of true Christians through the Lord Jesus Christ.

- **Colossians 3:15**
"And <u>let the peace of God rule in your hearts</u>, to the which also ye are called in one body; and be ye thankful."

God's peace should rule in the hearts of every genuine Christian.

- **1 Thessalonians 5:13**
"And to esteem them very highly in love for their work's sake. *And* <u>be at peace among yourselves</u>."

BIBLE-BELIEVING CHURCHES SHOULD HAVE PEACE

Peace should be true in every Bible-believing church in the world. There should be peace in the churches based upon the teachings of God's Words.

James
Chapter Four

James 4:1

"From whence come wars and fightings among you? come they not hence, even of your lusts that war in your members?"

James is writing to Jews who have become Christians. Apparently there were problems of various kinds. He mentions that there were *"wars and fightings"* among them. These battles come from their own internal lusts.

> **LUST CAUSES WARS AND FIGHTINGS**
> The Greek Word for *"lust"* is HEDONE. Some of the meanings of this Greek Word are:
> *1) pleasure; 2) desires for pleasure*

These *"lusts"* within the bodies of these Jewish Christians are waging war.

> **MEANING OF THE GREEK WORD, "STRATEUOMAI."**
> The Greek Word for *"war"* is STRATEUOMAI. Some of the meanings of this Greek Word are:
> 1) to make a military expedition, to lead soldiers to war or to battle, (spoken of a commander); 2) to do military duty, be on active service, be a soldier; 3) to fight.

Verses On Lust

- **Romans 6:12-14**

"Let not sin therefore reign in your mortal body, that ye should obey it in the lusts thereof. Neither yield ye your members *as* instruments of unrighteousness unto sin: but yield yourselves unto God, as those that are alive from the dead, and your members *as* instruments of righteousness unto God. But put ye on the Lord Jesus Christ, and make not provision for the flesh, to *fulfil* the lusts *thereof.*"

THE SIN NATURE SHOULD NOT REIGN
The lusts of the sin nature should not reign in the bodies of genuine born-again Christians. They should yield their bodies unto the Lord Jesus Christ.

- **1 Peter 2:11**
"Dearly beloved, I beseech *you* as strangers and pilgrims, abstain from fleshly lusts, which war against the soul;"

YIELD HANDS, EYES, EARS, AND FEET TO THE LORD
Abstaining from fleshly lusts in the bodies of true Christians is God's command. Their two hands, their two eyes, their two ears, their two feet, and all the rest of the members of their bodies should be yielded to the Lord.

- **Colossians 3:5**
"Mortify therefore your members which are upon the earth; fornication, uncleanness, inordinate affection, evil concupiscence, and covetousness, which is idolatry:"

MORTIFY SINS IN THE LIFE
These sins, and all others should be mortified or put to death in the lives of genuine Christians.

James 4:2
"Ye lust, and have not: ye kill, and desire to have, and cannot obtain: ye fight and war, yet ye have not, because ye ask not."

James states that his readers lust, kill, desire to have, fight and war. However, they don't get the things they want. These are very evil pursuits. Instead of pursuing evil things, they should follow after the things of the Lord and ask from Him what to do.

Verses On Asking
- **Matthew 6:6-8**
"But thou, when thou prayest, enter into thy closet, and when thou hast shut thy door, pray to thy Father which is in secret; and thy Father which seeth in secret shall reward thee openly. But when ye pray, use not vain repetitions, as the heathen *do*: for they think that they shall be heard for their much speaking. Be not ye therefore like unto them: for your Father knoweth what things ye have need of, before ye ask him."

The Lord Jesus Christ told His disciples the proper method of praying to God their Father.

James–Preaching Verse By Verse

- **Matthew 7:7**

"<u>Ask, and it shall be given you</u>; seek, and ye shall find; knock, and it shall be opened unto you: For <u>every one that asketh receiveth</u>; and he that seeketh findeth; and to him that knocketh it shall be opened."

THE DISCIPLES WERE TO ASK OF THE LORD

The disciples were told to <u>ask of the Lord in order</u> to receive what is asked for.

- **Matthew 18:19**

"Again I say unto you, That if two of you shall agree on earth as touching any thing that <u>they shall ask, it shall be done for them of my Father which is in heaven</u>."

If two or three disciples agreed in a matter and asked, God would fulfill their requests.

- **Matthew 21:22**

"And all things, <u>whatsoever ye shall ask in prayer, believing, ye shall receive</u>."

The Lord Jesus Christ told this to His disciples. <u>Ask, believe, and receive</u>.

- **John 14:13**

"And <u>whatsoever ye shall ask in my name, that will I do</u>, that the Father may be glorified in the Son. If ye shall ask any thing in my name, I will do *it*."

The Lord Jesus Christ again told His disciples to ask in His Name and He will do it.

- **John 16:23-24**

"And in that day (after the Lord Jesus has gone back to heaven) ye shall ask me nothing. Verily, verily, I say unto you, Whatsoever ye shall ask the Father in my name, he will give *it* you. Hitherto have ye asked nothing in my name: <u>ask, and ye shall receive, that your joy may be full</u>."

RECEIVING ANSWERS TO PRAYER BRINGS FULL JOY

The result of asking God the Father in prayer is receiving fullness of joy.

- **Ephesians 3:20**

"Now unto him that is <u>able to do exceeding abundantly above all that we ask</u> or think, according to the power that worketh in us,"

The Lord Jesus Christ has the power, if He wishes, to give that which genuine Christians ask for. <u>Sometimes He says 'No,' but He still wants them to ask Him</u>.

- **James 1:5**

"If any of you lack wisdom, let him ask of God, that giveth to all men liberally, and upbraideth not; and it shall be given him."

True Christians who lack wisdom should ask of God.

- **1 John 3:22**

"And whatsoever we ask, we receive of him, because we keep his commandments, and do those things that are pleasing in his sight."

Genuine Christians who keep His commandments and ask for His wisdom will receive it.

- **1 John 5:14-15**

"And this is the confidence that we have in him, that, if we ask any thing according to his will, he heareth us: And if we know that he hear us, whatsoever we ask, we know that we have the petitions that we desired of him."

God hears the prayers of every true Christian with all their sins confessed in accord with 1 John 1:9.

James 4:3

"Ye ask, and receive not, because ye ask amiss, that ye may consume it upon your lusts."

James' readers asked things from the Lord, but they asked amiss so they could consume it upon their lusts.

THE MEANING OF THE GREEK WORD, "KAKOS."

The Greek Word for *"amiss"* is KAKOS. Some of the meanings of this Greek Word are:

"1) miserable, to be ill; 2) improperly, wrongly; 3) to speak ill of, revile, one"

The reason that these people asked was to consume it on their lusts.

THE MEANING OF THE GREEK WORD, "DAPANAO."

The Greek Word for *"consume"* is DAPANAO. Some of the meanings of this Greek Word are:

1) to incur expense, expend, spend; 2) in a bad sense: to waste, squander, consume."

The reason for these people asking amiss is to consume it on their lusts.

THE MEANING OF THE GREEK WORD, "HEDONE."

The Greek Word for *"lusts"* is HEDONE. Some of the meanings of this Greek Word are:

"1) pleasure; 2) desires for pleasure"

James–Preaching Verse By Verse

Verses On Amiss

- **2 Chronicles 6:37b**

"We have sinned, we have done amiss, and have dealt wickedly;" Solomon, in his prayer, was referring to the nation of Israel doing wickedly.

- **Daniel 3:29**

"Therefore I make a decree, That every people, nation, and language, which speak any thing amiss against the God of Shadrach, Meshach, and Abednego, shall be cut in pieces, and their houses shall be made a dunghill: because there is no other God that can deliver after this sort."

THE BABYLONIANS WERE NOT TO BLASPHEME GOD

The people of Babylon were not to ask "amiss" against the true God of Shadrach, Meshach, and Abednego. Otherwise they would be slain.

- **Luke 23:41**

"And we indeed justly; for we receive the due reward of our deeds: but this man hath done nothing amiss."

At the crucifixion, one of the two thieves said that the Lord Jesus Christ had done nothing "amiss."

James 4:4

"Ye adulterers and adulteresses, know ye not that the friendship of the world is enmity with God? whosoever therefore will be a friend of the world is the enemy of God."

Loving this evil world is like being a spiritual adulterer or an adulteress.

THE MEANING OF THE GREEK WORD, "MOICHOS."

The Greek Words for "adulterer" is MOICHOS (masculine) and MOICHALIS (feminine). Some of the meanings of these Words are:

ADULTERER

1) an adulterer; 2) metaph. one who is faithless toward God, ungodly.

ADULTERESS

1) an adulteress; 2) as the intimate alliance of God with the people of Israel was likened to a marriage, those who relapse into idolatry are

> *said to commit adultery or play the harlot; 2a) fig. equiv. to faithless to God, unclean, apostate."*

Verses On Adultery
- **Exodus 20:14**

"Thou shalt not commit adultery."
God told His people in the Old Testament not to commit this sin of adultery.

- **Deuteronomy 5:18**

"Neither shalt thou commit adultery."
This command is repeated to the new generation of Israelites.

- **Jeremiah 3:8-9**

"And I saw, when for all the causes whereby backsliding Israel committed adultery I had put her away, and given her a bill of divorce; yet her treacherous sister Judah feared not, but went and played the harlot also. And it came to pass through the lightness of her whoredom, that she defiled the land, and committed adultery with stones and with stocks."
This implicates both northen Israel and southern Judah with spiritual adultery and whoredom.

Verses On Friends And Friendship
- **Proverbs 22:24**

"Make no friendship with an angry man; and with a furious man thou shalt not go:"

MAKE NO FRIENDS WITH ANGRY PEOPLE

If true Christians make friendships with angry and furious people, they're going to turn into furious people yourselves. God says to stay clear of these angry and furious people.

- **Proverbs 17:17**

"A friend loveth at all times, and a brother is born for adversity."
This is a good definition of what true "friends" are.

- **Proverbs 18:24**

"A man *that hath* friends must shew himself friendly: and there is a friend *that* sticketh closer than a brother."

FRIENDLINESS BRINGS FRIENDS

Friendliness will bring you friends. The Lord Jesus Christ is a Friend Who sticks close to genuine Christians.

- **Proverbs 19:4**

"Wealth maketh many friends; but the poor is separated from his neighbour."

James–Preaching Verse By Verse

If it is wealth that makes these "friends," it is not true friendship.
- **Proverbs 19:6**
"Many will intreat the favour of the prince: and every man *is* a friend to him that giveth gifts."

Once the gifts stop, the friendship will usually stop as well.
- **Proverbs 27:17**
"Iron sharpeneth iron; so a man sharpeneth the countenance of his friend."

DIFFERENCES OFTEN SHARPEN THE MIND
The iron might refer to differences of opinions between people. This sharpening might be good for the countenance and the mind if properly used.

- **Luke 23:12**
"And the same day Pilate and Herod were made friends together: for before they were at enmity between themselves."

Pilate and Herod were former enemies, but in despising the Lord Jesus Christ, they were made friends.
- **John 15:14**
"Ye are my friends, if ye do whatsoever I command you."

The Lord Jesus Christ was talking to His disciples. If true Christians don't do what the Lord Jesus Christ tells them to do, then they are no longer friends.
- **James 2:23**
"And the scripture was fulfilled which saith, Abraham believed God, and it was imputed unto him for righteousness: and he was called the Friend of God."

What an honor! May it be shared with every obedient Christian.

Verses On The World
- **1 John 2:15**
"Love not the world, neither the things *that are* in the world. If any man love the world, the love of the Father is not in him."

CHRISTIANS SHOULD NOT LOVE THE WORLD'S SINS
Genuine Christians should not love anything that is of the evil world, including the lust of the eyes, the flesh, and the pride of life.

- **Matthew 13:22**
"He also that received seed among the thorns is he that heareth the word; and the care of this world, and the deceitfulness of riches, choke the word, and he becometh unfruitful."

The care of this world rather than the care for God's Words choke the Word leading to unfruitfulness.

- **Mark 8:36**

"For what shall it profit a man, if he shall gain the whole world, and lose his own soul?"

Gaining the whole world and losing the soul is a serious and an eternal error.

- **Luke 4:5-8**

"And the devil, taking him up into an high mountain, shewed unto him all the kingdoms of the world in a moment of time. And the devil said unto him, All this power will I give thee, and the glory of them: for that is delivered unto me; and to whomsoever I will I give it. If thou therefore wilt worship me, all shall be thine. And Jesus answered and said unto him, Get thee behind me, Satan: for it is written, Thou shalt worship the Lord thy God, and him only shalt thou serve."

THE DEVIL LIED TO THE LORD JESUS CHRIST

The Devil lied (as usual). He promised the Lord Jesus Christ all the kingdoms of the world if He worshipped him. The Devil does not own these worldly kingdoms and couldn't give them to the Saviour. The Lord Jesus Christ owns all these kingdoms.

- **Luke 12:29-31**

"And seek not ye what ye shall eat, or what ye shall drink, neither be ye of doubtful mind. For all these things do the nations of the world seek after: and your Father knoweth that ye have need of these things. But rather seek ye the kingdom of God; and all these things shall be added unto you."

The world around is concerned only about eating and other material things.

- **John 1:10**

"He was in the world, and the world was made by him, and the world knew him not."

The Lord Jesus Christ created the physical world, but wicked people in that world rejected Him and did not receive Him.

- **John 3:16-17**

"For God so loved the world, that he gave his only begotten Son, that whosoever believeth in him should not perish, but have everlasting life. For God sent not his Son into the world to condemn the world; but that the world through him might be saved."

James–Preaching Verse By Verse

> **GOD LOVED THE ENTIRE WORLD OF PEOPLE**
>
> This refers to the physical world of people. God the Father loved all the people in the world and sent His Son, the Lord Jesus Christ to die for their sins so that if they trust in Him as their Saviour, they might have everlasting life.

- **John 7:7**

"The world cannot hate you; but me it hateth, because I testify of it, that the works thereof are evil."

The world of unsaved and non-Christian people hates the Lord Jesus Christ because He shows them that their works are evil.

- **John 8:23**

"And he said unto them, Ye are from beneath; I am from above: ye are of this world; I am not of this world."

The Lord Jesus Christ told the Pharisees that they were of the world. He was not of this world.

- **John 12:31**

"Now is the judgment of this world: now shall the prince of this world be cast out."

The prince of the world is the Devil. One day he will be judged and sent to the Lake of Fife.

- **John 14:17**

"*Even* the Spirit of truth; whom the world cannot receive, because it seeth him not, neither knoweth him: but ye know him; for he dwelleth with you, and shall be in you."

This evil world cannot receive the Holy Spirit until they come to the Lord Jesus Christ as their Saviour.

- **John 14:30**

"Hereafter I will not talk much with you: for the prince of this world cometh, and hath nothing in me."

> **SATAN IS THE PRINCE OF THIS WORLD**
>
> The prince of this world is Satan. He has nothing to do with the Lord Jesus Christ.

The Lord Jesus said to his disciples,

- **John 15:19**

"If ye were of the world, the world would love his own: but because ye are not of the world, but I have chosen you out of the world, therefore the world hateth you."

The Lord Jesus Christ told His disciples that the world hates them because they belong to Christ.

- **John 16:11**

"Of judgment, because the prince of this world is judged."

Satan was judged at the cross. The fulfillment of that judgment will be when he is sent to the Lake of Fire.

- **John 17:14**
  "I have given them thy word; and the <u>world hath hated them, because they are not of the world</u>, even as I am not of the world."

The Lord Jesus Christ, in His High Priestly prayer, told God the Father that He had warned His disciples that the world would hate them because they are not of the world.

- **John 17:16**
  "<u>They are not of the world, even as I am not of the world.</u>"

The disciples of the Lord Jesus Christ and genuine Christians today are not of the world, but are of God.

- **Romans 12:1-2**
  "I beseech you therefore, brethren, by the mercies of God, that ye present your bodies a living sacrifice, holy, acceptable unto God, *which is* your reasonable service. And <u>be not conformed to this world</u>: but be ye transformed by the renewing of your mind, that ye may prove what *is* that good, and acceptable, and perfect, will of God."

True Christians should not be conformed to this evil world. This world wants them to sin by means of their eyes, their minds, their actions, and their bodies.

- **1 Corinthians 3:19**
  "For <u>the wisdom of this world is foolishness with God</u>. For it is written, He taketh the wise in their own craftiness."

The wisdom of this world is foolishness to God. Genuine Christians should not follow such false wisdom.

- **2 Corinthians 4:4**
  "In whom <u>the god of this world</u> hath blinded the minds of them which believe not, lest the light of the glorious gospel of Christ, who is the image of God, should shine unto them."

The god of this world is Satan. He blinds the minds of people to prevent them from becoming true Christians.

- **Galatians 1:4**
  "Who gave himself for our sins, <u>that he might deliver us from this present evil world</u>, according to the will of God and our Father:"

CHRIST DIED TO DELIVER CHRISTIANS FROM SINS

The Lord Jesus Christ died on the cross to deliver genuine Christians from the evil world that includes crimes, criminals, murderers, rapes, adulteries, and many other evils.

- **Ephesians 2:2**
"Wherein in time past ye walked according to the course of this world, according to the prince of the power of the air, the spirit that now worketh in the children of disobedience:"

Genuine Christians at Ephesus had walked according to the course of this evil world, but now were to walk in God's way and will.

- **Ephesians 6:12**
"For we wrestle not against flesh and blood, but against principalities, against powers, against the rulers of the darkness of this world, against spiritual wickedness in high *places*."

True Christians wrestle with the rulers of the darkness of this world led by Satan.

- **Colossians 2:8**
"Beware lest any man spoil you through philosophy and vain deceit, after the tradition of men, after the rudiments of the world, and not after Christ."

> **BEWARE OF THE EVIL TRADITIONS OF MEN**
> Genuine Christians must beware of the rudiments and traditions of this evil world.

- **2 Timothy 4:10**
"For Demas hath forsaken me, having loved this present world, and is departed unto Thessalonica; Crescens to Galatia, Titus unto Dalmatia."

The reason Demas forsook Paul was because Demas loved this present evil world.

- **Titus 2:12**
"Teaching us that, denying ungodliness and worldly lusts, we should live soberly, righteously, and godly, in this present world;"

This present world has many worldly lusts. They should be denied in the lives of true Christians.

- **James 1:27**
"Pure religion and undefiled before God and the Father is this, To visit the fatherless and widows in their affliction, *and* to keep himself unspotted from the world."

Unspotted from the world indicates that the genuine Christians should strive for purity from the spots of the world.

- **1 John 2:15**
"Love not the world, neither the things *that are* in the world. If any man love the world, the love of the Father is not in him."

> **LOVE FOR THE WORLD SHOWS NO LOVE FOR GOD**
> True Christians are to stop loving the evil world with all of its sins. If this does not happen, it shows that the love for God the Father is not in them.

- 1 John 4:3

"And every spirit that confesseth not that Jesus Christ is come in the flesh is not of God: and this is <u>that *spirit* of antichrist</u>, whereof ye have heard that it should come; and <u>even now already is it in the world</u>."

The spirit of Antichrist has been in the world from the time the Bible was written. That evil spirit is still with us today–and even to a greater degree.

- 1 John 5:4-5

"For <u>whatsoever is born of God overcometh the world</u>: and this is <u>the victory that overcometh the world, *even* our faith</u>. Who is he that overcometh the world, but he that believeth that Jesus is the Son of God?"

True born-again Christians can overcome the world by genuine faith in their Saviour that they have. That's overcoming power to be victors over this world and all the world wants us to do.

- **Revelation 12:9**

"And the great dragon was cast out, that old serpent, called the Devil, and <u>Satan, which deceiveth the whole world</u>: he was cast out into the earth, and his angels were cast out with him."

This verse tells how Satan, who deceived the whole world, was cast out of Heaven onto the earth.

- **Genesis 3:15**

"And I will put <u>enmity between thee and the woman</u>, and between thy seed and her seed; it shall bruise thy head, and thou shalt bruise his heel."

> **CHRIST AND SATAN ARE ENEMIES**
> God was talking to Satan the serpent. He promised Satan that he would put enmity between him and the seed of the woman.

James 4:5

"Do ye think that the scripture saith in vain, The spirit that dwelleth in us lusteth to envy."

> **GOD THE HOLY SPIRIT INDWELLS CHRISTIANS**
> All genuine Christians have God the Holy Spirit indwelling them. Those who are lost have no Spirit of God inside of them at all but only true Christians have God's Spirit dwelling in them.

The Holy Spirit is envious that we not be found in the wickedness of the world. He wants us to follow the Lord. He's envious and anyone that is faithless to the Father and faithful to this wicked world, a friend of the world, the Holy Spirit is not happy, not pleased.

Verses On The Indwelling Of The Holy Spirit

- **Romans 8:11**

"But if <u>the Spirit</u> of him that raised up Jesus from the dead <u>dwell in you</u>, he that raised up Christ from the dead shall also quicken your mortal bodies by <u>his Spirit that dwelleth in you</u>."

The Holy Spirit indwells every genuine Christian.

- **1 Corinthians 3:16**

"Know ye not that ye are the temple of God, and *that* <u>the Spirit of God dwelleth in you</u>?"

All true Christians are called the temple of God and are indwelled by the Holy Spirit.

- **1 Corinthians 6:19**

"What? know ye not that <u>your body is the temple of the Holy Ghost *which is* in you</u>, which ye have of God, and ye are not your own?"

The bodies of genuine Christians are the temple of the indwelling Holy Spirit.

- **2 Timothy 1:14**

"That good thing which was committed unto thee <u>keep by the Holy Ghost which dwelleth in us</u>."

> **CHRISTIANS SHOULD KEEP ALL BIBLE TRUTH**
> Timothy was a pastor at the church of Ephesus. He urged his Christian followers to keep the truth that was committed to them by the power of the indwelling Holy Spirit.

James 4:6

"**But he giveth more grace. Wherefore he saith, God resisteth the proud, but giveth grace unto the humble.**"

God gives His grace to those who are genuine Christians. Since "resisteth" is the Greek present tense, it indicates that God resists the proud at all times.

> **MEANING OF THE GREEK WORD, "ANTITASSOMAI."**
>
> The Greek Word for "*resist*" is ANTITASSOMAI. Some of the meanings of "*resist*" are:
>> "*1) to range in battle against; 2) to oppose one's self, resist.*"

Are you proud? Am I proud? You may say, I'm proud to be a Christian. Well, that's a different kind of proud. The pride here refers to egotism and exalting of self.

> **MEANING OF THE GREEK WORD, "HUPEREPHANOS."**
>
> The Greek Word for pride is HUPEREPHANOS. Some of the meanings of "*pride*" are:
>> "*1) showing one's self above others, overtopping, conspicuous above others, pre-eminent; 2) with an overweening estimate of one's means or merits, despising others or even treating them with contempt, haughty.*"

Though God resists the proud, He gives His grace to those who are humble.

> **THE MEANING OF THE GREEK WORD, "TAPEINOS."**
>
> The Greek Word for "humble" is TAPEINOS. Some of the meanings of that Greek Word are:
>> "*1) not rising far from the ground; 2) metaph.; 2a) as a condition, lowly, of low degree; 2b) brought low with grief, depressed; 2c) lowly in spirit, humble; 2d) in a bad sense, deporting one's self abjectly, deferring servilely to others.*"

Verses On Pride And Proud

- **1 Peter 5:5**

"Likewise, ye younger, submit yourselves unto the elder. Yea, all *of you* be subject one to another, and be clothed with humility:

for God resisteth the proud, and giveth grace to the humble."
Peter repeats the phrase used by James as well.
- **Proverbs 16:19**
"Better *it is to be* of an humble spirit with the lowly, than to divide the spoil with the proud."

Though the proud might have much spoil, a lowly and humble spirit is far better than the proud and their goods.
- **Proverbs 29:23**
"A man's pride shall bring him low: but honour shall uphold the humble in spirit."

Somebody who is up high in his pride, that pride shall bring him down very low.
- **Matthew 23:12**
"And whosoever shall exalt himself shall be abased; and he that shall humble himself shall be exalted."

PRIDEFUL PEOPLE WILL BE BROUGHT LOW
Those who exalt themselves in prideful looks and actions shall be bought down low and abased.

James 4:7

"Submit yourselves therefore to God. Resist the devil, and he will flee from you."

God wants genuine Christians to submit themselves to God and all His will for their lives. God's will is found within the pages of the Bible. In English, the only accurate translation of that Bible is the King James Bible which is based on the only accurate Hebrew, Aramaic, and Greek Words.

THE MEANING OF THE GREEK WORD, "HUPOTASSO"

The Greek Word for "submit" is HUPOTASSO. Some of the meanings of "*submit*" are:

> "*1) to arrange under, to subordinate; 2) to subject, put in subjection; 3) to subject one's self, obey; 4) to submit to one's control; 5) to yield to one's admonition or advice; 6) to obey, be subject; A Greek military term meaning "to arrange [troop divisions] in a miliary fashion under the command of a leader". In non-military use, it was "a voluntary attitude of giving in, cooperating, assuming responsibility, and carrying a*

> *burden."*

The second imperative in this verse to these true Christians is to resist the Devil. If this is done in a satisfactory manner, he will flee from them. The Lord Jesus Christ resisted the Devil as He said, *"Get thee behind me Satan."*

Verses On Submission
- **Ephesians 5:22**

"Wives, submit yourselves unto your own husbands, as unto the Lord."

> **WIVES SHOULD SUBMIT TO THEIR HUSBANDS**
> This is God's will for every Christian wife. They are to be in submission to their own husbands. The only exception to this submission is when the husband wants the wife to so something contrary to God's will found in the Bible.

- **Colossians 3:18**

"Wives, submit yourselves unto your own husbands, as it is fit in the Lord."

The wives' submission should be as it is proper in the Lord.

- **Hebrews 13:17**

"Obey them that have the rule over you, and submit yourselves: for they watch for your souls, as they that must give account, that they may do it with joy, and not with grief: for that *is* unprofitable for you."

This probably refers to submission to a person's pastor or other leader as far as he is faithful to God's Words.

- **1 Peter 5:5**

"Likewise, ye younger, submit yourselves unto the elder. Yea, all *of you* be subject one to another, and be clothed with humility: for God resisteth the proud, and giveth grace to the humble."

There should also be a proper type of submission between true Christians who are following the will of God.

James 4:8

"Draw nigh to God, and he will draw nigh to you. Cleanse your hands, ye sinners; and purify your hearts, ye double minded."

Make close contact with the Lord and then He'll draw nigh to you. Draw nigh to him, he'll draw nigh to you. There's fellowship between those that are saved and those that are with the Lord.

Then it says cleanse your hands and purify your hearts. The

hands do things that people can see. The heart nobody can see. God says make them both clean. True Christians should have clean hands and pure hearts.

Verses On Clean Things

- **Psalms 19:12**

"Who can understand *his* errors? cleanse thou me from secret *faults*."

David prayed to be cleansed from secret faults.

- **Psalms 51:2**

"Wash me throughly from mine iniquity, and cleanse me from my sin."

DAVID COMMITTED ADULTERY AND MURDER

David committed adultery with Bathsheba and then he had Bathsheba's husband murdered. Afterward, he prayed for God's cleansing.

- **Psalms 119:9**

"BETH. Wherewithal shall a young man cleanse his way? by taking heed *thereto* according to thy word."

When read from Genesis through Revelation, understood, and followed completely, the Words of God can cleanse our ways.

- **Matthew 23:26**

"*Thou* blind Pharisee, cleanse first that *which is* within the cup and platter, that the outside of them may be clean also."

THE PHARISEES WERE UNCLEAN IN THEIR HEARTS

Though absolutely true, the Lord Jesus Christ was not "politically correct" when He called the Pharisees unclean in their hearts.

- **2 Corinthians 7:1**

"Having therefore these promises, dearly beloved, let us cleanse ourselves from all filthiness of the flesh and spirit, perfecting holiness in the fear of God."

Genuine Christians must be clean in both their flesh and their spirit.

- **Ephesians 5:25-27**

"Husbands, love your wives, even as Christ also loved the church, and gave himself for it; That he might sanctify and cleanse it with the washing of water by the word, That he might present it to himself a glorious church, not having spot, or wrinkle, or any such thing; but that it should be holy and without blemish."

The true Christians in the true church, which is the body of Christ, should be cleansed and clean for service by the washing by the Words of God.

- **1 John 1:9**
"If we confess our sins, he is faithful and just to forgive us *our* sins, and to cleanse us from all unrighteousness."

> **THE MEANING OF THE GREEK WORD, "HOMOLOGEO"**
> The word, "confess" comes from the Greek Word HOMOLOGEO. The Word means literally, *"to say the same thing, or to agree."* Real confession on the part of genuine Christians must include that they say the same thing about their sin they're confessing as God says. They must agree with God that it is sin. Only then true confession takes place and God will then forgive them and cleanse them.

Verses On The Need For Clean Hands
- **Psalms 7:3**
"O LORD my God, if I have done this; if there be iniquity in my hands;"

Hands should be clean from iniquity.

- **Psalms 24:3-4**
"Who shall ascend into the hill of the LORD? or who shall stand in his holy place? He that hath clean hands, and a pure heart; who hath not lifted up his soul unto vanity, nor sworn deceitfully."

Only those who have been redeemed by genuine faith in the Lord Jesus Christ can have clean hands.

Verses On The Need For Clean Hearts
- **Psalms 19:14**
"Let the words of my mouth, and the meditation of my heart, be acceptable in thy sight, O LORD, my strength, and my redeemer."

The meditation of the hearts of true Christians should be acceptable in the sight of God.

- **Psalms 26:2**
"Examine me, O LORD, and prove me; try my reins and my heart."

The Psalmist asked God to examine, prove, and try his heart that it would be acceptable in His sight.

- **Psalms 51:10**
"Create in me a clean heart, O God; and renew a right spirit within me."

God wants people's hearts to be clean.

- **Psalms 119:11**
"Thy word have I hid in mine heart, that I might not sin against thee."

When God's Words are in persons' hearts, they will help them not to sin against the Lord.

James 4:9

"Be afflicted, and mourn, and weep: let your laughter be turned to mourning, and your joy to heaviness."

CHRISTIANS SHOULD NOT BE DOUBLE MINDED
James tells his readers to be afflicted, mourn, and weep because they were double minded. Their laughter should be turned to mourning and their joy should be turned to heaviness. It appears like James is wishing judgment to come on his readers.

Verses On Affliction
- **Psalms 119:67**
"Before I was afflicted I went astray: but now have I kept thy word."

It looks like David's afflictions were caused by his going astray. I'm glad he began keeping God's Words after that affliction.

- **Psalms 119:71**
"*It is* good for me that I have been afflicted; that I might learn thy statutes."

David knew that his afflictions came because he was not learning God's Words.

- **Psalms 119:75**
"I know, O LORD, that thy judgments *are* right, and *that* thou in faithfulness hast afflicted me."

God is always faithful when He afflicts His true Christians.

Verses On Mourning
- **Ecclesiastes 3:4**
"A time to weep, and a time to laugh; a time to mourn, and a time to dance;"

SOMETIMES THERE IS A TIME TO MOURN
There are different times in life. One of these times is a time to mourn. So there are different times of our lives that we do different things.

Verses On Weeping, Laughter, And Heaviness
- **Jeremiah 9:1**

"Oh that my head were waters, and mine eyes a fountain of tears, <u>that I might weep</u> day and night for the slain of the daughter of my people!"

Jeremiah is called the weeping prophet. He had great sorrow for Israel's perpetual sinning and backsliding.

- **Ecclesiastes 7:3**

"<u>Sorrow *is* better than laughter</u>: for by the sadness of the countenance the heart is made better."

Many people don't agree with this, but after the sorrow, often, the heart is made better.

- **Ezra 9:5**

"And at the evening sacrifice <u>I arose up from my heaviness</u>; and having rent my garment and my mantle, I fell upon my knees, and spread out my hands unto the LORD my God,"

Ezra rose up from his heaviness, fell on his knees, and prayed unto the Lord. True Christians should do the same.

James 4:10

"Humble yourselves in the sight of the Lord, and he shall lift you up."

GOD WILL LIFT UP HUMBLE CHRISTIANS

This humility on the part of genuine Christians is not in the sight of other people. It is in the sight of the Lord. Then He will lift them up. The Pharisees humbled themselves in the sight of other people to make a scene. They used sackcloth and other things, but this humility was not in the sight of the Lord.

Verses On Humble And Humility
- **Psalms 9:12**

"When he maketh inquisition for blood, he remembereth them: <u>he forgetteth not the cry of the humble</u>."

God understands and remembers the cry of the humble.

- **Proverbs 16:19**

"<u>Better *it is to be* of an humble spirit</u> with the lowly, than to divide the spoil with the proud."

A humble spirit is considered by the Lord to be far better than pride, even if the proud have great riches.

- **Matthew 18:4**

James–Preaching Verse By Verse   137

"Whosoever therefore shall humble himself as this little child, the same is greatest in the kingdom of heaven."
Childlike humility is considered great in the eyes of the Lord.
- **Matthew 23:12**
"And whosoever shall exalt himself shall be abased; and he that shall humble himself shall be exalted."
When true Christians humble themselves, God will lift them up and exalt them.
- 1 Peter 5:5
"Likewise, ye younger, submit yourselves unto the elder. Yea, all *of you* be subject one to another, and be clothed with humility: for God resisteth the proud, and giveth grace to the humble."

CHRISTIANS SHOULD BE CLOTHED WITH HUMILITY
Humility should surround genuine Christians like clothing. If this is true, God promises them His grace.

- 1 Peter 5:6
"Humble yourselves therefore under the mighty hand of God, that he may exalt you in due time:"
If genuine Christians humble themselves, God will exalt them.

James 4:11

"Speak not evil one of another, brethren. He that speaketh evil of his brother, and judgeth his brother, speaketh evil of the law, and judgeth the law: but if thou judge the law, thou art not a doer of the law, but a judge."

This phrase, "*speak not*," is a prohibition. If the prohibition is in the Greek present tense, it means to stop an action already in progress. It is in the Greek aorist tense, it means to not even begin the action. This verb is in the Greek present tense. Therefore it means to stop speaking evil one of another on the part of those who are true Christian brethren.

CHRISTIANS SHOULD LOVE ONE ANOTHER
Though genuine Christians might differ from one another's theology and Christian views, they should love one another as the Lord Jesus Christ loves them both. They should stop calling each other evil. To speak evil of fellow Christians would be the same as speaking evil of the law and judging the law.

Verses On Speaking Evil And Blaspheming
- **Mark 3:29**

"But he that shall blaspheme against the Holy Ghost hath never forgiveness, but is in danger of eternal damnation:"

One of the meanings of "*blaspheme*" is "*to speak evil.*" In the context, it speaks of attributing the works of the Holy Spirit to Satan.

- **Acts 26:11**

"And I punished them oft in every synagogue, and compelled *them* to blaspheme; and being exceedingly mad against them, I persecuted *them* even unto strange cities."

Paul compelled the Christians to blaspheme or speak evil of God and the Lord Jesus Christ.

Verses On Judge And Judging
- **Acts 10:42**

"And he commanded us to preach unto the people, and to testify that it is he which was ordained of God *to be* the Judge of quick and dead."

The Lord Jesus Christ is going to be the Judge at the Judgment Seat of Christ for genuine Christians as well as at the Great White Throne judgment of the non-Christians.

- **Acts 17:31**

"Because he hath appointed a day, in the which he will judge the world in righteousness by *that* man whom he hath ordained; *whereof* he hath given assurance unto all *men*, in that he hath raised him from the dead."

- **Romans 2:16**

"In the day when God shall judge the secrets of men by Jesus Christ according to my gospel."

The Lord Jesus Christ will judge the secrets of all people–both the saved at the Judgment Seat Of Christ and the lost at the Great White Throne.

CHRIST THE JUDGE KNOWS ALL THE FACTS

Sometimes judges in this world don't have all the facts. When people go before the court, the prosecuting attorney has one side of the case and the defense attorney has the other side. The judge must have all the facts ready when he makes his judgment. The Lord Jesus does have all the facts. Not only the external facts but the internal facts as he sees within the hearts.

James 4:12

"There is one lawgiver, who is able to save and to destroy: who art thou that judgest another?"

We don't have the facts. We cannot judge one another as believers. One lawgiver, the Lord Jesus Christ Himself. Notice what this Lawgiver is able to—to save and to destroy. Those that reject the Lord Jesus Christ will be judged and sent to Hell, the Lake of Fire.

Verses On Being Saved

- **Luke 19:10**

"For the Son of man is come to seek and to save that which was lost."

That's why the Lord Jesus Christ came into this world.

- **John 12:47**

"And if any man hear my words, and believe not, I judge him not: for I came not to judge the world, but to save the world."

> **CHRIST PROVIDES SALVATION TO TRUE BELIEVERS**
>
> Not that everybody in the world is saved. That was the mission of the Lord Jesus Christ to die for the sins of the world so that those who trust Him truly might be saved.

- **1 Corinthians 1:21**

"For after that in the wisdom of God the world by wisdom knew not God, it pleased God by the foolishness of preaching to save them that believe."

Salvation is by genuine faith in the Lord Jesus Christ.

- **1 Timothy 1:15**

"This *is* a faithful saying, and worthy of all acceptation, that Christ Jesus came into the world to save sinners; of whom I am chief."

That's why the Lord Jesus Christ came into the world—to save sinners.

- **Hebrews 7:25**

"Wherefore he is able also to save them to the uttermost that come unto God by him, seeing he ever liveth to make intercession for them."

The only way to God is through the Lord Jesus Christ. He can save completely—to the uttermost.

Verses On Judging

- **Matthew 7:1**

"Judge not, that ye be not judged."

People are not to render final judgment on other people. This is left only for The Lord Jesus Christ.

- **John 7:24**
"Judge not according to the appearance, but judge righteous judgment."

JUDGE NOT ON APPEARANCE ONLY
Appearance alone should not be the basis for judgment. It must be righteous.

- **Romans 14:3-4**
"Let not him that eateth despise him that eateth not; and let not him which eateth not judge him that eateth: for God hath received him. <u>Who art thou that judgest another man's servant?</u> to his own master he standeth or falleth. Yea, he shall be holden up: for God is able to make him stand."

The Lord Jesus Christ alone will be the Judge of all. Others should keep out of final judgment.

- **Romans 14:10**
"But <u>why dost thou judge thy brother?</u> or why dost thou set at nought thy brother? for we shall all stand before the judgment seat of Christ."

CHRIST WILL JUDGE CHRISTIANS RIGHTEOUSLY
This is the task of the Lord Jesus Christ at the Judgment Seat of Christ.

- **Romans 14:13**
"<u>Let us not therefore judge one another any more</u>: but judge this rather, that no man put a stumblingblock or an occasion to fall in *his* brother's way."

Genuine Christians must be careful that they do not stumble one another.

James 4:13

"Go to now, ye that say, To day or to morrow we will go into such a city, and continue there a year, and buy and sell, and get gain:"

Today, there are many things, some things people need to do. Some of them can wait until tomorrow, other things cannot.

Verses On Today, Not Tomorrow

- **Luke 19:5**
"And when Jesus came to the place, he looked up, and saw him, and said unto him, Zacchaeus, make haste, and come down; for <u>to day I must abide at thy house</u>."

The Lord Jesus Christ told Zacchaeus that He was coming to his house today–not tomorrow.

James–Preaching Verse By Verse

- **Luke 23:42**

"And he said unto Jesus, Lord, remember me when thou comest into thy kingdom. And Jesus said unto him, Verily I say unto thee, To day shalt thou be with me in paradise."

> **THE BELIEVING THIEF WOULD BE WITH CHRIST**
>
> The repentant thief had faith in the Lord Jesus Christ. The Lord knew the thief was going to die that day. The Lord Jesus Christ also knew He was going to die that day. This thief was told that on that very day he would be with the Lord Jesus Christ in paradise.

- **2 Corinthians 6:2**

"(For he saith, I have heard thee in a time accepted, and in the day of salvation have I succoured thee: behold, now *is* the accepted time; behold, now *is the day of salvation*.)"

For lost people, there should be no putting off of salvation until some other day. It should be done today.

- **Hebrews 3:13**

"But exhort one another daily, while it is called To day; lest any of you be hardened through the deceitfulness of sin."

Fellow Christians should exhort one another today, before there might be a hardening of their hearts.

- **Hebrews 13:8**

"Jesus Christ the same yesterday, and to day, and for ever."

> **THE LORD JESUS CHRIST IS CHANGELESS**
>
> The Lord Jesus Christ does not change. He is the same yesterday, today and forever.

- **Proverbs 27:1**

"Boast not thyself of to morrow; for thou knowest not what a day may bring forth."

Tomorrow might be altogether different than today. Don't boast or brag about tomorrow. It is an unknown.

- **1 Corinthians 15:32**

"If after the manner of men I have fought with beasts at Ephesus, what advantageth it me, if the dead rise not? let us eat and drink; for to morrow we die."

There should be no excuse for eating and drinking evil things that should not be eaten or drunk by using the excuse that they are going to die tomorrow and will no longer be able to eat or drink.

James 4:14

"Whereas ye know not what shall be on the morrow. For what is your life? It is even a vapour, that appeareth for a little time, and then vanisheth away."

Life is very short. It is like "*vapour*" that appears for a little time and then vanishes away. It's just like a puff of smoke.

Verses On The Shortness Of Life

- Job 7:1

"<u>Is there</u> not an appointed time to man upon earth? *are not* his days also like the days of an hireling?"

EVERY PERSON HAS AN APPOINTMENT FOR DEATH

There is an appointed time to die for every person on this earth. No one but the Lord knows when that time of life is up for any person on earth.

- Job 7:6

"<u>My days are swifter than a weaver's shuttle</u>, and are spent without hope."

MAN'S DAYS ARE FASTER THAN A SHUTTLE

I'm not a weaver, I don't weave anything but I understand that a person is weaving with a weaving machine that the shuttle goes back and forth until the weaving is done. Then it stops. So with the life of all people. They do not know when their life will stop.

- Job 8:9

"(For we *are but of* yesterday, and know nothing, because <u>our days upon earth</u> *are* <u>a shadow:</u>)"

People's days are like a shadow. Shadows are not visible unless there is some light that is shining. When the light appears, the shadow is no more. Such is the life of people on earth.

- Job 9:25

"Now <u>my days are swifter than a post: they flee away</u>, they see no good."

A post would refer to someone carrying letters. They used to deliver the mail by horses. It was like the pony express. When the letters are delivered, the postman flees away. So people's lives.

- Job 10:20

"<u>*Are* not my days few</u>? cease *then, and* let me alone, that I may take comfort a little,"

Job was in much physical pain. Compared with eternity, he and all

James–Preaching Verse By Verse

of us have very few days on earth. Methuselah lived 969 years, but even those years, compared to eternity, are few.
- **Job 14:1**
"Man *that is* born of a woman *is* of few days, and full of trouble."
This is another verse that mentions the fewness of people's days on earth.
- **Job 14:5**
"Seeing his days *are* determined, the number of his months *are* with thee, thou hast appointed his bounds that he cannot pass;"

GOD KNOWS HOW MANY MONTHS PEOPLE HAVE

God has determined the number of people's months that they have to live on this earth.

- **Job 14:14**
"If a man die, shall he live *again*? all the days of my appointed time will I wait, till my change come."
Job was waiting until his appointed time to die would come.
- **Psalms 39:4**
"LORD, make me to know mine end, and the measure of my days, what it *is; that* I may know how frail I *am*. Behold, thou hast made my days *as* an handbreadth; and mine age *is* as nothing before thee: verily every man at his best state *is* altogether vanity. Selah."
No one knows the end of their days. Their days are as short as the width of a hand.
- **Psalms 90:10**
"The days of our years *are* threescore years and ten; and if by reason of strength *they be* fourscore years, yet *is* their strength labour and sorrow; for it is soon cut off, and we fly away."

PEOPLE GO EITHER TO HEAVEN OR TO HELL

Though some live 70 years, some 80 years, some 90 years, and others live longer, their life is soon cut off and they fly away, either to Heaven or to Hell.

- **Psalms 90:12**
"So teach *us* to number our days, that we may apply *our* hearts unto wisdom."
Every day that people live upon earth should be used in the right, honourable, and wise way.
- **Psalms 102:11**
"My days *are* like a shadow that declineth; and I am withered like grass."
This is another verse that compares life to a shadow that declines and vanishes away.

- **Psalms 102:23**

"He weakened my strength in the way; he shortened my days. I said, O my God, take me not away in the midst of my days: thy years *are* throughout all generations."

David's days were shortened. So people's days today might also be shortened by something that happens to them.

- **Psalms 103:15**

"*As for* man, his days *are* as grass: as a flower of the field, so he flourisheth."

OUR DAYS ARE AS BRIEF AS THE GRASS

Grass doesn't last very long. In a few months, when winter arrives, it becomes dry and often changes its color. In a very real sense, it doesn't look the same.

- **Psalms 119:84**

"How many *are* the days of thy servant? when wilt thou execute judgment on them that persecute me?"

The Psalmist asks this question. He doesn't know the answer, nor does anyone living today.

- **Psalms 144:4**

"Man is like to vanity: his days *are* as a shadow that passeth away."

This is another verse comparing people's days as a shadow that passes away.

- **Luke 12:16-21**

"And he spake a parable unto them, saying, The ground of a certain rich man brought forth plentifully: And he thought within himself, saying, What shall I do, because I have no room where to bestow my fruits? And he said, This will I do: I will pull down my barns, and build greater; and there will I bestow all my fruits and my goods. And I will say to my soul, Soul, thou hast much goods laid up for many years; take thine ease, eat, drink, *and* be merry. But God said unto him, *Thou* fool, this night thy soul shall be required of thee: then whose shall those things be, which thou hast provided? So *is* he that layeth up treasure for himself, and is not rich toward God."

The rich man in this parable was going to die on that very night, yet, though he had made provisions for his earthly treasures, he made no provision for his soul.

James 4:15

"For that ye ought to say, If the Lord will, we shall live, and do this, or that."

He says we're going tomorrow, we're going to go living and shopping and gaining, make gain, if the Lord will. That's what we should say. That's what he is saying here. If the Lord will. If the Lord will we shall live and do this or that.

Verses On The Will Of The Lord

- **Luke 12:47**

"And <u>that servant, which knew his lord's will, and prepared not himself</u>, neither did according to his will, shall be beaten with many *stripes*."

Every person must first know God's will which is revealed in the Bible as well as in various circumstances. Then they must prepare to fulfill that will immediately.

- **1 Corinthians 4:19**

"But I will come to you shortly, <u>if the Lord will</u>, and will know, not the speech of them which are puffed up, but the power."

Genuine Christians should always be sure it is the Lord's will before they do anything.

- **1 John 5:14**

"And this is the confidence that we have in him, that, <u>if we ask any thing according to his will, he heareth us</u>:"

God will hear true Christians requests if they are in His will.

James 4:16

"But now ye rejoice in your boastings: all such rejoicing is evil."

The Greek Word for "***boastings***" is ALADZONIA. Some of the meanings of this Greek Word are:

> "1) empty, braggart talk; 2) an insolent and empty assurance, which trusts in its own power and resources and shamefully despises and violates divine laws and human rights; 3) an impious and empty presumption which trusts in the stability of earthy things."

ALL BOASTINGS ARE EVIL

The Galatians were rejoicing in some of their boastings. The boastings might have something to do with trying to keep the law of Moses. It is not clear. In any event, these boastings were and are evil.

Verses On Boasting
- **Romans 3:27**

"Where *is* boasting then? It is excluded. By what law? of works? Nay: but by the law of faith."

> **CHRISTIANS SHOULDN'T BOAST, BUT BE THANKFUL**
>
> We should not boast and brag of the things God has given to us. We should be thankful to Him for these things.

- **2 Corinthians 10:15**

"Not boasting of things without *our* measure, *that is*, of other men's labours; but having hope, when your faith is increased, that we shall be enlarged by you according to our rule abundantly,"

Paul does not want to boast and brag as he mentioned in this verse. This quality should be also found among true Christians today.

James 4:17

"Therefore to him that knoweth to do good, and doeth it not, to him it is sin."

It's a sad situation if genuine Christians read their entire Bibles from Genesis through Revelation every year (though, sad to say, there are very few of these in our day) and yet do not follow the truths that they read. James labels this situation as sin. It's one thing to know God's Words, but it quite another to follow these Words.

James
Chapter Five

James 5:1

"Go to now, ye rich men, weep and howl for your miseries that shall come upon you."

These first six verses are talking about rich people who are not using their riches well. They are wicked rich people. Not all rich people are wicked but these are wicked. They are persecuting the Christians that James is writing to. Because these rich men are misusing their riches, they will weep because of the miseries that will come upon them.

Verses On Riches

- **1 Samuel 2:7**

The LORD maketh poor, and maketh rich: he bringeth low, and lifteth up."

For genuine Christians, the Lord permits them to be either poor or rich.

- **Proverbs 10:4**

"He becometh poor that dealeth *with* a slack hand: but the hand of the diligent maketh rich."

If people are lazy, they're not going to get much money. But diligence can give them riches.

- **Proverbs 10:22**

"The blessing of the LORD, it maketh rich, and he addeth no sorrow with it."

Blessings come from the LORD, including riches without sorrow. These are the riches true Christians should strive for and thank the Lord for.

- **Proverbs 13:7**

"There is that maketh himself rich, yet *hath* nothing: *there is* that maketh himself poor, yet *hath* great riches."

Here are two kinds of riches. There are those who have riches but have nothing and those who are poor, but if they are genuine Christians, they have great riches in the Lord Jesus Christ.

148   James–Preaching Verse By Verse

- **Proverbs 23:4**

"<u>Labour not to be rich</u>: cease from thine own wisdom."
Riches shouldn't be your main desire and goal; otherwise you'll throw out everything else. True Christians should take much of their time to serve the Lord Jesus Christ.

- **Jeremiah 9:23**

"Thus saith the LORD, Let not the wise *man* glory in his wisdom, neither let the mighty *man* glory in his might, <u>let not the rich *man* glory in his riches</u>:
Genuine Christians should not glory in their riches, but in the Lord Jesus Christ.

- **Matthew 19:23-24**

"Then said Jesus unto his disciples, Verily I say unto you, That a <u>rich man shall hardly enter into the kingdom of heaven</u>. And again I say unto you, It is easier for a camel to go through the eye of a needle, than for a rich man to enter into the kingdom of God."
Though all things are possible, many of those who are rich do not care for the things of the Lord.

- **Matthew 27:57**

"When the even was come, there came a rich man of Arimathaea, named Joseph, who also himself was Jesus' disciple:"
The Lord used that rich man, Joseph of Arimathaea, with the tomb, to help the Lord Jesus Christ.

- **Luke 12:16, 20-21**

"And he spake a parable unto them, saying, <u>The ground of a certain rich man brought forth plentifully</u>: ... But God said unto him, *Thou* fool, this night thy soul shall be required of thee: then whose shall those things be, which thou hast provided? <u>So *is* he that layeth up treasure for himself, and is not rich toward God.</u>"

BEING RICH TOWARD GOD IS IMPORTANT

No matter how much treasure people have, they should not fail to be rich toward God by trusting in the Lord Jesus Christ as their Saviour and be rich toward God.

- **Luke 19:2-3**

"And, behold, *there was* a man named <u>Zacchaeus</u>, which was the chief among the publicans, and he <u>was rich</u>. And he sought to see Jesus who he was; and could not for the press, because he was little of stature. ... And when Jesus came to the place, he looked up, and saw him, and said unto him, Zacchaeus, make haste, and come down; for to day I must abide at thy house."

CHRIST CAME TO RICH ZACCHAEUS' HOUSE

The rich man, Zacchaeus, climbed a tree to see the Lord Jesus Christ. When the Lord looked up, He told Zacchaeus that he must come to his house that day. Zacchaeus apparently trusted in the Lord Jesus Christ and received His great riches.

- **2 Corinthians 6:10**

"As sorrowful, yet alway rejoicing; <u>as poor, yet making many rich; as having nothing, and</u> *yet* <u>possessing all things.</u>"

Paul was indeed poor. Yet he possessed all things in Christ and made many rich by leading them to salvation by genuine faith in the Saviour.

- **2 Corinthians 8:9**

"For ye know the grace of our Lord Jesus Christ, that, <u>though he was rich</u>, yet for your sakes he became poor, that ye through his poverty might be rich."

CHRIST BECAME POOR TO MAKE BELIEVERS RICH

This is a wonderful picture of riches. The Lord Jesus Christ, rich in Heaven throughout all eternity past, yet took upon Himself a body, came to this earth, left His riches and became poor, dying for the sins of every person whoever lived. Through trust in Him sincerely, people can be spiritually rich and joint-heirs with the Lord Jesus Christ.

Paul cautions Pastor Timothy,

- **1 Timothy 6:9**

"But <u>they that will be rich fall into temptation and a snare</u>, and *into* many foolish and hurtful lusts, which drown men in destruction and perdition."

Those people who will to be rich with strong desire will fall into a snare and many foolish lusts.

- **1 Timothy 6:17**

"<u>Charge them that are rich in this world, that they be not highminded</u>, nor trust in uncertain riches, but in the living God, who giveth us richly all things to enjoy;"

Those genuine Christians who are rich in this world must be very careful of being highminded, or in trusting in those uncertain riches rather than in the living God Who gives great spiritual riches.

James 5:2

"Your riches are corrupted, and your garments are motheaten."

Today, our "riches" based on paper money are corrupt as well. Genuine "riches" and material wealth is found in gold or silver, not in paper. Article One Section Eight, clause Five in our U.S. Constitution says very clearly that Congress (not the phony Federal Reserve System) shall have power **to coin money**, not to PRINT WORTHLESS PAPER and call it "money."

In the German inflationary time of 1922-1923, we read that after World War I, Germany was plunged into one of the worse inflations ever to hit a Western country. The government struggled with truly massive punitive damages demanded by the Treaty of Versailles, during the brief period of hyper-inflation. That's what our country has plunged itself into leading to the same hyper-inflation.

In Germany, many bank accounts were closed because even large pre-war sums, of 100,000 marks, were no longer worth even the price of a postage stamp. That's what we are getting into in our country. When the paper dollar originated in about the 1920's, it was worth 100 cents. It is very true for us in the USA that our riches are corrupted.

James 5:3

"Your gold and silver is cankered; and the rust of them shall be a witness against you, and shall eat your flesh as it were fire. Ye have heaped treasure together for the last days."

Notice your gold and silver. They had gold and silver. How many of us have gold and silver? We may have a few gold things and articles and a few silver things. Mainly, with few exceptions, people have paper money. The people James was writing to had their gold and silver cankered. Their riches also have "rust" on them.

THE MEANING OF THE GREEK WORD, "IOS"

The Greek Word for "*rust*" is IOS. Some of the meanings of that Greek Word are:

> *1) poison (of animals); 1a) poison of asps is under their lips; 1b) spoken of men given to reviling and calumniating and thereby injuring others; 2) rust.*

The Lord Jesus Christ had something to say about treasures on this earth.
- **Matthew 6:19-21**
"Lay not up for yourselves treasures upon earth, where moth and rust doth corrupt, and where thieves break through and steal: But lay up for yourselves treasures in heaven, where neither moth nor rust doth corrupt, and where thieves do not break through nor steal: For where your treasure is, there will your heart be also."

> **LAY UP TREASURES IN HEAVEN**
> Since this is in the Greek present tense, the meaning is to stop an action that was already going on. They should stop laying up for themselves treasure on this earth, but they should lay up treasures in Heaven.

You might think of all the millionaires and billionaires who have died and have left all of their millions or billions here on earth. They cannot take those kind of riches to Heaven.

James 5:4

"Behold, the hire of the labourers who have reaped down your fields, which is of you kept back by fraud, crieth: and the cries of them which have reaped are entered into the ears of the Lord of sabaoth."

James is scolding those who own the fields because of their holding back, by fraud, the hire of those who reaped down their fields.

> **THE MEANING OF THE GREEK WORD, "MISTHOS"**
> The Greek Word for *"hire"* (or *"wages"*) is MISTHOS. Some of the meanings of this Greek Word are:
> *"dues paid for work; 1a) wages, hire; 2) reward: used of the fruit naturally resulting from toils and endeavours; 2a) in both senses, rewards and punishments; 2b) of the rewards which God bestows, or will bestow, upon good deeds and endeavours; 2c) of punishments."*

These wages were held back from the laborers because of the fraud of the owners.

> **THE MEANING OF THE GREEK WORD, "APOSTEREO"**
>
> The Greek Word for "*fraud*" is APOSTEREO. Some of the meanings of that Greek Word are:
> 1) *to defraud, rob, despoil*

This a serious charge against these rich owners who are doing this to their employees.

> **THE MEANING OF THE GREEK WORD, "KRAZO"**
>
> The Greek Word for "*cry*" is KRAZO. Some of the meanings of that Greek Word are:
> "*1) to croak; 1a) of the cry of a raven; 1b) hence, to cry out, cry aloud, vociferate; 1c) to cry or pray for vengeance; 2) to cry; 2a) cry out aloud, speak with a loud voice.*"

Verses On Wages

- **Leviticus 19:13**

"Thou shalt not defraud thy neighbour, neither rob *him*: the wages of him that is hired shall not abide with thee all night until the morning."

Day laborers were to be paid at the end of the working day in the Old Testament.

- **Jeremiah 22:13**

"Woe unto him that buildeth his house by unrighteousness, and his chambers by wrong; *that* useth his neighbour's service without wages, and giveth him not for his work;"

In this case, the owners were making their laborers to work without any wages at all.

- **Haggai 1:6**

"Ye have sown much, and bring in little; ye eat, but ye have not enough; ye drink, but ye are not filled with drink; ye clothe you, but there is none warm; and he that earneth wages earneth wages *to put it* into a bag with holes."

It is a foolish thing to put wages into a bag with holes in it. This would be a very insecure location for wages.

- **Malachi 3:5**

"And I will come near to you to judgment; and I will be a swift witness against the sorcerers, and against the adulterers, and against false swearers, and against those that oppress the hireling in *his* wages, the widow, and the fatherless, and that turn aside the stranger *from his right*, and fear not me, saith the LORD of hosts."

James–Preaching Verse By Verse

Here is a wrong use of oppression of the hirelings regarding their wages as well as other oppressions.

James 5:5

"Ye have lived in pleasure on the earth, and been wanton; ye have nourished your hearts, as in a day of slaughter."

These wealthy people have lived in pleasure and been wanton. Their hearts have been nourished like they were in a day of slaughter.

THE MEANING OF THE GREEK WORD, "SPATALAO"

The Greek Word for *"wanton"* is SPATALAO. Some of the meanings of that Greek Word are:

"1) to live luxuriously, lead a voluptuous life, (give one's self to pleasure)"

These rich people have not only lived in pleasure and been wanton, but they have nourished their hearts.

THE MEANING OF THE GREEK WORD, "TREPHO"

The Greek Word for *"nourish"* is TREPHO. Some of the meanings of that Greek Word are:

"1) to nourish, support; 2) feed; 3) to give suck, to fatten; 4) to bring up, nurture."

It is difficult to see what kind of heart-nourishment these people will partake in this day of slaughter.

Verses On Pleasure

- **Proverbs 21:17**

"He that loveth pleasure *shall be* a poor man: he that loveth wine and oil shall not be rich."

Things that bring people pleasure (whether good or evil) usually cost a lot of money. Therefore, those who indulge in these things often become poor both in physical things and in their spirit.

- **Romans 1:32**

"Who knowing the judgment of God, that they which commit such things are worthy of death, not only do the same, but have pleasure in them that do them."

These evil people have pleasure in those who do sinful and wicked things.

- **2 Thessalonians 2:12**

"That they all might be damned who believed not the truth, but had pleasure in unrighteousness."

Those who do not believe the truth have pleasure in unrighteousness.

- **1 Timothy 5:6**
"But she that liveth in pleasure is dead while she liveth."

> **CHURCHES NOT TO SUPPORT LOOSE WIDOWS**
>
> **This is speaking about the young widow who leaves the support of the local church and goes back into the world. She is spiritually dead while she is living.**

- **2 Peter 2:13**
"And shall receive the reward of unrighteousness, *as* they that count it pleasure to riot in the day time. Spots *they are* and blemishes, sporting themselves with their own deceivings while they feast with you;"

These are people who find pleasure in rioting in the day time.

Verses On Wantonness

- **Romans 13:13**
"Let us walk honestly, as in the day; not in rioting and drunkenness, not in chambering and wantonness, not in strife and envying."

Genuine Christians should walk honestly, not in the sin of wantonness.

- **1 Timothy 5:11**
"But the younger widows refuse: for when they have begun to wax wanton against Christ, they will marry;"

The churches should not support the younger widows because they will likely marry again perhaps live sinful lives.

- **2 Peter 2:18**
"For when they speak great swelling *words* of vanity, they allure through the lusts of the flesh, *through much* wantonness, those that were clean escaped from them who live in error."

False teachers allure others through the lusts of the flesh and much wantonness and sin.

James 5:6

"Ye have condemned and killed the just; and he doth not resist you."

These rich people have condemned and killed just and righteous people who do not resist them.

James 5:7

"Be patient therefore, brethren, unto the coming of the Lord. Behold, the husbandman waiteth for the precious fruit of the earth, and hath long patience for it, until he receive the early and latter rain."

James is now talking to true Christians who are being hurt by these rich people. They are to be as patient as the farmer who sows his seed and waits for the precious fruit of the earth. He has to be patient because he can't plant and have the crops the next day, the next week, or probably not even the next month.

MEANING OF THE GREEK WORD, "MAKROTHUMEO"

The Greek Word for *"patience"* is MAKROTHUMEO. Some of the meanings of that Greek Word are:

"1) to be of a long spirit, not to lose heart; 1a) to persevere patiently and bravely in enduring misfortunes and troubles; 1b) to be patient in bearing the offenses and injuries of others; 1b1) to be mild and slow in avenging; 1b2) to be longsuffering, slow to anger, slow to punish."

Still More Verses On Patience

- **Ecclesiastes 7:8**

"Better *is* the end of a thing than the beginning thereof: *and* the patient in spirit *is* better than the proud in spirit."

Patient in spirit should be what genuine Christians should be like rather than to be proud in spirit.

- **Romans 12:12**

"Rejoicing in hope; patient in tribulation; continuing instant in prayer;"

Even though true Christians will undergo persecutions for their Biblical faith and practice, they should be patient through all of them.

1 Thessalonians 5:14

"Now we exhort you, brethren, warn them that are unruly, comfort the feebleminded, support the weak, be patient toward all *men*."

Though circumstances are sometimes very difficult, genuine Christians should be patient toward all who are involved in such problems.

- **2 Thessalonians 3:5**
"And the Lord direct your hearts into the love of God, and into the patient waiting for Christ."

God wants to direct true Christians' hearts to wait patiently for the return of the Lord Jesus Christ for them in the rapture.

- **1 Timothy 3:3**
"Not given to wine, no striker, not greedy of filthy lucre; but patient, not a brawler, not covetous;"

PASTORS MUST BE PATIENT TO QUALIFY

To be patient is one of the qualifications of a true pastor. If he is not patient, he does not meet these qualifications and should not be a pastor.

- **2 Timothy 2:24**
"And the servant of the Lord must not strive; but be gentle unto all *men*, apt to teach, patient."

Patience is uncommon in people, even in true Christian people, yet it is extremely necessary for the servants of the Lord Jesus Christ.

James 5:8

"Be ye also patient; stablish your hearts: for the coming of the Lord draweth nigh."

James commends patience in the hearts that are established because "*the coming of the Lord draweth nigh.*" Here are 17 verses about the coming of the Lord Jesus Christ. Approximately nine of them refer to the second phase of His coming, here on earth, in order to establish His millennial reign. The other eight verses refer to the first phase of His coming--the Rapture--the snatching away of the genuine Christians into Heaven before any part of the Tribulation.

Verses On Christ's Return

- **Matthew 24:3**
"And as he sat upon the mount of Olives, the disciples came unto him privately, saying, Tell us, when shall these things be? and what *shall be* the sign of thy coming, and of the end of the world?"

SIGNS WILL PRECEDE CHRIST'S COMING TO REIGN

This refers to the second phase of Christ's coming to earth to set up the Millennium. There are no signs prior to the Rapture, but this second phase of Christ's return to earth will be preceded by signs.

James-Preaching Verse By Verse

- **Matthew 24:27**

"For as the lightning cometh out of the east, and shineth even unto the west; <u>so shall also the coming of the Son of man be.</u>"

This also refers to the second phase of Christ's coming. It will be as the lightning.

- **Matthew 24:30**

"And then shall appear the sign of the Son of man in heaven: and then shall all the tribes of the earth mourn, and <u>they shall see the Son of man coming in the clouds of heaven with power and great glory.</u>"

This refers to the second phase of Christ's coming. All the tribes of the earth will see it.

- **Matthew 24:37**

"But as the days of Noe *were*, <u>so shall also the coming of the Son of man be.</u>"

This refers to the second phase of Christ's coming. The sins and wickedness of people will be just as bad as in the days of Noah.

- **Matthew 24:39**

"And knew not until the flood came, and took them all away; <u>so shall also the coming of the Son of man be.</u>"

This refers to the second phase of Christ's coming. No one will believe it until it happens and judgement comes upon those on the earth.

- **Matthew 26:64**

"Jesus saith unto him, Thou hast said: nevertheless I say unto you, Hereafter shall ye see the Son of man sitting on the right hand of power, and <u>coming in the clouds of heaven.</u>"

This refers to the second phase of Christ's coming. People on earth will see the Lord Jesus before he comes back to set up His millennial kingdom.

- **John 5:28**

"Marvel not at this: for the hour is coming, in the which <u>all that are in the graves shall hear his voice,</u>"

This will occur at the first phase of His coming–at the rapture of the genuine Christians as well as for the non-Christians at the second phase of His coming.

- **John 5:29**

"And shall come forth; <u>they that have done good, unto the resurrection of life;</u> and <u>they that have done evil, unto the resurrection of damnation.</u>"

As the verse before, this verse refers both to the first phase of His coming–at the rapture of the genuine Christians--as well as later for the non-Christians at the second phase of His coming.

- 1 Corinthians 1:7
"So that ye come behind in no gift; waiting for the coming of our Lord Jesus Christ:"

> **THE DEFINITION OF CHRIST'S "RAPTURE"**
> This refers to the first phase of the Coming of the Lord Jesus Christ–at the Rapture. It will not be only a partial rapture of true Christians–some walking after the Spirit, and some walking after the flesh. But very born-again Christian will be raptured by their Saviour. This event will take place before any part of the Tribulation period. It will be a pre-tribulation Rapture and not either a mid-tribulation rapture, or a post-tribulation, or a pre-wrath rapture.

- 1 Corinthians 15:23
"But every man in his own order: Christ the firstfruits; afterward they that are Christ's at his coming."
This again refers to the first phase of the Coming of the Lord Jesus Christ–at the Rapture.
- 1 Thessalonians 2:19
"For what *is* our hope, or joy, or crown of rejoicing? Are not even ye in the presence of our Lord Jesus Christ at his coming?"
This again refers to the first phase of the Coming of the Lord Jesus Christ–at the Rapture.
- 1 Thessalonians 3:13
"To the end he may stablish your hearts unblameable in holiness before God, even our Father, at the coming of our Lord Jesus Christ with all his saints."

> **CHRIST'S REIGN IS 7 YEARS AFTER THE RAPTURE**
> This refers to the second phase of his coming back to earth with all His saints who were raptured seven years before. The Rapture takes all the genuine Christians to Heaven. Then, seven years later, the Lord Jesus Christ will come, with these true Christians, back to the earth to reign with Him during the thousand-year Millennium.

- 1 Thessalonians 4:15-17
"For this we say unto you by the word of the Lord, that we which are alive *and* remain unto the coming of the Lord shall not prevent them which are asleep. For the Lord himself shall descend from heaven with a shout, with the voice of the archangel, and with the trump of God: and the dead in Christ shall rise first: Then we which are alive *and* remain shall be caught up together with them in the clouds, to meet the Lord in

James–Preaching Verse By Verse

the air: and so shall we ever be with the Lord."
This is the order at the rapture of the genuine Christians, both the dead and the living.

- **1 Thessalonians 5:23**
"And the very God of peace sanctify you wholly; and *I pray God* your whole spirit and soul and body be preserved blameless unto the coming of our Lord Jesus Christ."

This refers to the first phase of Christ's return–the rapture.

- **2 Thessalonians 2:1**
"Now we beseech you, brethren, by the coming of our Lord Jesus Christ, and *by* our gathering together unto him,"

This refers to the first phase of Christ's return–the rapture.

- **2 Thessalonians 2:8**
"And then shall that Wicked be revealed, [that antichrist] whom the Lord shall consume with the spirit of his mouth, and shall destroy with the brightness of his coming:"

> **CHRIST KILLS THE ANTICHRIST AT ARMAGEDDON**
> This refers to the second phase of Christ's coming. He will come back to earth at the battle of Armageddon and destroy the Antichrist and his followers with the brightness of his coming.

- **2 Peter 3:4**
"And saying, Where is the promise of his coming? for since the fathers fell asleep, all things continue as *they were* from the beginning of the creation."

This refers also to the second phase of His coming.

- **1 John 2:28**
"And now, little children, abide in him; that, when he shall appear, we may have confidence, and not be ashamed before him at his coming."

This refers to the coming of the Lord Jesus Christ for the genuine Christians to take them to Heaven at the Rapture. The true Christians should abide in Him so as not to be ashamed before Him at His coming.

James 5:9

"Grudge not one against another, brethren, lest ye be condemned: behold, the judge standeth before the door."

"*Grudge not.*" This is a negative prohibition. It is in the Greek present tense. As such, it means to stop an action already in progress. James is telling his readers to stop grudging their brethren so they won't be condemned. The Lord Jesus Christ, the Divine Judge, is standing at the door to judge those who are continually grudging, sighing, and groaning.

> **THE MEANING OF THE GREEK WORD, "STENAZO"**
> The Greek Word for *"judging"* is STENAZO. Some of the meanings of this Greek Word are:
> *"1) a sigh, to groan"*

Verses About Grudging
- **Leviticus 19:18**

"Thou shalt not avenge, nor bear any grudge against the children of thy people, but thou shalt love thy neighbour as thyself: I *am* the LORD."

James tells his readers to not hold a grudge against any one. This is sometimes very difficult to perform. If a grudge occurs, try to dismiss it as soon as possible.

- **2 Corinthians 9:7**

"Every man according as he purposeth in his heart, *so let him give*; not grudgingly, or of necessity: for God loveth a cheerful giver."

> **CHRISTIAN GIVING IS WITH A CHEERFUL HEART**
> Genuine Christians should give to the Lord's work with a purposeful and cheerful heart. It should not be done grudgingly or of necessity.

- **1 Peter 4:9**

"Use hospitality one to another without grudging."

True Christians should welcome fellow Christians into their home without grudging.

Verses On Judge And Judging
- **Genesis 18:25**

"That be far from thee to do after this manner, to slay the righteous with the wicked: and that the righteous should be as the wicked, that be far from thee: Shall not the Judge of all the earth do right?"

Abraham stated this truth as he contemplated God's coming judgment of Sodom and Gomorrah. It is so true. God's judgments are always right. He has a perfect standard. He will always do right at all times, though many people doubt this.

- **Psalms 7:8**

"The LORD shall judge the people: judge me, O LORD, according to my righteousness, and according to mine integrity *that is* in me."

In this present dispensation of grace, the Lord Jesus Christ has been given by God the Father complete and total judgment.

- **Psalms 9:8**
"And he shall judge the world in righteousness, he shall minister judgment to the people in uprightness."

Unlike many human judges in this world, God always judges in absolute righteousness.

- **John 5:22**
"For the Father judgeth no man, but hath committed all judgment unto the Son:"

CHRIST WILL JUDGE THE SAVED AND THE LOST

All judgment, whether of the genuine Christians at the Judgment Seat of Christ, or of the non-Christian at the Great White Throne Judgment will be by the Lord Jesus Christ.

- **John 5:27**
"And hath given him authority to execute judgment also, because he is the Son of man."

God, the Father, has given the Lord Jesus Christ the authority to execute judgment.

- **John 12:47**
"And if any man hear my words, and believe not, I judge him not: for I came not to judge the world, but to save the world."

That wasn't the Lord Jesus Christ's mission to judge the world, but to save it.

- **Acts 10:42**
"And he commanded us to preach unto the people, and to testify that it is he which was ordained of God *to be* the Judge of quick and dead."

The Lord Jesus Christ will be the judge of both the quick, the living, or Genuine Christians as well as the dead, the non-Christians.

- **Acts 17:31**
"Because he hath appointed a day, in the which he will judge the world in righteousness by *that* man whom he hath ordained; *whereof* he hath given assurance unto all *men*, in that he hath raised him from the dead."

The resurrected Saviour will be the judge of all people, both the saved and the lost.

- **Romans 2:16**
"In the day when God shall judge the secrets of men by Jesus Christ according to my gospel."

The Lord Jesus Christ will judge even the secrets of men. All will be revealed.

- **Romans 14:10**
"But why dost thou judge thy brother? or why dost thou set at nought thy brother? for <u>we shall all stand before the judgment seat of Christ</u>."

GNOSTIC-BASED VERSIONS DENY CHRIST AS JUDGE
The Gnostic Critical-based Bible versions wrongly change the *"judgment seat of Christ"* to the *"judgment seat of God."* The Gnostic heretics don't believe Christ could do anything. They teach that He was just a man so this couldn't be the judgment seat of "Christ." They didn't believe Christ was Deity.

- **2 Timothy 4:1**
"I charge *thee* therefore before God, and <u>the Lord Jesus Christ, who shall judge the quick and the dead</u> at his appearing and his kingdom;"

WHERE CHRIST JUDGES THE SAVED AND THE LOST
This verse shows the two phases of the coming of the Lord Jesus Christ. The Lord Jesus will judge the genuine Christians at His appearing--the Rapture. This will be the judgment seat of Christ. At the second phase of His coming, at the end of His millennial reign, He will judge all of the lost non-Christians at the Great White Throne.

- **2 Timothy 4:8**
"Henceforth there is laid up for me a crown of righteousness, which <u>the Lord, the righteous judge</u>, shall give me at that day: and not to me only, but unto all them also that love his appearing."

The Lord Jesus Christ is a righteous Judge. He will never judge anyone wrongfully.

- **Hebrews 9:27**
"And as it is appointed unto men once to die, but <u>after this the judgment</u>:"

After the death of every person in the world, they will be judged by the Lord Jesus Christ.

- **1 Peter 4:5**
"Who shall give account <u>to him that is ready to judge the quick and the dead</u>."

It's the Lord Jesus Christ who will judge the saved and the lost.

- **2 Peter 2:9**
"The Lord knoweth how to deliver the godly out of temptations, and to reserve <u>the unjust unto the day of judgment to be punished</u>:"

James–Preaching Verse By Verse

The unjust, lost non-Christians will for all eternity will endure their conscious judgment in Hell, the Lake of Fire.
- **2 Peter 3:7**
"But the heavens and the earth, which are now, by the same word are kept in store, reserved unto fire against <u>the day of judgment and perdition of ungodly men</u>."

There will be a judgment and perdition of all ungodly people.
- **Jude 1:6**
"And <u>the angels which kept not their first estate</u>, but left their own habitation, <u>he hath reserved</u> in everlasting chains under darkness <u>unto the judgment of the great day</u>."

The Lord Jesus Christ will judge the fallen angels as well as all the people.
- **Jude 1:14-15**
"And Enoch also, the seventh from Adam, prophesied of these, saying, Behold, <u>the Lord cometh</u> with ten thousands of his saints, <u>To execute judgment upon all</u>, and to convince all that are ungodly among them of all their ungodly deeds which they have ungodly committed, and of all their hard *speeches* which ungodly sinners have spoken against him."

NO ESCAPE FROM CHRIST'S RIGHTEOUS JUDGMENT
No person who ever lived on this earth will escape the righteous judgment of the Lord Jesus Christ.

- **Revelation 19:11**
"And I saw heaven opened, and behold a white horse; and he that sat upon him *was* called Faithful and True, and <u>in righteousness he doth judge</u> and make war."

This is speaking about the battle of Armageddon. The Lord Jesus Christ is going to put down these evil nations who are seeking to take over Jerusalem and slay millions of people. The Lord Jesus Christ will judge these evil nations in righteousness and destroy them because of their wicked actions.
- **Revelation 20:11-15**
"And <u>I saw a great white throne</u>, and him that sat on it, from whose face the earth and the heaven fled away; and there was found no place for them. And I saw the dead, small and great, stand before God; and the books were opened: and another book was opened, which is *the book* of life: and <u>the dead were judged out of those things which were written in the books</u>, according to their works. And the sea gave up the dead which were in it; and death and hell delivered up the dead which were in them: and <u>they were judged every man according to their works</u>. And death and hell were cast into the lake of fire. This is the second

death. And whosoever was not found written in the book of life was cast into the lake of fire."

> **GREAT WHITE THRONE JUDGMENT OF THE LOST**
> This is the Great White Throne judgment of all the unsaved, lost people from everywhere on earth from the beginning to the end of time. They will be judged according to their works, beginning with their wicked work of rejecting the Lord Jesus Christ as their Saviour. Because of this rejection, they will be cast into Hell's Lake Of Fire. I believe this is literal and everlasting fire.

James 5:10

"Take, my brethren, the prophets, who have spoken in the name of the Lord, for an example of suffering affliction, and of patience."

These Old Testament prophets spoke to the nation of Israel in the Name of the Lord. They were an example of suffering affliction, but also of patience. Both the 10 northern tribes of Israel and the 2 tribes of the southern tribes of Judah failed to follow the Words of the Lord which were proclaimed by their prophets.

May genuine Christians today hearken to the Words of the Lord in our days and be obedient. As with the Old Testament prophets, faithful preachers of the proper Words of God in the faithful translations of those Words, will bring some suffering and affliction. If and when this comes to these preachers, it should be accompanied by patience.

Verses On Prophets

- **1 Kings 18:13**

"Was it not told my lord what I did when <u>Jezebel slew the prophets of the LORD, how I hid an hundred men of the LORD'S prophets by fifty in a cave, and fed them with bread and water</u>?"

Jezebel slew many of God's prophets. Fortunately fifty prophets were hidden in a cave and escaped death.

- **2 Kings 9:7**

"And thou shalt smite the house of Ahab thy master, <u>that I may avenge the blood of my servants the prophets</u>, and the blood of all the servants of the LORD, at the hand of Jezebel."

Jezebel and Ahab slew many of God's prophets. Because of Ahab's slaughter of these prophets, his house would be smitten.

- **2 Chronicles 36:14-16**

"Moreover all the chief of the priests, and the people,

transgressed very much after all the abominations of the heathen; and polluted the house of the LORD which he had hallowed in Jerusalem. And the LORD God of their fathers sent to them by his messengers, rising up betimes, and sending; because he had compassion on his people, and on his dwelling place: But <u>they mocked the messengers of God</u>, and despised his words, and <u>misused his prophets</u>, until the wrath of the LORD arose against his people, till *there was* no remedy."

Because the chief of the priests and the people who sinned against God's Words and God's prophets, God sent His wrath upon these people without any remedy at all.

- **Nehemiah 9:26**

"Nevertheless they were disobedient, and rebelled against thee, and cast thy law behind their backs, and <u>slew thy prophets which testified against</u> them to turn them to thee, and they wrought great provocations."

Nehemiah went back to Jerusalem after being in the captivity in Babylon. The Jews in Jerusalem were disobedient to the Lord and slew some of God's prophets.

- **Psalms 105:15**

"*Saying*, Touch not mine anointed, and <u>do my prophets no harm</u>."

God does not want His prophets to be harmed.

- **Jeremiah 2:30**

"In vain have I smitten your children; they received no correction: <u>your own sword hath devoured your prophets, like a destroying lion</u>."

ISRAEL DESTROYED THEIR PROPHETS

Jeremiah told the Israelites that they devoured their prophets like a hungry and destroying lion.

Verses On Prophets By Christ

- **Matthew 5:11-12**

"Blessed are ye, when *men* shall revile you, and persecute *you*, and shall say all manner of evil against you falsely, for my sake. Rejoice, and be exceeding glad: for great *is* your reward in heaven: for <u>so persecuted they the prophets which were before you</u>."

True Christians who had been reviled and persecuted falsely for the Lord's sake, should rejoice and be very glad. This is what evil people did to the prophets in the Old Testament.

- **Matthew 23:31**

"Wherefore ye be witnesses unto yourselves, that <u>ye are the children of them which killed the prophets</u>."

James–Preaching Verse By Verse

> **CHRIST BLASTED THE PAGAN PHARISEES**
> The Lord Jesus Christ spoke very plainly to the ungodly Pharisees who were related to the Old Testament Jews who killed their prophets.

- **Matthew 23:34**

"Wherefore, behold, I send unto you prophets, and wise men, and scribes: and *some* of them ye shall kill and crucify; and *some* of them shall ye scourge in your synagogues, and persecute *them* from city to city:"

The Lord Jesus Christ predicted what these Pharisees would do to the prophets which will be sent to them. They will scourge, persecute, kill, and crucify them.

- **Matthew 23:37**

"O Jerusalem, Jerusalem, *thou* that killest the prophets, and stonest them which are sent unto thee, how often would I have gathered thy children together, even as a hen gathereth her chickens under *her* wings, and ye would not!"

The Pharisees stoned and killed the prophets sent to them.

- **Luke 11:47**

"Woe unto you! for ye build the sepulchres of the prophets, and your fathers killed them."

The Pharisees were building the sepulchers for the prophets, but their Old Testament fathers actually killed them.

- **Luke 11:49**

"Therefore also said the wisdom of God, I will send them prophets and apostles, and *some* of them they shall slay and persecute: That the blood of all the prophets, which was shed from the foundation of the world, may be required of this generation;"

> **THE BLOOD OF THE O.T. PROPHETS REQUIRED**
> All the blood of the prophets of the Old Testament will be required of the generation alive in Christ's day.

More N.T. Verses About Prophets

- **Acts 7:52**

"Which of the prophets have not your fathers persecuted? and they have slain them which shewed before of the coming of the Just One; of whom ye have been now the betrayers and murderers:"

The Jews of the Old Testament persecuted and slew many of their prophets.

- **Romans 11:3**
  "Lord, <u>they have killed thy prophets</u>, and digged down thine altars; and I am left alone, and they seek my life."

Elijah told the LORD that these Old Testament Jews had killed God's prophets and digged down His altars.

- **1 Thessalonians 2:15**
  "<u>Who both killed the Lord Jesus, and their own prophets</u>, and have persecuted us; and they please not God, and are contrary to all men:"

These Israelites of old, and in the New Testament times had killed their prophets and crucified the Lord Jesus Christ.

James 5:11

"**Behold, we count them happy which endure. Ye have heard of the patience of Job, and have seen the end of the Lord; that the Lord is very pitiful, and of tender mercy.**"

James said that he and others count them happy which endure their trials and hardships.

THE MEANING OF THE GREEK WORD, "HUPOMONE"

The Greek Word for "*endure*" is HUPOMONE. Some of the meanings of that Greek Word are:

"*1) steadfastness, constancy, endurance; 1a) in the NT the characteristic of a man who is not swerved from his deliberate purpose and his loyalty to faith and piety by even the greatest trials and sufferings; 1b) patiently, and steadfastly; 2) a patient, steadfast waiting for; 3) a patient enduring, sustaining, perseverance*"

Job had this endurance for a very long time. In the New Testament, Here we see one of the characteristics of men or women who have not swerved from their deliberate purpose and loyalty to their faith and piety, even when suffering the greatest of trials. Those who endure such things are counted as happy.

Verses On Happiness

- **Psalms 144:15**
  "Happy *is that* people, that is in such a case: *yea*, <u>happy *is that* people, whose God *is* the LORD</u>."

Those who are genuine Christians have happiness in their Saviour,

the Lord Jesus Christ. This is one of the fruits of the Holy Spirit.
- **Proverbs 16:20**
"He that handleth a matter wisely shall find good: and whoso trusteth in the LORD, happy *is* he."

> **HAPPINESS BY CHRIST FOR TRUE CHRISTIANS**
> True Christians don't have to be sad or filled with gloom, but happiness is theirs as they trust in the Lord Jesus Christ and walk with Him day by day.

- **Proverbs 29:18**
"Where *there is* no vision, the people perish: but he that keepeth the law, happy *is* he."

Having the accurate Bible such as the King James Bible in English, reading it from Genesis through Revelation, understanding it, and following it completely gives happiness.

- **John 13:17**
"If ye know these things, happy are ye if ye do them."

What if a genuine Christian does not follow God's Words? If so, there is no real happiness given by the Lord.

- **1 Peter 3:14**
"But and if ye suffer for righteousness' sake, happy *are ye*: and be not afraid of their terror, neither be troubled;"

Even if true Christians suffer for righteousness' sake, (not for their own errors), happiness in the Lord can be their portion.

- **1 Peter 4:14**
"If ye be reproached for the name of Christ, happy *are ye*; for the spirit of glory and of God resteth upon you: on their part he is evil spoken of, but on your part he is glorified."

If you are a genuine Christian and are reproached for the Name of the Lord Jesus Christ, you should be "*happy*" as Peter stated.

Verses On Endurance

- **2 Thessalonians 1:4**
"So that we ourselves glory in you in the churches of God for your patience and faith in all your persecutions and tribulations that ye endure:"

The Thessalonian Christians endured all the persecutions they were going through.

- **2 Timothy 2:3**
"Thou therefore endure hardness, as a good soldier of Jesus Christ."

> **GOOD CHRISTIAN SOLDIERS ENDURE HARDNESS**
> Soldiers endure hardness as they train for the battles

James–Preaching Verse By Verse

> and afterward pursue those battles. I was a Navy Chaplin in the Marines with an infantry division for about nine months in Okinawa. I went out with my battalion on maneuvers. We went out in the field, sleeping in the rain and enduring all the other hardships of those maneuvers.

- **2 Timothy 4:5**

"But watch thou in all things, <u>endure afflictions</u>, do the work of an evangelist, make full proof of thy ministry."

Afflictions come into the lives of those who are born-again and true Christians. Such afflictions must be endured.

- **1 Peter 2:19**

"For <u>this is thankworthy, if a man for conscience toward God endure grief, suffering wrongfully</u>."

It is indeed thankworthy when genuine Christians suffer wrongfully and still endure the grief.

Verses On Patience

- **Romans 15:4**

"For whatsoever things were written aforetime were written for our learning, that we <u>through patience and comfort of the scriptures might have hope</u>."

> **SCRIPTURES GIVE PATIENCE, COMFORT & HOPE**
> The Scriptures, both the Old and the New Testaments, if read and believed, can give true Christians patience, comfort, and hope.

- **Colossians 1:11**

"Strengthened with all might, according to his glorious power, <u>unto all patience</u> and longsuffering with joyfulness;"

Many people are impatient people–including genuine Christians. God wants them to have patience.

- **Hebrews 10:36**

"For <u>ye have need of patience</u>, that, after ye have done the will of God, ye might receive the promise."

God knows that even true Christians need patience. God doesn't always answer immediately–in fact, He very seldom does.

- **Hebrews 12:1**

"Wherefore seeing we also are compassed about with so great a cloud of witnesses, let us lay aside every weight, and the sin which doth so easily beset *us*, and <u>let us run with patience the race that is set before us</u>,"

Every genuine Christian has a different race in their lives. They must run their race with patience until that race is over.

Verses On The Patience Of Job

We see from Job's life, in Job chapter one, that he was a man who was perfect, upright, feared God, and despised evil. He had seven sons and three daughters. His property at first consisted of seven thousand sheep, three thousand camels, five hundred yoke of oxen, (one thousand animals), five hundred she asses, and a great household. He was the greatest of all men of the East in his day.

- **Job 1:6**

"Now there was a day when <u>the sons of God came to present themselves before the LORD, and Satan came also among them</u>."

The "*sons of God*" in the Old Testament were angels (as in Job 1:6; 2:1; and 38:7). That's why I believe in Genesis 6, when the sons of God married daughters of men, they were fallen angels, cohabiting with women and producing terrible giants and corrupt people. At that time, Satan, a fallen angel, was able to come into the presence of God. God asked a question to Satan. He said: "*<u>Hast thou considered my servant Job there is none like him in the earth, a perfect and upright man, one that feareth God, and escheweth evil</u>*?"

- **Job 1:9-11**

"<u>Then Satan answered the LORD, and said, Doth Job fear God for nought? Hast not thou made an hedge about him</u>, and about his house, and about all that he hath on every side? thou hast blessed the work of his hands, and his substance is increased in the land. But put forth thine hand now, and touch all that he hath, and he will curse thee to thy face."

This referred to all the many possessions that he had.

- **Job 1:13-22**

"And there was a day when his sons and his daughters *were* eating and drinking wine in their eldest brother's house: And <u>there came a messenger unto Job</u>, and said, The oxen were plowing, and the asses feeding beside them: And the Sabeans fell *upon them*, and took them away; yea, they have slain the servants with the edge of the sword; and I only am escaped alone to tell thee. While he *was* yet speaking, there came also another, and said, The fire of God is fallen from heaven, and hath burned up the sheep, and the servants, and consumed them; and I only am escaped alone to tell thee. While he *was* yet speaking, there came also another, and said, The Chaldeans made out three bands, and fell upon the camels, and have carried them away, yea, and slain the servants with the edge of the sword; and I only am escaped alone to tell thee. While he *was* yet speaking, there came also another, and said, Thy sons and thy daughters *were* eating and drinking wine in their eldest brother's house: And, behold, there came a great wind from the

wilderness, and smote the four corners of the house, and it fell upon the young men, and they are dead; and I only am escaped alone to tell thee. Then Job arose, and rent his mantle, and shaved his head, and fell down upon the ground, and worshipped, And said, Naked came I out of my mother's womb, and naked shall I return thither: the LORD gave, and the LORD hath taken away; blessed be the name of the LORD. In all this Job sinned not, nor charged God foolishly."
Job's seven sons and three daughters were eating together.

JOB'S FIVE DEVASTATING LOSSES
Five devastating things happened while they were eating.
1. Event #1–Job's oxen and asses and servants were slain.
2. Event #2–Job's sheep and servants were slain.
3. Event #3–Job's camels and servants were slain.
4. Event #4–Job's sons and daughters were slain.
5. Event #5–Job's body was afflicted with serious illnesses.

Those are the serious events that happened to Job. Satan told God to touch all that Job has and *"he will curse thee to thy face."* Did Satan's words come true? No, his words did not come true.

GOD THWARTED SATAN'S ATTACK ON JOB
So Satan's will and his ways were thwarted by the Lord and Job didn't do as Satan thought he would do. It certainly shows *"the patience of Job."* When similar things happen in the lives of genuine Christians, I hope they have the same testimony as Job did when he lost almost all of the things he held dear, including his family and his health.

- Job 2:1-5

"Again there was a day when the sons of God came to present themselves before the LORD, and Satan came also among them to present himself before the LORD. And the LORD said unto Satan, From whence comest thou? And Satan answered the LORD, and said, From going to and fro in the earth, and from walking up and down in it. And the LORD said unto Satan, Hast thou considered my servant Job, that *there is* none like him in the earth, a perfect and an upright man, one that feareth God, and escheweth evil? and still he holdeth fast his integrity, although thou movedst me against him, to destroy him without cause.

And Satan answered the LORD, and said, Skin for skin, yea, all that a man hath will he give for his life. But <u>put forth thine hand now, and touch his bone and his flesh, and he will curse thee to thy face</u>."

Satan wanted God to smite Job in his body. If this happened, Satan thought Job would curse God. But Job did never cursed God.

- **Job 2:6-10**

"And the LORD said unto Satan, Behold, he *is* in thine hand; but save his life. So went Satan forth from the presence of the LORD, and <u>smote Job with sore boils from the sole of his foot unto his crown</u>. Then said his wife unto him, Dost thou still retain thine integrity? curse God, and die. But he said unto her, Thou speakest as one of the foolish women speaketh. What? shall we receive good at the hand of God, and shall we not receive evil? In all this did not Job sin with his lips."

Job did not curse God, even though he was in serious pain every hour of the day. He said, *"Shall we receive good at the hand of God, and shall we not receive evil?"*

JOB'S WIFE WANTED HIM TO CURSE GOD

Job's wife looked at him with all his boils, completely defaced, ugly, probably smelly, and now very thin, and told him to *"Curse God and Die!"* He did not do this. He maintained his patience.

Verses On Mercy

- **Psalms 85:10**

"<u>Mercy and truth are met together</u>; righteousness and peace have kissed *each other*."

At the cross of Calvary, God's mercy and truth were united. In mercy the Lord Jesus Christ bore the sins of the world. This is the truth and is a fact.

- **Psalms 86:13**

"For <u>great *is* thy mercy toward me</u>: and thou hast delivered my soul from the lowest hell."

God's mercy is great toward all the sins of men and women on the earth. It is sad that all do not realize His mercy and receive His Son as their Saviour.

- **Psalms 86:15**

"But thou, O Lord, *art* a God full of compassion, and gracious, longsuffering, and <u>plenteous in mercy</u> and truth."

God has abundance of His mercy. Some have stated: *"Grace is getting something that we <u>don't deserve</u>, mercy is <u>not getting something</u> that we <u>do deserve</u>."*

GOD HEALED JOB AND BLESSED HIM GREATLY
God healed Job and blessed him greatly after Satan's requested trial and serious testing. He had ten more children. He had double the number of animals. It was a double blessing. I think Job might have also doubled his age. Though it is not certain, he was seventy when he suffered and he might well have lived until he was one hundred and forty. Many in his day lived much longer than we do today.

James 5:12

"But above all things, my brethren, swear not, neither by heaven, neither by the earth, neither by any other oath: but let your yea be yea; and your nay, nay; lest ye fall into condemnation."

STOP ANY KIND OF SWEARING!
This is a present tense prohibition in the Greek. As such, it means to stop an action already in progress. It means for James' audience to stop their swearing and taking oaths. The New Testament applies this to genuine Christians even today.

Verses On Taking Oaths Or Swearing
- Leviticus 5:4

"Or if a soul swear, pronouncing with *his* lips to do evil, or to do good, whatsoever *it be* that a man shall pronounce with an oath, and it be hid from him; when he knoweth *of it*, then he shall be guilty in one of these."

No swearing of oaths were to be used in the Old Testament or in the New Testament.

- 1 Kings 8:31

"If any man trespass against his neighbour, and an oath be laid upon him to cause him to swear, and the oath come before thine altar in this house:"

This verse speaks of swearing by oaths.

- Matthew 5:34-37

"But I say unto you, Swear not at all; neither by heaven; for it is God's throne: Nor by the earth; for it is his footstool: neither by Jerusalem; for it is the city of the great King. Neither shalt thou swear by thy head, because thou canst not make one hair white or black. But let your communication be, Yea, yea; Nay, nay: for

whatsoever is more than these cometh of evil."
Every time I go into a court of law, they say *"will, you swear"*? As soon as I raise my hand, I say *"I will affirm, I don't swear."*

James 5:13

"Is any among you afflicted? let him pray. Is any merry? let him sing psalms."

Afflictions and troubles come to everyone. All people have them at one time or another in their lives.

Verses On Afflictions And Problems
- **Psalms 119:67**

"Before I was afflicted I went astray: but now have I kept thy word."

God used affliction to keep David from going astray. Afflictions sometimes are sent to us to keep us where we should be according to the Scripture.

- **Psalms 119:71**

"*It is* good for me that I have been afflicted; that I might learn thy statutes."

Sometimes God afflicts genuine Christians in order for them to learn His ways.

Verses On Merry
- **Proverbs 15:13**

"A merry heart maketh a cheerful countenance: but by sorrow of the heart the spirit is broken."

A MERRY HEART CHANGES THE APPEARANCE

This is interesting that a merry heart will change peoples' faces and looks. So what does that do with a heart that is not merry? It will probably end up with an ugly countenance.

- **Proverbs 15:15**

"All the days of the afflicted *are* evil: but he that is of a merry heart *hath* a continual feast."

A merry heart makes possible a continual feast.

- **Proverbs 17:22**

"A merry heart doeth good *like* a medicine: but a broken spirit drieth the bones."

A merry heart is medicinal. Everyone should try it and see its results.

James 5:14

"Is any sick among you? let him call for the elders of the church; and let them pray over him, anointing him with oil in the name of the Lord:"

This is the idea of prayer for the sick. The gifts of the New Testament were certainly prevalent and there during the apostolic times. After the apostolic times, we believe most of these special gifts have disappeared. They're no longer here. This includes the special miracle of Divine healing, the gift of speaking in tongues, and many other gifts. After the Bible was completed in 90 or 100 A.D., these special gifts ceased. James was written in 60 A.D. which was before the Bible was completed and before these special gifts had ceased.

Verses On Healing During New Testament Times
- **Matthew 10:8**

"<u>Heal the sick</u>, cleanse the lepers, raise the dead, cast out devils: freely ye have received, freely give."

This special miracle of healing was a provision given by the Lord Jesus Christ to His apostles during the apostolic times. He gave the apostles that power. He did not give genuine Christians that miraculous power after the entire New Testament was completed in 90 to 100 A.D.

- **Mark 6:13**

"And they cast out many devils, and <u>anointed with oil many that were sick, and healed *them*</u>."

The apostles were given this power to heal the sick in the apostolic times.

- **Mark 16:18**

"They shall take up serpents; and if they drink any deadly thing, it shall not hurt them; <u>they shall lay hands on the sick, and they shall recover.</u>"

APOSTOLIC MIRACLES CEASED IN 90-100 A.D.

Apostolic miracles of healing of the sick were there in the apostolic times up until 90-100 A.D. before the Bible was completed. After that time, these special miracles have ceased, despite the teaching of the Pentecostals and Charismatics.

- **Luke 9:1-2**

"Then <u>he called his twelve disciples together, and gave them power</u> and authority over all devils, and <u>to cure diseases</u>. And he sent them to preach the kingdom of God, and to <u>heal the sick</u>."

This was apostolic power given by the Lord Jesus Christ in the time of James.

- **Acts 5:15-16**
"Insomuch that they brought forth the sick into the streets, and laid *them* on beds and couches, that at the least the shadow of Peter passing by might overshadow some of them. There came also a multitude *out* of the cities round about unto Jerusalem, bringing sick folks, and them which were vexed with unclean spirits: and they were healed every one."

The apostles were given the power to heal sicknesses of all kinds.

- **2 Corinthians 12:8-9**
"For this thing I besought the Lord thrice, that it might depart from me. And he said unto me, My grace is sufficient for thee: for my strength is made perfect in weakness. Most gladly therefore will I rather glory in my infirmities, that the power of Christ may rest upon me."

EVEN IN PAUL'S DAY, GOD DID NOT ALWAYS HEAL.

God did not always heal, even in Paul's day. Paul asked the Lord three times to heal him of the sickness that he had. God told Paul that His grace was sufficient for him. Paul accepted God's Words. He was an apostle, but even in apostolic times, God did not always answer our prayers. So James said, in his day, that they might call for the elders of the church to pray for the sick, anointing them with oil which was a balm to soothe the wounds.

James 5:15

" And the prayer of faith shall save the sick, and the Lord shall raise him up; and if he have committed sins, they shall be forgiven him."

In James' day, the prayer of faith--believing prayer--shall save the sick, deliver them from their sickness, bring them health, *"and the Lord shall raise him up."* If the sickness is a result of sins, God can forgive them.

As far as believing prayer, prayer of faith shall save the sick. We ask the Lord so many times in sicknesses, could the Lord hear us as well as answer us, but certainly we can pray that the Lord will cure us and raise us up from the sickness.

Verses On Praying In Faith
- **Matthew 17:20**

"And Jesus said unto them, Because of your unbelief: for verily I say unto you, <u>If ye have faith</u> as a grain of mustard seed, <u>ye shall say unto this mountain, Remove hence to yonder place; and it shall remove; and nothing shall be impossible unto you.</u>"

The apostles were given this possible miracle provided that they had strong faith rather than unbelief.

- **Matthew 21:22**

"And all things, whatsoever ye shall <u>ask in prayer, believing, ye shall receive.</u>"

BELIEVING PRAYER NEEDED FOR ANSWERS

The Lord Jesus Christ told this to His apostles while He was on earth. They had to believe when they were praying in order to receive answered prayer.

- **Mark 11:23**

"For verily I say unto you, That <u>whosoever shall say unto this mountain, Be thou removed</u>, and be thou cast into the sea; and shall not doubt in his heart, <u>but shall believe</u> that those things which he saith shall come to pass; <u>he shall have whatsoever he saith</u>."

The Lord Jesus Christ told His apostles that if they had sincere faith, their prayers would be answered, even to remove mountains. This was great power in these apostolic times.

Other Verses On The Apostles Praying & Receiving
- **John 14:13**

"And <u>whatsoever ye shall ask in my name, that will I do</u>, that the Father may be glorified in the Son."

The Lord Jesus Christ promised to do what the apostles asked for in His Name.

- **John 15:16b**

"That <u>whatsoever ye shall ask of the Father</u> in my name, <u>he may give it you</u>."

PRAYER MUST BE IN CHRIST'S NAME

The apostles were to ask God the Father in the Name of the Lord Jesus Christ in their prayers. If so, their request would be given them.

- **John 16:23b**

"<u>Whatsoever ye shall ask the Father</u> in my name, <u>he will give *it* you</u>."

The apostles were to ask God the Father in the name of the Lord Jesus Christ in their prayers. If so, their request would be given them.
- 1 John 3:22

"And whatsoever we ask, we receive of him, because we keep his commandments, and do those things that are pleasing in his sight."

The apostles were to ask God the Father in the name of the Lord Jesus Christ in their prayers. If so, their request would be given them.
- 1 John 5:15

"And if we know that he hear us, whatsoever we ask, we know that we have the petitions that we desired of him."

The apostles were to ask God the Father in the name of the Lord Jesus Christ in their prayers. If so, their request would be given them.
- 1 John 1:9

"If we confess our sins, he is faithful and just to forgive us *our* sins, and to cleanse us from all unrighteousness."

CONFESSION IS AGREEING WITH GOD ABOUT SIN

Forgiveness and cleansing by the Lord is only possible if it is preceded by confessing to Him of our sins. That Greek Word for "*confess*" is HOMOLOGEO. It means literally "*to say the same thing*" about our sins as God says, that is, to agree with God that it is sin.

James 5:16

"Confess your faults one to another, and pray one for another, that ye may be healed. The effectual fervent prayer of a righteous man availeth much."

The modern Bible versions have a wrong translation for the word, "*faults*." They render it "*sins*."

THE MEANING OF THE GREEK WORD, "PARAPTOMA"

The Greek Word used here is PARAPTOMA. Some of the meanings of this Greek Word are:

"*1) to fall beside or near something; 2) a lapse or deviation from truth and uprightness;*"

It is better and more clear to use the word, "*faults*," as the King James Bible does. If it is translated "*sins*," it might lend support for

James–Preaching Verse By Verse 179

the Roman Catholic error of people confessing the sins to a human and sinful priest rather than directly to God alone.

Other Verses On Faults

- **Genesis 41:9**

"Then spake the chief butler unto Pharaoh, saying, <u>I do remember my faults</u> this day:"

The butler's "faults" were that he forgot to mention Joseph to the Pharaoh and tell him that Joseph interpreted a dream for him.

- **1 Peter 2:20**

"For <u>what glory *is it*, if, when ye be buffeted for your faults</u>, ye shall take it patiently? but if, when ye do well, and suffer *for it*, ye take it patiently, this *is* acceptable with God."

This verse shows that true Christians have faults or errors.

Verses On Prayer

INTERCESSORY PRAYER IS NEEDED

This verse 16 says that, in the Apostolic times, genuine Christians were to pray for one another that they might be healed. In the times of the apostles (around 90 to 100 A.D.), God gave them the power to pray for healing.

Also in verse 17, James tells his readers that *"the effectual fervent prayer of a righteous man availeth much."* This was true in apostolic times as well as post-apostolic times.

- **Acts 12:1-16**

"Now about that time Herod the king stretched forth *his* hands to vex certain of the church. And he killed James the brother of John with the sword. And because he saw it pleased the Jews, he proceeded further to take Peter also. (Then were the days of unleavened bread.) And when he had apprehended him, he put *him* in prison, and delivered *him* to four quaternions of soldiers to keep him; intending after Easter to bring him forth to the people. Peter therefore was kept in prison: but <u>prayer was made without ceasing of the church unto God for him</u>. And when Herod would have brought him forth, the same night Peter was sleeping between two soldiers, bound with two chains: and the keepers before the door kept the prison. And, behold, the angel of the Lord came upon *him*, and a light shined in the prison: and he smote Peter on the side, and raised him up, saying, Arise up quickly. And his chains fell off from *his* hands. And the angel said unto him, Gird thyself, and bind on thy sandals. And so he did. And he saith unto him, Cast thy garment about thee, and follow me. And he went out, and followed him; and wist not that it was true which was done by the angel; but thought he saw a vision. When they were past the first and the second ward, they came unto the iron gate that leadeth unto the city; which opened to them of his own accord: and they went out, and passed on through one street; and forthwith the angel departed from him. And when Peter was come to himself, he said, Now I know of a surety, that the Lord hath sent his angel, and hath delivered me out of the hand of Herod, and *from* all the expectation of the people of the Jews. The angel of the Lord smote the chains and the chains left him. And when he had considered *the thing*, he came to the house of Mary the mother of John, whose surname was Mark; where many were gathered together praying. And as Peter knocked at the door of the gate, a damsel came to hearken, named Rhoda. And when she knew Peter's voice, she opened not the gate for gladness, but ran in, and told how Peter stood before the gate. And they said unto her, Thou art mad. But she constantly affirmed that it was even so. Then said they, It is his angel. But Peter continued knocking: and <u>when they had opened *the door*, and saw him, they were astonished</u>."

Though the disciples did not believe that Peter was out of the Roman prison, yet God, through faithful prayer by these Christians, delivered him from that prison. Many times, when God answers the prayers of genuine Christians, they are astonished like these disciples were. The effectual fervent prayer of a righteous man, or a righteous woman, availeth much.

GOD FREED PETER FROM PRISON THROUGH PRAYER

Consider Peter's difficult situation. Herod was intending to kill Peter. He was chained and had four quaternions of soldiers guarding him. Every fourth watch of each day, four soldiers came to guard Peter. This was daily, around the clock, day and night that these soldiers came in order to prevent Peter from escaping. Peter was kept in prison but <u>prayer was made without ceasing of the church unto God for him</u>.

<u>John Mark and his mother, Mary, had a prayer meeting</u> at that time. <u>They were praying for Peter's release</u>. They were praying that Peter, the apostle, would be set free from Herod's prison. God answered their prayers. Peter appeared at the door where they had been praying for Peter's release, but those who were praying refused to believe that it was Peter. They refused to believe that he had been

James–Preaching Verse By Verse

released by God's miracle and was knocking at their door.

More Verses On Prayer

- **Romans 12:12**

"Rejoicing in hope; patient in tribulation; <u>continuing instant in prayer</u>;"

Paul urged continuing in prayer to the Lord.

- **Colossians 4:2**

"<u>Continue in prayer, and watch in the same with thanksgiving;</u>"

Paul told the Colossian Christians to continue in prayer and be thankful in it.

- **1 Thessalonians 5:17**

"<u>Pray without ceasing.</u>"

Paul wanted those in Thessalonica to pray without any ceasing. They were not to stop their prayers.

James 5:17

"Elias was a man subject to like passions as we are, and he prayed earnestly that it might not rain: and it rained not on the earth by the space of three years and six months."

"ELIJAH" IN O.T. HEBREW, "ELIAS" IN N.T. GREEK

Nearly all of the modern English Bible versions–even some that are called the "King James Bible" change "Elias" to "Elijah." That's not a correct translation, and that certainly does not follow the correct and historic King James Bible's translation. The name is a transliteration, letter for letter. In the Old Testament Hebrew language, is "Elijah." In the New Testament Greek language, it is "Elias." Our *Defined King James Bible* uses the proper Greek text and rightly has "Elias" in its translation.

Though Elias was a prophet, he was nevertheless "a man subject to like passions as we are." He's a prophet. He prayed earnestly. He prayed fervently. The earnest, fervent, effectual prayer of a righteous man availeth much. Now Elias, or Elijah, prayed that it might not rain and it rained not for a space of three years and six months.

The following verses show us what happened as a result of Elijah's prayers.

- **1 Kings 17:1**

"And <u>Elijah the Tishbite</u>, *who was* of the inhabitants of Gilead, said unto Ahab, *As* the LORD God of Israel liveth, before whom I stand, <u>there shall not be dew nor rain these years, but according to my word.</u>"

- **1 Kings 17:7**
  "And it came to pass after a while, that the brook dried up, because there had been no rain in the land."
God answered his prayer. No rain.
  - **1 Kings 17:14**
  "For thus saith the LORD God of Israel, The barrel of meal shall not waste, neither shall the cruse of oil fail, until the day *that* the LORD sendeth rain upon the earth."
  - **1 Kings 18:1**
  "And it came to pass *after* many days, that the word of the LORD came to Elijah in the third year, saying, Go, shew thyself unto Ahab; and I will send rain upon the earth."
  - **1 Kings 18:41**
  "And Elijah said unto Ahab, Get thee up, eat and drink; for *there is* a sound of abundance of rain."
  - **1 Kings 18:44-45**
  "And it came to pass at the seventh time, that he said, Behold, there ariseth a little cloud out of the sea, like a man's hand. And he said, Go up, say unto Ahab, Prepare *thy chariot*, and get thee down, that the rain stop thee not. And it came to pass in the mean while, that the heaven was black with clouds and wind, and there was a great rain. And Ahab rode, and went to Jezreel."

GOD'S ANSWER TO ELIJAH'S PRAYER FOR RAIN

This is a summary of this prophet Elijah as he prayed believingly that it might rain. God answered his prayer and sent an abundance of rain to the land of Israel.

James 5:18

"**And he prayed again, and the heaven gave rain, and the earth brought forth her fruit.**"

Elijah did pray for rain and the Lord answered and rain came. This is a very important answer to prayer in Elijah's life.

James 5:19

"**Brethren, if any of you do err from the truth, and one convert him;** "

Here is a verse that warns genuine Christians not to err either in heart, or life, from the truth of God's Words.

Verses On Erring

- **Proverbs 19:27**
  "Cease, my son, to hear the instruction *that causeth* to err from the words of knowledge."

James–Preaching Verse By Verse

DEALING WITH INSTRUCTIONS CAUSING ERRORS

If there is some instruction or teaching that would cause a true Christian to err from God's Words and truth, they should not give heed to it. They should not ever go back to the place that gave such false instruction. Such erring and false instruction is given in television, in newspapers, in magazines, on the Internet, in most theological seminaries, in most colleges, in most churches in the United States, and all around the world. Genuine Christians should separate from all such erring instruction and expose it whenever and wherever possible.

- Isaiah 3:12

"*As for* my people, children *are* their oppressors, and women rule over them. O my people, they which lead thee cause *thee* to err, and destroy the way of thy paths."

The leaders are often the people who cause people to err. This is sad that we have many of such leaders. Sin that is contrary to God's Words is praised by leaders all around our country. Whether it be the sin of lesbianism, male homosexuality, cross-dressing, bestiality, fornication, adultery, or many other sins.

ERRING ON BIBLE DOCTRINES

Not only do leaders cause people to err in immorality, but also to err in Bible doctrines. These false leaders are pastors of many apostate or compromise churches who teach doctrines that are totally contrary to the Bible, thus causing their followers to err in Bible doctrines.

- Jeremiah 23:32

"Behold, I *am* against them that prophesy false dreams, saith the LORD, and do tell them, and cause my people to err by their lies, and by their lightness; yet I sent them not, nor commanded them: therefore they shall not profit this people at all, saith the LORD."

God is against people who cause people to err by their lies. This can be said of the many news outlets who give people fake and false news in the newspapers, magazines, Internet, TV, or any other way.

- Matthew 22:29

"Jesus answered and said unto them, Ye do err, not knowing the scriptures, nor the power of God."

The Lord Jesus Christ told these Pharisees and others that they didn't know the Old Testament Scriptures, or God's power. Because of this, they were teaching many errors and heresies to the people.

James 5:20

"**Let him know, that he which converteth the sinner from the error of his way shall save a soul from death, and shall hide a multitude of sins.**"

Converting the sinners from the errors of their ways is very important. If left alone without being saved by genuine faith in the Lord Jesus Christ, lost people around the world are bound for eternal death in Hell. Salvation by genuine faith in the Lord Jesus Christ as their Saviour is the only way their sins can be forgiven.

Verses On Saving People's Souls

- **Luke 19:10**

"For the Son of man is come to seek and to save that which was lost."

It was the mission of the Lord Jesus Christ to seek and save the lost people who would truly trust in Him for their salvation.

- **Matthew 18:11**

"For the Son of man is come to save that which was lost."

This was Christ's purpose and mission. This verse is eliminated from the many of the Gnostic critical Greek texts and the modern Bible versions which are based upon those false texts

- **John 12:47b**

"For I came not to judge the world, but to save the world."

Not that everybody is saved, but they can be saved by trusting the Lord Jesus Christ as their Saviour.

- **1 Corinthians 1:21**

"For after that in the wisdom of God the world by wisdom knew not God, it pleased God by the foolishness of preaching to save them that believe."

Genuinely believing in the Lord Jesus Christ alone can save people.

- **1 Timothy 1:15**

"This *is* a faithful saying, and worthy of all acceptation, that Christ Jesus came into the world to save sinners; of whom I am chief."

That was the purpose and mission of the Lord Jesus Christ–to save sinners who genuinely trust in Him as their Saviour.

- **Hebrews 7:25**

"Wherefore he is able also to save them to the uttermost that come unto God by him, seeing he ever liveth to make intercession for them."

The Lord Jesus Christ is able to save all those who come to God through true faith in Him and He does this.

- **James 1:21**

"Wherefore lay apart all filthiness and superfluity of naughtiness, and <u>receive with meekness the engrafted word, which is able to save your souls</u>."

> **ETERNAL LIFE FOUND ONLY IN THE WORDS OF GOD**
>
> The way of salvation and eternal life is found in the Words of God. In English, the only faithful Words of God are found in the King James Bible. Those Words are accurately translated from the inspired, inerrant, and preserved Words of the Hebrew, Aramaic, and Greek that underlie our King James Bible.

Index of Words and Phrases

1 John 1:9. .... 120, 134, 178
85 verses per day. 104
90-100 A.D.. 175
A CONTROLLED TONGUE AVOIDS MUCH TROUBLE........ 91
A DIRTY TONGUE CAN DEFILE THE WHOLE BODY......... 92
A MERRY HEART CHANGES THE APPEARANCE........... 174
A Verse On Wrath. 34
A VIRTUOUS WOMAN HAS A KIND TONGUE.............. 41
abide forever.. 17, 26
ABRAHAM AND IMPUTED RIGHTEOUSNESS. 79
ABRAHAM'S ACTIONS–AN EVIDENCE OF HIS FAITH....... 73
accurate Bibles... 33
ACTION ALREADY IN PROGRESS. ... 22, 28, 45, 83, 137, 159, 173
Adam... 17, 23, 163
ADAM'S SIN BROUGHT PHYSICAL DEATH TO ALL. 17
ADULTERER. 60, 61, 121
adulterers. 61, 121, 152
adultery................. 16, 25, 56, 58, 60-62, 97, 122, 133, 183
affliction. 3, 22, 42, 43, 127, 135, 164, 174
afflictions. 6, 21, 22, 103, 135, 169, 174
agreeing with God. 178
ALL BOASTINGS ARE EVIL. 145
amiss... 120, 121
anger. 34, 43, 44, 54, 55, 63, 93, 138, 152, 155
angry people... 122
Antichrist. 128, 159
APOSTOLIC MIRACLES CEASED IN 90-100 A.D.. 175
appearance... 140, 174
appointment for death. 142
Armageddon.................................... 94, 159, 163
asking.............................. 9, 47, 63, 90, 118-120
AT ARMAGEDDON, FLAMING FIRE WILL BE USED......... 94
BAD USE OF THE TONGUE IS LIKE A SHARP RAZOR. 41
battle. 15, 25, 94, 97, 117, 130, 159, 163
bear fruit... 42, 82
BEING RICH TOWARD GOD IS IMPORTANT. 148
BELIEVING PRAYER NEEDED FOR ANSWERS..............177
bestiality. 107, 183
BEWARE OF THE EVIL TRADITIONS OF MEN............. 127
BFT Phone: 856-854-4452................................. I
Bible For Today Baptist Church........................ I, iv

Bible truth. 129
BIBLE-BELIEVING CHURCHES. 61, 107, 115
BIBLE-BELIEVING CHURCHES SHOULD HAVE PEACE. . . . 115
blaspheme. 55, 56, 99, 121, 138
blaspheming. 138
blasphemy. 55, 56
blessing. 47, 98-100, 104, 147, 173
blessing and cursing. 100
boast. 66, 68, 87, 141, 146
boasting. 105, 146
bodily resurrection. 2, 12, 32, 75
Bodily Resurrection In The Old Testament. 2
born of God. 31, 128
BOTH SAVED AND LOST WILL CONFESS TO CHRIST. 91
BRETHREN SOMETIMES ERR FROM THE TRUTH. 29
bridle. 40, 84-86, 88, 91
bridled. 86, 89
Canter, Patty. iv
change. 13, 16, 30, 38, 141, 143, 162, 174, 181
changeless. 141
Chaplain Waite, U. S. Navy. 71, 72, 95, 96
chasten. 21
chastening. 21, 113
cheerful heart. 160
CHRIST AND SATAN ARE ENEMIES. 128
CHRIST BECAME POOR TO MAKE BELIEVERS RICH. 149
CHRIST BECAME POOR TO MAKE CHRISTIANS RICH. 49
CHRIST BECAME POOR TO MAKE PEOPLE RICH. 53
CHRIST CAME TO RICH ZACCHAEUS' HOUSE. 149
CHRIST DIED TO DELIVER CHRISTIANS FROM SINS. 126
Christ is changeless. 141
CHRIST IS MADE WISDOM TO TRUE CHRISTIANS. 10
CHRIST KILLS THE ANTICHRIST AT ARMAGEDDON. 159
CHRIST PROVIDES SALVATION TO TRUE BELIEVERS. 139
CHRIST SAID ANGER IS OFTEN SPIRITUAL MURDER. 63
CHRIST SAID LOOKING WITH LUST IS ADULTERY. 62
CHRIST THE FIRST TO BE BODILY RESURRECTED. 32
Christ the judge. 138
CHRIST THE JUDGE KNOWS ALL THE FACTS. 138
CHRIST UPBRAIDED NON-REPENTANT CITIES. 12
CHRIST WAS BOTH PERFECT GOD & PERFECT MAN. 103
CHRIST WILL JUDGE CHRISTIANS RIGHTEOUSLY. 140
CHRIST WILL JUDGE THE SAVED AND THE LOST. 161
CHRISTIAN GIVING IS WITH A CHEERFUL HEART. 160

Christian love. 53, 92
CHRISTIAN LOVE SHOWN BY WORDS AND DEEDS.. 92
CHRISTIANS ARE GOD'S FIRSTFRUITS. 30
CHRISTIANS HAVE THE FIRSTFRUITS OF THE SPIRIT. 32
CHRISTIANS MUST BE HEARERS AND DOERS ALSO. 37
CHRISTIANS MUST BEAR GOOD FRUIT. 82
CHRISTIANS MUST WALK IN GOD'S WISDOM. 11
CHRISTIANS NEED WISDOM FROM GOD'S WORDS. 104
CHRISTIANS SHOULD BE CLOTHED WITH HUMILITY..... 137
CHRISTIANS SHOULD BE LED BY THE LORD. 97
CHRISTIANS SHOULD BE MATURE IN CHRIST.. 86
CHRISTIANS SHOULD BE RIGHTEOUS. 112, 113
CHRISTIANS SHOULD BE RIGHTEOUS AND HOLY. 112
CHRISTIANS SHOULD BEAR PERMANENT FRUIT.......... 82
CHRISTIANS SHOULD CLEANSE FROM FILTHINESS. 37
CHRISTIANS SHOULD DIFFER FROM UNBELIEVERS....... 26
CHRISTIANS SHOULD KEEP ALL BIBLE TRUTH.. 129
CHRISTIANS SHOULD LOVE ONE ANOTHER. 137
CHRISTIANS SHOULD NOT BE DOUBLE MINDED. 135
CHRISTIANS SHOULD NOT LOVE THE WORLD'S SINS..... 123
CHRISTIANS SHOULD NOT RESPECT PERSONS........... 46
CHRISTIANS SHOULD PLEASE CHRIST. 37
CHRISTIANS SHOULDN'T BOAST, BUT BE THANKFUL..... 146
CHRISTIANS SUPPORTED POOR CHRISTIANS. 52
CHRISTIANS WERE TOLD TO BLESS PERSECUTORS........ 99
CHRISTIANS' MOUTHS MUST BE GUARDED............... 34
CHRISTIANS' TEMPTATIONS ARE NOT FROM GOD........ 22
CHRISTIANS' TWO NATURES–FLESH & HOLY SPIRIT. 26
CHRISTIANS--LOVE OTHERS AS THEMSELVES. 57
Christ's coming.. .... 156, 157, 159
Christ's coming to reign in the Millennium. 156
Christ's Name. 177
CHRIST'S REIGN IS 7 YEARS AFTER THE RAPTURE. 158
Christ's reign for 1,000 years in the Millennium. 158
Christ's return. 156
Christ's righteous judgment. 163
Christ's Words. 33
church leaders. 29
CHURCH LEADERS OFTEN CAUSE PEOPLE TO ERR. 29
Church Phone: 856-854-4747. I
CHURCHES NOT TO SUPPORT LOOSE WIDOWS. 154
clean.. .... 19, 36, 42, 71, 72, 92, 95, 110, 122, 133, 134, 154, 176
clean hands. 133, 134
clean hearts. 134

cleanse.. . . . . 15, 36, 37, 96, 132-134, 175, 178
comfort. 6, 76, 114, 142, 155, 169
confession. 112, 134, 178
CONFESSION IS AGREEING WITH GOD ABOUT SIN. 178
confusion. 107-109
CONTROL OF THE TONGUE KEEPS FROM TROUBLE. 41
converted. 1, 36, 99
CONVERTED JEWS WILL BE CLEAN WITH GOD. 36
COOPERATION WITHOUT COMPROMISE, Navy Chaplain. 71, 95
Crown Of Glory. 20
Crown of Life. 19-21
Crown of Rejoicing. 21, 158
Crown Of Righteousness.. . . . . 20, 162
D. A. Waite, Th.D.,Ph.D.. 1
David the King. 15, 40, 88, 99, 108, 133, 135, 174
DAVID COMMITTED ADULTERY AND MURDER.. 133
days. . . 5, 17, 21-23, 74, 91, 92, 142-144, 150, 157, 164, 174, 179, 182
DEALING WITH INSTRUCTIONS CAUSING ERRORS. 183
death. 17, 21, 27-29, 41, 60, 81, 90, 103, 108, 114, 118, 142, 153,
162-164, 184
DEATH DEFINED–THE BODY WITHOUT THE SPIRIT.. 81
deeds cannot save. 59
DEEDS CANNOT SAVE THE SOUL OF ANYONE. 59
descendants. 75, 78
Devil. 3, 21, 22, 24, 70, 93, 95, 114, 124, 125, 128, 131, 132
devils. 70-73, 95, 101, 175
DIFFERENCES OFTEN SHARPEN THE MIND. 123
diligence. 47, 147
diligent. 47, 92, 147
DISCIPLES PREACHED THE GOSPEL TO THE POOR. 52
doctrinal faith.. . . . . 5, 13
doers. 37
DON'T MEDDLE WITH PEOPLE WHO CHANGE. 30
DON'T OPPRESS THE WIDOWS AND FATHERLESS. 44
DON'T SUCCUMB TO LYING HARLOTS. 90
double hearts. 15
double minded. 14, 15, 132, 135
double minds. 15
DOUBLE-HEARTEDNESS IS EXPOSED. 15
drawn away.. 23-25
Easy to be intreated. 109, 110
Elias, letter for letter in the Greek N.T. 181
Elijah, letter for letter in the Hebrew O.T. 167, 181, 182
endurance. 5, 167, 168

endure. 20-22, 163, 167-169
ENDURE AFFLICTIONS HAPPILY. 22
ENDURE HARDNESS LIKE GOOD SOLDIERS. 21
enduring. 5, 20, 21, 155, 167, 169
entice. 25-27
envy. 63, 105, 129
envying. 12, 105-107, 154
err.. . . . . 3, 28, 29, 182, 183
erred in heart. 29
erring. 28, 182, 183
ERRING ON BIBLE DOCTRINES.. 183
eternal life. 16, 27, 49, 51, 65, 66, 185
ETERNAL LIFE FOUND ONLY IN THE WORDS OF GOD. . . . 185
EVEN IN PAUL'S DAY, GOD DID NOT ALWAYS HEAL. 176
everlasting Hell, the Lake Of Fire. 63, 93
EVERLASTING HELL FIRE AWAITS THE LOST PEOPLE. 93
EVERY PERSON HAS AN APPOINTMENT FOR DEATH. 142
evil thoughts. 50, 51
evil traditions. 127
evil works. 70, 107, 109
e-mail: BFT@BibleForToday.org. I
faith in Christ. 20, 35, 60, 67, 68, 70
faith in God. 75
FAITH IN GOD LED ABRAHAM TO OBEDIENCE. 75
FAITH THAT LACKS WORKS IS FALSE FAITH. 66
false faith. 66
false prophets. 61
fatherless. 42-44, 55, 127, 152
faults. 39, 83, 133, 178, 179
FAX: 856-854-2464. I
fervent heat. 18, 94
filthiness. 35-37, 96, 133, 185
filthy.. . . . . 19, 35, 88, 156
filthy mouths. 88
fire. . . 13, 26, 28, 41, 42, 63-65, 74, 87, 89, 92-94, 101, 126, 139, 150,
163, 164, 170
firstfruits. 30-32, 158
flesh. . . . 2, 4, 7, 15, 17, 24-26, 28, 31, 37, 42, 62, 68, 70, 85, 92, 94,
96, 97, 109, 112, 117, 123, 127, 128, 133, 150, 154,
158, 171
flesh and Spirit. 37, 96, 133
foolishness. 10, 11, 41, 90, 126, 139, 184
foolishness of preaching. 10, 139, 184
friend. . . . . iii, 26, 57, 77, 99, 121-123, 129

FRIENDLINESS BRINGS FRIENDS. 122
friends. 48, 122, 123
friendship. 121-123
FROM THE SAME MOUTH--BLESSING AND CURSING. 100
fruit. . . 27, 28, 41, 42, 66, 70, 81, 82, 90, 100, 101, 111, 113, 114, 151,
155, 182
full joy. 119
Full of good fruits. 110
Full of mercy.. . . . . 109, 110
gentle.. . . . . 109, 110, 156
genuine Christians.. . . . iv, 1, 4, 6, 8-13, 16, 21-24, 26, 27, 30-34, 36-
39, 41, 42, 46, 52, 60, 62-64, 66, 67, 76, 77, 82, 85,
86, 91, 92, 97, 99-101, 104-106, 112, 113, 118-120,
122, 123, 126, 127, 129-131, 133, 134, 136-138, 140,
145-149, 154-162, 164, 167, 169, 171, 173-175, 179,
180, 182, 183
GENUINE CHRISTIANS ARE BORN OF GOD.. 31
Gnostic. 162, 184
GNOSTIC-BASED VERSIONS DENY CHRIST AS JUDGE.. . . . 162
GOD ALWAYS JUDGES RIGHTEOUSLY. 112
GOD CALLS BESTIALITY A WICKED SIN. 107
GOD CALLS FOOLISH THE WISDOM OF THIS WORLD. 10
GOD CONSIDERS WORLDLY WISDOM FOOLISHNESS. 11
GOD FREED PETER FROM PRISON THROUGH PRAYER. . . 180
GOD HEALED JOB AND BLESSED HIM GREATLY. 173
GOD IS A FATHER TO FATHERLESS AND WIDOWS.. 44
GOD IS NO RESPECTER OF PERSONS. 46
GOD KNOWS HOW MANY MONTHS PEOPLE HAVE. 143
GOD LOVED THE ENTIRE WORLD OF PEOPLE.. 125
GOD PROMISED ABRAHAM SEED AS THE STARS. 74
GOD RECOGNIZES ALL PERSONS ALIKE. 46
GOD SENT CHRIST FOR PEOPLE TO TRUST IN HIM. 66
GOD SPEAKS TODAY THROUGH ACCURATE BIBLES. 33
GOD THE HOLY SPIRIT INDWELLS CHRISTIANS.. 129
GOD THWARTED SATAN'S ATTACK ON JOB. 171
GOD USES THE "FOOLISHNESS" OF PREACHING. 10
GOD WANTS CHRISTIANS TO BE MATURE. 76
GOD WILL LIFT UP HUMBLE CHRISTIANS. 136
godly works.. . . . . 70, 73
GOD'S ANSWER TO ELIJAH'S PRAYER FOR RAIN. 182
GOD'S PERFECT WILL IS FOUND IN GOD'S WORDS. 8
GOD'S STRENGTH IS MADE PERFECT IN WEAKNESS.. 85
GOD'S TRUTH IS FOUND ONLY IN THE RIGHT BIBLE. 102
GOD'S WAY TO ESCAPE IN TEMPTATIONS.. 23

God's will.................... 15, 19, 76, 86, 104, 131, 132, 145
God's wisdom......................... 8-11, 14, 103-105, 109
God's Words... iv, 8, 16, 17, 30, 33, 34, 37-39, 51, 76, 85, 104, 108, 110, 115, 123, 132, 135, 146, 165, 168, 176, 182, 183
GOD'S WORDS SHOW HIS GLORY....................... 38
GOOD CHRISTIAN SOLDIERS ENDURE HARDNESS....... 168
good fruit.. 27, 82, 101
good soldier....................................... 21, 168
good works........ 8, 50, 66, 67, 70, 73, 76, 78, 81, 82, 86, 111, 113
gospel............................. 52, 94, 103, 126, 138, 161
Great White Throne...................... 63, 91, 138, 161-164
GREAT WHITE THRONE JUDGMENT OF THE LOST....... 164
GREEK PRESENT TENSE.... 14, 22, 28, 45, 59, 83, 105, 130, 137, 151, 159
grudging... 159, 160
happiness.. 167, 168
HAPPINESS BY CHRIST FOR TRUE CHRISTIANS.......... 168
happy..................... 19, 20, 22, 40, 72, 98, 129, 167, 168
hardness.. 12, 21, 168
harlots... 90
hay, wood, and stubble............................... 64, 93
HAY, WOOD, AND STUBBLE WORKS ARE BURNED UP...... 64
heal... 175, 176
healing.. 175, 179
hearers.. 37
hearing.. 33, 34, 36, 37
HEARING CHRIST'S WORDS USING SOUND BIBLES........ 33
heart.. 3, 12, 14-16, 25, 28, 29, 40, 44, 55, 57, 62, 69, 72, 73, 90, 91, 109, 112, 132, 134, 136, 151, 153, 155, 160, 174, 177, 182
hearts...... 11, 12, 15, 29, 33, 36, 40, 67, 81, 104, 105, 115, 132-135, 138, 141, 143, 153, 156, 158
HEARTS CAN BE PURIFIED BY FAITH IN CHRIST.......... 67
heart-adultery... 62
Heaven... 18, 32, 46, 49, 56, 66, 67, 73, 74, 78, 81, 85, 94, 101, 109, 119, 128, 136, 143, 148, 149, 151, 156-159, 163, 165, 170, 173, 182
heaven and earth.................................... 18, 94
HEAVEN AND EARTH WILL PERISH BY FIRE.............. 94
heaviness.. 135, 136
HEBREW & GREEK BIBLE WORDS ARE PRESERVED....... 18
Hell................... 42, 63, 65, 92-94, 139, 143, 163, 172, 184
Hell fire.. 63, 93
hold fast.. 12, 20

holy. . 7, 18, 26, 28, 32, 38, 42, 44, 62, 78, 94, 96-98, 103, 107, 112, 113, 125, 126, 129, 133, 134, 138, 167
Holy Spirit. . . 7, 18, 26, 28, 32, 38, 42, 62, 78, 96, 97, 107, 125, 129, 138, 167
Holy Spirit indwelling. 32, 129
HOMOSEXUALITY AND LESBIANISM ARE ALSO SINS. 108
hope. . . . . iv, 2, 5, 6, 13, 21, 56, 142, 146, 155, 158, 169, 171, 181
HOW GOD'S RIGHTEOUSNESS CAN BE RECEIVED. 111
HOW TO STOP AN ACTION ALREADY IN PROGRESS. 83
humble. 130-132, 136, 137
humility. 130, 132, 136, 137
husbands. 132
hypocrisy. 37, 109, 110
IF YOU LOVE PEOPLE, YOU WON'T HURT THEM. 58
IN THE WILDERNESS ISRAEL ERRED IN HEART. 29
Incorruptible Crown. 20
Index of Words and Phrases. . . . . v, 187
indwelling. 32, 129
indwelling of the Holy Spirit. 129
INIQUITIES REMOVE PEOPLE FROM GOD'S WILL. 19
instructions. 73, 183
intercessory prayer. 179
INTERCESSORY PRAYER IS NEEDED. 179
intreated. 109, 110
Israel. 1, 2, 4, 26, 29, 30, 54, 61, 80, 84, 121, 122, 164, 165, 181, 182
ISRAEL DESTROYED THEIR PROPHETS. 165
James Chapter Five. v
James Chapter Four. v
James Chapter One. v
James Chapter Three. v
James Chapter Two. v
Jews. 1, 2, 25, 36, 57, 61, 67, 72, 117, 165-167, 179, 180
Job. 2, 22, 38, 142, 143, 167, 169-173
JOB'S FIVE DEVASTATING LOSSES. 171
JOB'S WIFE WANTED HIM TO CURSE GOD. 172
joy. 2, 21, 114, 119, 132, 135, 158
JUDAS ISCARIOT WANTED MONEY TO STEAL. 52
judge. 2, 20, 44, 51, 77, 83, 112, 137-140, 159-163, 184
JUDGE NOT ON APPEARANCE ONLY. 140
judging. 2, 137-139, 160
judgment seat of Christ. 63, 64, 93, 138, 140, 161, 162
JUDGMENT SEAT OF CHRIST'S SIX MATERIALS. 64
justification. 60, 73, 79, 80

JUSTIFICATION BEFORE GOD BY FAITH. 79, 80
JUSTIFIED IN THE EYES OF GOD IS NEEDED. 68
knowledge. . . . . iii, 9, 11, 41, 76, 82, 85, 90, 101-104, 182
Lake Of Fire. 28, 92, 126, 139, 163, 164
laughter. 89, 135, 136
law of Moses. 59, 61, 79, 145
LAY UP TREASURES IN HEAVEN.. 151
laziness. 47
lazy. 147
led by the Lord. 97
LOOKING WITH HEART LUST IS ADULTERY. 25
looking with lust.. 62
love. 2, 15, 19-21, 41, 51, 53, 57, 58, 76, 85, 90-92, 114, 115, 123,
                125, 127, 128, 133, 137, 156, 160, 162
LOVE FOR THE WORLD SHOWS NO LOVE FOR GOD.. 128
love one another.. 137
loving neighbors.. 57
lust. 15, 19, 23-27, 42, 62, 97, 117, 118, 123
LUST BY MEN AND WOMEN SHOULD NOT EXIST. 25
LUST CAUSES WARS AND FIGHTINGS. 117
MADE PERFECT AND MATURE AFTER SUFFERING. 8
MAKE NO FRIENDS WITH ANGRY PEOPLE. 122
MANY UNCHRISTIAN MOUTHS ARE FILTHY. 88
man's days.. . . . . 17, 142
MAN'S DAYS ARE FASTER THAN A SHUTTLE. 142
master. 46, 57, 64, 84, 140, 164
mature. 7, 8, 75-77, 85, 86
maturity.. . . . . 8, 76, 84
MAY OUR TONGUES SPEAK OF PRAISE TO GOD. 88
MEANING OF THE GREEK WORD, "CHALINAGOGEO.".. 40,
                                                                                                    84
MEANING OF THE GREEK WORD, "HUPEREPHANOS.". . . . 130
MEANING OF THE GREEK WORD, "MAKROTHUMEO.". 155
merciful. 30, 65, 66
mercy. 22, 51, 65, 66, 109, 110, 113, 167, 172
merry. 144, 174
merry heart. 174
Miracles ceased. 175
mirror. 37-39
MODERN BIBLE VERSIONS. 16, 178, 184
money. 16, 20, 48, 52, 147, 150, 153
More N.T. Verses About Prophets. 166
More Verses On Prayer. 181
MORTIFY SINS IN THE LIFE. 118

Moses. 3, 4, 59, 61, 79, 145
motto of the Navy Chaplaincy, cooperation, not compromise. . . . 71
mourn. 135, 157
mourning. 135
mouth. 19, 40, 41, 56, 59, 86-91, 96, 99, 100, 112, 134, 159
murder. 44, 61-63, 133
Naval Chaplain, Pastor Waite was for five years. 71, 95
New Testament Crowns, five of them. 20
NO ESCAPE FROM CHRIST'S RIGHTEOUS JUDGMENT. . . . 163
NO HUMAN BEING CAN TAME THE TONGUE. 96
no respecter of persons, God is not. 46
NON-CHRISTIANS ARE JUDGED AND SENT TO HELL. 63
O.T. prophets. 166
oaths, not to use. 173
obedience. 27, 39, 74, 75
OBEDIENCE TO GOD'S WORDS IS BLESSED BY GOD. 39
obey. 27, 38, 87, 94, 117, 131
obey God's Words. 38
offend. 59, 84, 85, 93
OLD TESTAMENT ADULTERERS WERE SLAIN. 61
ONE DAY THE HEAVENS WILL PASS AWAY. 18
oppression. 54, 55, 153
orderly. 109
Orders: 1-800-John 10:9. I
Other Verses On Faults. 179
OUR DAYS ARE AS BRIEF AS THE GRASS. 144
OUR DOCTRINAL FAITH MUST BE HELD FAST. 13
OUR TONGUES SHOULD EXALT GODS WORDS. 89
pass away. 16, 18, 19, 26
passing away. 17
Pastors. 107, 108, 156, 183
PASTORS MUST BE PATIENT TO QUALIFY. 156
patience. 5-7, 22, 24, 155, 156, 164, 167-169, 171, 172
patience of Job. 22, 167, 169, 171
patient. 5, 6, 155, 156, 167, 181
Patricia Canter. iv
Paul. . . . 2, 6, 7, 11, 21, 23, 27, 53, 56, 64, 82, 99, 103, 104, 109, 127,
138, 146, 149, 176, 181
PAUL HAD MUCH PATIENCE. 6
PAUL MADE CHRISTIANS BLASPHEME CHRIST. 56
PAUL WAS READY TO GO HOME TO HEAVEN. 109
peace. 8, 28, 56, 68, 69, 76, 80, 85, 108-111, 113-115, 159, 172
Peaceable. 109, 110, 113
PEOPLE GO EITHER TO HEAVEN OR TO HELL. 143

PEOPLE SHOULD BE EXERCISED BY CHASTENING.	113
people who change.	30
perfect.	3, 7, 8, 11, 29, 35, 39, 53, 75-77, 84-86, 94, 103, 104, 113, 114, 126, 160, 169-171, 176
PERFECT GOD & PERFECT MAN.	103
perfect will of God.	7
persecutors.	99
PETER.	4, 8, 12, 16-18, 20, 31, 46, 51, 62, 77, 82, 91, 94, 106, 118, 130-132, 137, 154, 159, 160, 162, 163, 168, 169, 176, 179, 180
Pharisees.	29, 31, 36, 125, 133, 136, 166, 183
pleasure.	48, 117, 120, 153, 154
pleasures.	48
poor.	16, 43, 44, 47-55, 122, 147, 149, 153
poor Christians.	52
praise.	40, 51, 88, 94, 98, 99, 113
pray.	4, 34, 81, 98, 99, 103, 104, 118, 152, 159, 174-176, 178, 179, 181, 182
prayer.	4, 8, 12-14, 66, 119, 121, 126, 155, 175-182
PRAYER MUST BE IN CHRIST'S NAME.	177
praying.	103, 118, 177, 180
preserved.	18, 76, 159, 185
pride.	15, 26, 123, 130, 131, 136
PRIDEFUL PEOPLE WILL BE BROUGHT LOW.	131
prince of this world.	125
problems.	49, 117, 155, 174
PROPER CHASTENING IS OFTEN NECESSARY.	21
prophets.	22, 58, 59, 61, 164-167
PROTECT THE FATHERLESS AND WIDOWS.	43
proud.	88, 130-132, 136, 137, 155
PROVOKING AND ENVYING ARE NOT GOOD.	106
pure.	36, 42, 64, 65, 109, 110, 133, 134
purity.	36, 55, 111, 127
PURITY IN OUR OWN EYES DOESN'T MEAN PURITY.	36
Rahab the harlot helped the Israel's messengers.	80
rapture of the Lord Jesus Christ.	32, 156-159, 162
read the Bible daily.	104
READ THE BIBLE IN ONE YEAR.	104
READ THE BIBLE IN ONE YEAR=85 VERSES PER DAY.	104
RECEIVING ANSWERS TO PRAYER BRINGS FULL JOY.	119
rejoice.	16, 97, 99, 145, 165
rejoicing.	16, 21, 53, 145, 149, 158
REJOICING EVEN WHEN MADE LOW.	16
respect of persons, we're not to have.	45-47, 50, 58, 59

respecting persons should not be done.. 59
resurrection, bodily. 2, 12, 32, 52, 75, 157
resurrections. 32
rich. . . . 4, 16, 17, 19, 45, 47-51, 53-56, 58, 104, 144, 147-149, 152-155
riches. 16, 17, 47-51, 123, 136, 147-151
right Bible is necessary. 102
righteous. . . 20, 49, 59, 68, 79, 89, 111-113, 140, 154, 160, 162, 163, 178-181
righteous judgment. 140, 163
righteousness. . . 8, 10, 20, 27, 35, 40, 59, 60, 67, 68, 77-79, 88, 89, 111-114, 117, 123, 138, 160-163, 172
RIGHTEOUSNESS IS ONLY BY FAITH IN CHRIST. 60
salvation. . . 46, 65, 66, 68, 70, 101, 112, 114, 139, 141, 149, 184, 185
Satan. 23, 106, 124-128, 132, 138, 170-172
SATAN FAILED IN HIS TEMPTATION OF CHRIST. 23
SATAN IS THE PRINCE OF THIS WORLD. 125
SATAN'S DESIRE TO TEMPT CHURCHES. 23
save. 10, 29, 35-37, 59, 66, 81, 139, 161, 172, 176, 184, 185
saved. . . . 2, 32, 60, 66-68, 91, 101, 103, 113, 124, 132, 138, 139, 161, 162, 184
saving people's souls. 184
SCRIPTURES GIVE PATIENCE, COMFORT & HOPE. 169
Scriptures preserved in Hebrew, Aramaic, and Greek Words. . . . 76
SCRIPTURES PRESERVED TO ENABLE MATURITY. 76
seed as the stars, Abraham's descendants. 74
seven years of the Tribulation period. 158
shortness of life. 142
SIGNS WILL PRECEDE CHRIST'S COMING TO REIGN. 156
sin. . . . 2, 3, 10, 16, 17, 23, 24, 27-29, 34, 35, 40, 43, 45, 46, 58, 59, 62, 66, 67, 71-73, 78, 79, 81, 82, 86, 88, 103-105, 107, 108, 110, 117, 118, 122, 126, 130, 133-135, 141, 146, 149, 151, 154, 159, 169, 172, 177, 178, 183
sin nature. 118
sinning.. . . . . 40, 60, 136
SINNING IN ANY AREA MAKES YOU A SINNER. 60
sins. . . 16, 28, 29, 36, 37, 49, 53, 66, 69, 96, 105, 106, 108, 118, 120, 123, 125, 126, 128, 134, 139, 149, 157, 172, 176, 178, 179, 183, 184
sleep.. . . . . 4, 49, 158, 159
SOME CHRISTIANS REFUSE TO OBEY GOD'S WORDS. 38
SOME FALSE PROPHETS WERE ADULTERERS. 61
SOME HAVE EYES FULL OF HEART-ADULTERY. 62
SOMETIMES THERE IS A TIME TO MOURN. 135
speaking. . 4, 14, 16, 33, 34, 40, 61, 72, 86, 88, 91-93, 109, 113, 118,

James–Preaching Verse By Verse

                                          137, 138, 154, 163, 170, 175
speaking evil. 91, 137, 138
spiritual fruit.. 101
SPIRITUAL FRUIT SHOULD ACCOMPANY SALVATION..... 101
spiritual mindedness. 28
SPIRITUAL MINDEDNESS BRINGS LIFE AND PEACE. 28
spiritual values. 48
Still More Verses On Patience. 155
STOP ANY KIND OF SWEARING!. 173
strength. 7, 15, 26, 85, 134, 143, 144, 176
submission. 132
submit. 130-132, 137
suffering. 8, 22, 77, 94, 164, 167, 169
swearing. 173
Table of Contents. v
Taming The Untamed Man.. 95
temptation. 3, 4, 19, 21-23, 149
TESTING BIBLE DOCTRINES. 5
thankful. 115, 146, 181
THE APOSTLES DOUBTED CHRIST'S RESURRECTION. 12
THE APOSTLES–POOR AND MAKING MANY RICH. 53
THE BABYLONIANS WERE NOT TO BLASPHEME GOD..... 121
THE BELIEVING THIEF WOULD BE WITH CHRIST. 141
THE BIBLE AND EVIL THOUGHTS. 51
THE BIBLE CAN MAKE CHRISTIANS MATURE. 86
THE BIBLE FOR TODAY PRESS. I
THE BIBLE IS LIKE A MIRROR. 38
THE BLOOD OF THE O.T. PROPHETS REQUIRED. 166
THE CHRISTIAN BATTLE BETWEEN FLESH & SPIRIT.. 97
THE DEFINITION OF CHRIST'S "RAPTURE". 158
THE DEVIL LIED TO THE LORD JESUS CHRIST. 124
THE DISCIPLES WERE TO ASK OF THE LORD. 119
The Eight Characteristics Of God's Wisdom. 109
THE ELEMENTS WILL MELT WITH FERVENT HEAT.. 94
THE EPHESUS CHURCH NEEDED GOD'S WISDOM. 103
THE FORM FOR "THINK" MEANS "STOP THINKING". 14
THE HIGH COST OF PLEASURES.. 48
the Holy Spirit. . . 7, 18, 26, 28, 32, 38, 42, 62, 78, 96, 97, 107, 125,
                                                     129, 138, 167
THE INFLUENCE OF MONEY AND FRIENDS. 48
THE INSTABILITY OF MODERN BIBLE VERSIONS. 16
THE LAKE OF FIRE FOR CHRIST-REJECTERS. 28
THE LORD JESUS CHRIST IS CHANGELESS. 141
THE LOST WILL BE SENT TO EVERLASTING FIRE. 92

THE MEANING OF THE 8 GREEK WORDS BELOW......... 109
THE MEANING OF THE GREEK PRESENT TENSE.......... 45
THE MEANING OF THE GREEK WORD, "APOSTEREO"..... 152
THE MEANING OF THE GREEK WORD, "DOULOS".......... 1
THE MEANING OF THE GREEK WORD, "HOMOLOGEO"... 134
THE MEANING OF THE GREEK WORD, "HUPOMONE".... 167
THE MEANING OF THE GREEK WORD, "HUPOTASSO".... 131
THE MEANING OF THE GREEK WORD, "IOS".............. 150
THE MEANING OF THE GREEK WORD, "KAKOS.".......... 120
THE MEANING OF THE GREEK WORD, "KRAZO".......... 152
THE MEANING OF THE GREEK WORD, "MISTHOS"....... 151
THE MEANING OF THE GREEK WORD, "PARAPTOMA".... 178
THE MEANING OF THE GREEK WORD, "PEGE.".......... 100
THE MEANING OF THE GREEK WORD, "PEIRASMOS"....... 2
THE MEANING OF THE GREEK WORD, "PIKROS"......... 100
THE MEANING OF THE GREEK WORD, "SPATALAO"...... 153
THE MEANING OF THE GREEK WORD, "STENAZO"....... 160
THE MEANING OF THE GREEK WORD, "TAPEINOS"...... 130
THE MEANING OF THE GREEK WORD, "TREPHO"........ 153
THE NEED TO FIND THE PERFECT WILL OF GOD........... 7
THE PHARISEES WERE UNCLEAN IN THEIR HEARTS..... 133
THE POOR IN THE WORLD CAN BE RICH IN FAITH........ 51
THE RESULTS OF LAZINESS AND DILIGENCE............. 47
THE SIN NATURE SHOULD NOT REIGN.................. 118
THE SLEEP PROBLEMS OF THE RICH..................... 49
THE SMALL TONGUE CAN BRING BIG TROUBLE........... 42
THE SMALL TONGUE CAN DO HUGE DAMAGE............ 87
THE SPEECH OF THE POOR AND THE RICH............... 48
THE TONGUE NEEDS TO BE BRIDLED.................... 86
THE UNBRIDLED TONGUE DOES THREE THINGS......... 89
THE WORLD'S AND GOD'S WILL TOTALLY DIFFERENT..... 15
thief... 18, 141
Things Of Earth That Fail................................. 19
THIS WORLD IS FILLED WITH MURDER................... 63
THOUSANDS OF DESCENDANTS PROMISED............... 75
THREE STAGES OF CHRISTIANS' RESURRECTIONS......... 32
today.. I, iii, iv, 6, 16, 33, 34, 41, 61, 85, 88, 126, 140, 141, 144, 146, 150, 164, 173
tomorrow................................... 16, 140, 141, 145
tongue.................... 25, 40-42, 84, 86-92, 94, 96, 98, 100
tongues...................... 40-42, 86, 88-92, 95, 96, 109, 175
TONGUES SHOULD TALK OF GOD'S RIGHTEOUSNESS..... 40
treasures in Heaven..................................... 151
tribulation of seven years........... 6, 21, 32, 56, 155, 156, 158, 181

TRIBULATION CAN WORK PATIENCE. 6
true Christians. . . . 5-10, 12, 14, 16, 17, 22, 23, 26, 28, 31, 32, 34, 37,
                  38, 42, 50, 53, 63-67, 76-79, 81, 82, 85, 86, 91, 92,
                  96, 97, 99-101, 104, 105, 110, 112, 113, 115, 118, 120,
                  122, 123, 126-129, 132-137, 145-148, 155, 158-160,
                  165, 168, 169, 179
TRUE CHRISTIANS WILL ABIDE FOREVER. 17, 26
TRUE FAITH IN CHRIST BRINGS RIGHTEOUSNESS. 35
TRUE FAITH IN CHRIST RESULTS IN GODLY WORKS.. 70
TRUE FAITH IN CHRIST SAVED–NOT GOOD WORKS. 67
truth. . . . iv, 9, 12, 28-30, 65, 72, 90-92, 102, 105, 113, 125, 129, 153,
                  160, 172, 178, 182, 183
two natures. 26
Two Verses On Respect Of Persons. 59
unbridled tongue. 89
unstable. 13-16, 62
unstable seas. 13
upbraiding. 12
Verses About Devils. 70
Verses About Grudging. 160
Verses About Rahab. 80
Verses On Adultery. 60, 122
Verses On Affliction. 135
Verses On Afflictions And Problems. 174
Verses On Amiss. 121
Verses On Asking. 118
Verses On Being Born Of God. 31
Verses On Being Drawn Away. 25
Verses On Being Perfect Or Mature. 76
Verses On Being Saved. 139
Verses On Being Unstable. 15
Verses On Blessing. 98
Verses On Boasting. 146
Verses On Bridle. 86
Verses On Change. 30
Verses On Christ's Return. 156
Verses On Clean Things. 133
Verses On Confusion. 107
Verses On Death. 27
Verses On Double Hearts Or Double Minds. 15
Verses On Endurance. 168
Verses On Enduring. 21
Verses On Entice. 26
Verses On Envy And Envying. 105

Verses On Erring. 28, 182
Verses On Evil Works. 109
Verses On Filthiness. 36
Verses On Fire. 92, 94
Verses On Firstfruits. 31
Verses On Friends And Friendship. 122
Verses On Good Works. 81
Verses On Happiness. 167
Verses On Healing During New Testament Times. 175
Verses On Hearing. 33
Verses On Humble And Humility. 136
Verses On Judge And Judging. 138, 160
Verses On Judging. 139
Verses On Justification. 79
Verses On Knowledge. 102
Verses On Loving Neighbors. 57
Verses On Lust. 25, 117
Verses On Mercy. 65, 172
Verses On Mercy And Merciful. 65
Verses On Merry. 174
Verses On Mirrors. 38
Verses On Mourning. 135
Verses On Murder. 62
Verses On Name And Blaspheme. 56
Verses On Offend. 85
Verses On Oppression. 54
Verses On Patience. 6, 155, 169
Verses On Peace. 114
Verses On Perfect. 7, 85
Verses On Pleasure. 153
Verses On Prayer. 179, 181
Verses On Praying In Faith. 177
Verses On Pride And Proud. 130
Verses On Prophets. 164, 165
Verses On Prophets By Christ. 165
Verses On Respect Of Persons. 46, 59
Verses On Riches. 147
Verses On Righteousness. 35, 111
Verses On Saving People's Souls. 184
Verses On Speaking. 34, 138
Verses On Speaking Evil And Blaspheming. 138
Verses On Submission. 132
Verses On Taking Oaths Or Swearing. 173
Verses On Temptation. 3, 22

Verses On The Flesh And Tongue. 96
Verses On The Indwelling Of The Holy Spirit. 129
Verses On The Judgment Seat Of Christ.. 64
Verses On The Law Of Moses. 59
Verses On The Need For Clean Hands. 134
Verses On The Need For Clean Hearts. 134
Verses On The Patience Of Job. 169
Verses On The Poor. 51
Verses On The Shortness Of Life. 142
Verses On The Tongue.. . . . . 40, 88
Verses On The Tongue And Mouth. 40
Verses On The Will Of The Lord. 145
Verses On The World.. 123
Verses On Things Being Changed And Passing Away. 17
Verses On Today, Not Tomorrow. 140
Verses On Unstable Seas.. 13
Verses On Upbraiding. 12
Verses On Wages. 152
Verses On Wantonness. 154
Verses On Weeping, Laughter, And Heaviness. 136
Verses On Widows And The Fatherless. 43
Verses On Wisdom.. . . . . 10, 102
Verses Using The Word, Master.. 84
virtuous woman. 41, 91
wages. 27, 28, 151-153
Waite, Pastor D.A., Pastor Daniel, Mrs. Yvonne. . . . . . 1, I, iii, iv, 71
wantonness. 105, 154
WE CAN HEAR CHRIST THROUGH ACCURATE BIBLES. 33
weakness. 7, 85, 176
wealth. 47, 48, 73, 123, 150
WEALTH AND SPIRITUAL VALUES.. 48
Website: www.BibleForToday.org. I
weeping. 136
WHEN I BECAME A CHRISTIAN MY LIFE CHANGED. 70
WHEN IN EXISTENCE, TONGUES WERE ORDERLY. 109
WHERE CHRIST JUDGES THE SAVED AND THE LOST. 162
widows.. . . . . 42-44, 55, 103, 127, 154
will of God. 7, 8, 10, 15, 19, 26, 76, 86, 126, 132, 169
will of the Lord. 145
wisdom of this world. 10, 11, 126
without hypocrisy.. . . . . 109, 110
without partiality. 109, 110
wives. 61, 132, 133
WIVES SHOULD SUBMIT TO THEIR HUSBANDS. 132

world. . . . iv, 1, 2, 7, 9-11, 15, 16, 18, 19, 26, 31, 35, 42, 43, 46, 48-51, 53, 56, 59, 61, 63, 66, 70, 80, 85, 88, 89, 91, 92, 104, 109, 112, 115, 121, 123-129, 138, 139, 149, 150, 154, 156, 161, 162, 166, 172, 183, 184
worldly wisdom. 10, 11
wrath. 32, 34, 35, 97, 158, 165
yield. 27, 38, 100, 112, 117, 118, 131
YIELD HANDS, EYES, EARS, AND FEET TO THE LORD. 118

About The Author

The author of this book, Dr. D. A. Waite, received a B.A. (Bachelor of Arts) in classical Greek and Latin from the University of Michigan in 1948, a Th.M. (Master of Theology), with high honors, in New Testament Greek Literature and Exegesis from Dallas Theological Seminary in 1952, an M.A. (Master of Arts) in Speech from Southern Methodist University in 1953, a Th.D. (Doctor of Theology), with honors, in Bible Exposition from Dallas Theological Seminary in 1955, and a Ph.D. in Speech from Purdue University in 1961. He held both New Jersey and Pennsylvania teacher certificates in Greek and Language Arts.

He has been a teacher in the areas of Greek, Hebrew, Bible, Speech, and English for over thirty-five years in ten schools, including one junior high, one senior high, four Bible institutes, two colleges, two universities, and one seminary. He served his country as a Navy Chaplain for five years on active duty; pastored three churches; was Chairman and Director of the Radio and Audio-Film Commission of the American Council of Christian Churches; since 1969, has been Founder, President, and Director of THE BIBLE FOR TODAY; since 1978, has been Founder and President of the DEAN BURGON SOCIETY; has produced over 700 other studies, books, cassettes, VHS's, CD's, or VCR's on various topics; and is heard IN DEFENSE OF TRADITIONAL BIBLE TEXTS and verse-by-verse preaching, by streaming on the Internet at BibleForToday.org, 24/7/365 on the BROWN BOX.

Dr. and Mrs. Waite have been married since 1948; they have four sons, one daughter, and, at present, eight grandchildren, and seventeen great-grandchildren. Since October 4, 1998, he has been the Pastor of the Bible For Today Baptist Church in Collingswood, New Jersey. His sermons are heard on the Internet over www.BibleForToday.org on the BROWN BOX.

Order Blank (p. 1)

Name:_____
Address:_____
City & State:_____ Zip:_____
Credit Card #:_____ Expires:_____

Verse by Verse Preaching Books By Dr. D. A. Waite

[ ] Send James–Preaching Verse By Verse By Pastor D. A. Waite, (218 pages (16.00 + $7.00 S&H) fully indexed.

[ ] Send *1,2, & 3 John–Preaching Verse By Verse* By Pastor D. A. Waite, 202 pages ($14.00 + $7.00 S&H) fully indexed.

[ ] Send *2 Peter & Jude–Preaching Verse By Verse* By Pastor D. A. Waite, 237 pages ($16.00 +$7.00 S&H) fully indexed.

[ ] Send *1 & 2 Thessalonians–Preaching Verse By Verse* By Pastor D. A. Waite, 360 pages ($20.00 + $8.00 S&H) fully indexed.

[ ] Send *Hebrews–Preaching Verse by Verse*, By Pastor D. A. Waite, 616 pages ($34.00 +$10.00 S&H) fully indexed.

[ ] Send *Revelation–Preaching Verse by Verse*, By Pastor D. A. Waite, 1032 pages ($55.00 + $10.00 S&H) fully indexed.

[ ] Send *1 Timothy--Preaching Verse by Verse*, by Pastor D. A. Waite, 288 pages, hardback ($18+$7 S&H) fully indexed.

[ ] Send *2 Timothy--Preaching Verse by Verse*, by Pastor D. A. Waite, 250 pages, hardback ($16+$7 S&H) fully indexed.

[ ] Send *Romans--Preaching Verse by Verse* by Pastor D. A. Waite 736 pp. Hardback ($35+$8 S&H) fully indexed

[ ] Send *Colossians & Philemon--Preaching Verse by Verse* by Pastor D. A. Waite ($16+$7 S&H) hardback, 240 pages.

[ ] Send *Philippians--Preaching Verse by Verse* by Pastor D A. Waite ($14+$7 S&H) hardback, 176 pages. fully indexed.

[ ] Send *Ephesians--Preaching Verse by Verse* by Pastor D. A. Waite ($15+$7 S&H) hardback, 224 pages. fully indexed.

[ ] Send *Galatians--Preaching Verse By Verse* by Pastor D. A. Waite ($15+$7 S&H) hardback, 216 pages. fully indexed.

[ ] Send *1 Peter–Preaching Verse By Verse* by Pastor D. A. Waite ($15.00 + $7.00 S&H) hardback, 176 pages. fully indexed.

Send or Call Orders to:
THE BIBLE FOR TODAY
900 Park Ave., Collingswood, NJ 08108
Phone: 856-854-4452; FAX:--2464; Orders: 1-800 JOHN 10:9
E-Mail Orders: BFT@BibleForToday.org; Credit Cards OK

Order Blank (p. 2)

Name:_____
Address:_____
City & State:_____ Zip:_____
Credit Card #:_____ Expires:_____

Other Books By Dr. D. A. Waite

[ ] Send *A Critical Answer to God's Word Preserved* by Pastor D. A. Waite, 192 pp. perfect bound ($11.00+$4.00 S&H)

[ ] Send *Defending the King James Bible* by DAW ($12+$5 S&H) A hardback book, indexed with study questions.

[ ] Send *BJU's Errors on Bible Preservation* by Dr. D. A. Waite, 110 pages, paperback ($8+$4 S&H) fully indexed

Other Books By Dr. D. A. Waite (Continued)

[ ] Send *Fundamentalist Deception on Bible Preservation* by Dr. D. A. Waite, ($8+$4 S&H), paperback, fully indexed

[ ] Send *Fundamentalist MIS-INFORMATION on Bible Versions* by Dr. Waite ($7+$4 S&H) perfect bound, 136 pages

[ ] Send *Fundamentalist Distortions on Bible Versions* by Dr. Waite ($6+$3 S&H) A perfect bound book, 80 pages

[ ] Send *Fuzzy Facts From Fundamentalists* by Dr. D. A. Waite ($8.00 + $4.00) printed booklet

[ ] Send *Foes of the King James Bible Refuted* by DAW ($10 +$4 S&H) A perfect bound book, 164 pages in length.

[ ] Send *Central Seminary Refuted on Bible Versions* by Dr. Waite ($10+$4 S&H) A perfect bound book, 184 pages

[ ] Send *The Case for the King James Bible* by DAW ($7 +$3 S&H) A perfect bound book, 112 pages in length.

[ ] Send *Theological Heresies of Westcott and Hort* by Dr. D. A. Waite, ($7+$3 S&H) A printed booklet.

[ ] Send *Westcott's Denial of Resurrection*, Dr. Waite ($4+$3)

[ ] Send *Four Reasons for Defending KJB* by DAW ($3+$3)

Send or Call Orders to:
THE BIBLE FOR TODAY
900 Park Ave., Collingswood, NJ 08108
Phone: 856-854-4452; FAX:--2464; Orders: 1-800 JOHN 10:9
E-Mail Orders: BFT@BibleForToday.org; Credit Cards OK

Order Blank (p. 3)

Name:_____
Address:_____
City & State:_____Zip:_____
Credit Card #:_____Expires:_____

[ ] Send *Holes in the Holman Christian Standard Bible* by Dr. Waite ($3+$2 S&H) A printed booklet, 40 pages
[ ] Send *Contemporary Eng. Version Exposed*, DAW ($3+$2)
[ ] Send *NIV Inclusive Language Exposed* by DAW ($5+$3)
[ ] Send *26 Hours of KJB Seminar* (4 videos) by DAW($50.00)
[ ] Send *Making Marriage Melodious* by Pastor D. A. Waite ($7+$4 S&H), perfect bound, 112 pages.
[ ] Send *Burgon's Warnings on Revision* by DAW ($7+$4 S&H) A perfect bound book, 120 pages in length.
[ ] Send *The Superior Foundation of the KJB* By Dr. D. A. Waite ($10.00 + $7.00 S&H)

Other Books By Dr. D. A. Waite (Continued)

[ ] Send *Biblical Separation–1,896 Bible Verses About It* by Dr. D. A. Waite ($14.00 + $7.00 S&H)
[ ] Send *Westcott & Hort's Greek Text & Theory Refuted by Burgon's Revision Revised--Summarized* by Dr. D. A. Waite ($7.00+$4 S&H), 120 pages, perfect bound.
[ ] Send *Dean Burgon's Confidence in KJB* by DAW ($3+$3)
[ ] Send *Vindicating Mark 16:9-20* by Dr. Waite ($3+$3S&H)
[ ] Send *Summary of Traditional Text* by Dr. Waite ($3 +$3)
[ ] Send *Summary of Causes of Corruption*, DAW ($3+$3)
[ ] Send *Summary of Inspiration* by Dr. Waite ($3+$3 S&H)
[ ] Send *Soulwinning's Versions-Perversions* By Dr. D. A. Waite ($6.00 + $5.00 S&H)

Books By Dean John William Burgon

[ ] Send *The Revision Revised* by Dean Burgon ($25 + $5 S&H) A hardback book, 640 pages in length.
[ ] Send *The Last 12 verses of Mark* by Dean Burgon ($15+$5 S&H) A hardback book 400 pages.
[ ] Send *The Traditional Text* hardback by Burgon ($16+$5 S&H) A hardback book, 384 pages in length.

Send or Call Orders to:
THE BIBLE FOR TODAY
900 Park Ave., Collingswood, NJ 08108
Phone: 856-854-4452; FAX:--2464; Orders: 1-800 JOHN 10:9
E-Mail Orders: BFT@BibleForToday.org; Credit Cards OK

Order Blank (p. 4)

Name:_____

Address:_____

City & State:_____ Zip:_____

Credit Card #:_____ Expires:_____

[ ] Send *Causes of Corruption* by Burgon ($15+$5 S&H) A hardback book, 360 pages in length.

[ ] Send *Inspiration and Interpretation*, Dean Burgon ($25+$5 S&H) A hardback book, 610 pages in length.

Books By Dr. Jack Moorman

[ ] Send *Samuel P. Tregelles--The Man Who Made the Critical Text Acceptable to Bible Believers* by Dr. Moorman ($2+$1)

[ ] Send *8,000 Differences Between TR & CT* by Dr. Jack Moorman [$65 + $7.50 S&H] Over 500-large-pages of data

[ ] Send *356 Doctrinal Errors in the NIV & Other Modern Versions*, 100-large-pages, $10.00+$6 S&H.

More Books By Dr. Jack Moorman

[ ] Send *The Doctrinal Heart of the Bible--Removed from Modern Versions* by Dr. Jack Moorman, VCR, $15 +$4 S&H

[ ] Send *Modern Bibles--The Dark Secret* by Dr. Jack Moorman, $5+$3 S&H

[ ] Send *The Manuscript Digest of the N.T.* (721 pp.) By Dr. Jack Moorman, copy-machine bound ($50+$7 S&H)

[ ] *Early Manuscripts, Church Fathers, & the Authorized Version* by Dr. Jack Moorman, $18+$5 S&H. Hardback

[ ] Send *Forever Settled--Bible Documents & History Survey* by Dr. Jack Moorman, $20+$5 S&H. Hardback book.

[ ] Send *When the KJB Departs from the So-Called "Majority Text"* by Dr. Jack Moorman, $16+$5 S&H

[ ] Send *Missing in Modern Bibles--Nestle-Aland/NIV Errors* by Dr. Jack Moorman, $8+$4 S&H

Books By Miscellaneous Authors

[ ] Send *Guide to Textual Criticism* by Edward Miller ($7+$4) Hardback book

[ ] Send *Scrivener's Greek New Testament Underlying the King James Bible*, hardback, ($14+$5 S&H)

Send or Call Orders to:
THE BIBLE FOR TODAY
900 Park Ave., Collingswood, NJ 08108
Phone: 856-854-4452; FAX:--2464; Orders: 1-800 JOHN 10:9
E-Mail Orders: BFT@BibleForToday.org; Credit Cards OK

Order Blank (p. 5)

Name:_____

Address:_____

City & State:_____Zip:_____

Credit Card #:_____Expires:_____

[ ] Send *Scrivener's <u>Annotated</u> Greek New Testament,* by Dr. Frederick Scrivener: Hardback--($35+$5 S&H); Genuine Leather--($45+$5 S&H)

[ ] Send *Why Not the King James Bible?--An Answer to James White's KJVO Book* by Dr. K. D. DiVietro, $10+$5 S&H

[ ] Send Brochure #1: "*1000 Titles Defending the KJB/TR*" No Charge

[ ] Send *The LIE That Changed the Modern World* by Dr. H. D. Williams ($16+$5 S&H) Hardback book

[ ] Send *With Tears in My Heart* by Gertrude G. Sanborn. Hardback 414 pp. ($25+$5 S&H) 400 Christian Poems

More Books By Miscellaneous Authors

[ ] Send *Able To Bear It* By Gertrude Sanborn ($14.00 + $7.00 S&H

[ ] Send *Visitation In Action* By Mr. R. O. Sanborn ($10.00 + $7.00 S&H)

[ ] Send *Daily Bible Blessings From Daily Bible Readings* By Yvonne Sanborn Waite ($30.00 + $10.00 S&H)

[ ] Send *Husband-Loving Lessons* By Yvonne Sanborn Waite ($25.00 + $8.00 S&H)

[ ] Send *Gnosticism--The Doctrinal Foundation of New Bibles* by J. Moser ($20.00 + $8.00 S&H)

[ ] Send *Dean Burgon's Defense of the Authorised Version* By Dr. David Bennett ($14.0 + 8.00 S&H)

[ ] Send *Drift in Baptist Missions, Churches & Schools* by Dr. David Bennett ($12.00 + $8.00 S&H)

[ ] Send *God's Marvelous Book* By Dr. David Bennett ($15.00 + $8.00 S&H)

[ ] Send *CCM Not The Problem--Only A Symptom* By Dr. David Bennett ($12.00 + $7.00 S&H)

Send or Call Orders to:
THE BIBLE FOR TODAY
900 Park Ave., Collingswood, NJ 08108
Phone: 856-854-4452; FAX:--2464; Orders: 1-800 JOHN 10:9
E-Mail Orders: BFT@BibleForToday.org; Credit Cards OK

Order Blank (p. 6)

Name:_____
Address:_____
City & State:_____ Zip:_____
Credit Card #:_____ Expires:_____

[ ] Send *English Standard Bible (ESV) Deficiencies* By several authors ($7.00 + $4.00 S&H)
[ ] Send *Strong's Micro-Print Concordance* By the Sherbornes ($21.00 + $8.00 S&H)

Books by D. A. Waite, Jr.

[ ] Send *The Doctored New Testament* by D. A. Waite, Jr. ($25+$5 S&H) Greek MSS differences shown, hardback
[ ] Send *Readability of A.V. (KJB)* by D. A. Waite, Jr. ($6+$3)
[ ] Send *4,114 Definitions from the Defined King James Bible* by D. A. Waite, Jr. ($7.00+$4.00 S&H)

Question And Answer Books By Dr. D. A. Waite

[ ] Send *The First 200 Questions Answered* By Dr. D. A. Waite ($15.00 + $7.00 S&H)
[ ] Send *The Second 200 Questions Answered* By Dr. D. A. Waite ($15.00 + $7.00 S&H)
[ ] Send *The Third 200 Questions Answered* By Dr. D. A. Waite ($15.00 + $7.00 S&H)
[ ] Send *The Fourth 200 Questions Answered* By Dr. D. A. Waite ($15.00 + $7.00 S&H)
[ ] Send *The Fifth 200 Questions Answered* By Dr. D. A. Waite ($15.00 + $7.00 S&H)
[ ] Send *The Sixth 200 Questions Answered* By Dr. D. A. Waite ($15.00 + $7.00 S&H)

Send or Call Orders to:
THE BIBLE FOR TODAY
900 Park Ave., Collingswood, NJ 08108
Phone: 856-854-4452; FAX:--2464; Orders: 1-800 JOHN 10:9
E-Mail Orders: BFT@BibleForToday.org; Credit Cards OK

The Defined
King James Bible
Uncommon Words Defined Accurately

I. Deluxe Genuine Leather

✦Large Print--Black or Burgundy✦
1 for $44.00+$12.00 S&H
✦Case of 12 for✦
$34.00 each+$50.00 S&H

✦Medium Print--Black or Burgundy✦
1 for $39.00+$8.00 S&H
✦Case of 12 for✦
$29.00 each+$40.00 S&H

II. Deluxe Hardback Editions

1 for $22.00+12.00 S&H (Large Print)
✦Case of 12 for✦
$17.00 each+$40.00 S&H (Large Print)

1 for $19.50+$8.00 S&H (Medium Print)
✦Case of 12 for✦
$12.50 each+$30.00 S&H (Medium Print)

Order Phone: 1-800-JOHN 10:9
Credit Cards

Pastor D. A. Waite, Th.D., Ph.D.

Justification Before People

Two Kinds Of Justification In The New Testament.
One kind of justification is from the pen of the Apostle Paul (justification before God). The other kind is from the pen of the Book of James (justification before other people). Through the years, there has been much confusion and misunderstanding because of these differences.

Justification Before God By Genuine Faith In The Lord Jesus Christ.
Paul's letters are very clear that for people be justified in the sight of God, they must trust the Lord Jesus Christ as their Saviour by genuine heart-felt faith. By this action alone can they be declared righteous before God. They are not justified before God by any of their good works.

Justification Before Other People By Showing Them Good Works, The Fruits Of Salvation.
James speaks of this justification before other people so that, by the good works of genuine Christians, those who are not Christians can see that there is something wholesom about the lives of these true Christians which is a visible testimony to other people. Many times readers have misinterpreted the Book of James, believing wrongly that it teaches people can be saved merely by doing good works. This is a very false interpretation of the Book of James.

James Illustrates The Importance of Matthew 5:16.
The Lord Jesus Christ told His disciples: *"Let your light so shine before men, that they may see your good works, and glorify your Father which is in heaven."* The purpose of Christians' good works, after they have become genuine Christians, is for people to see these good works and glorify—not themselves, but--their *"Father which is in Heaven."*

www.BibleForToday.org

www.ingramcontent.com/pod-product-compliance
Lightning Source LLC
Chambersburg PA
CBHW062207080426
42734CB00010B/1821